The Advertising Research Handbook

The Advertising Research Handbook

by
Charles E. Young

SECOND EDITION
Ideas in Flight
Seattle, Washington
a division of Ad Essentials, LLC.

Second Edition, October, 2008

ISBN 978-0-615-24496-9

The author is grateful for permission to use exhibit material from Unilever, Sara Lee, IBM, United Dairy Association, and Hello Hello, Inc.

Acknowledgments

Several chapters are adapted from papers noted in the End Notes section of this book, with thanks to coauthors Michael Robinson, John Kastenholz, and Graham Kerr.

Front Page Cover Photo

Physicist Harold Edgerton used stop-action photography to freeze time and make the invisible visible. © Harold & Esther Edgerton Foundation, 2008, courtesy of Palm Press, Inc.

Back Page Cover Art

The Ameritest Flow of Attention® graph freezes time to study how audience attention flows through the moving pictures of film.

Illustrations, cover, and book layout and design by Patricia D. King.

Printed in the United States of America.

Contents

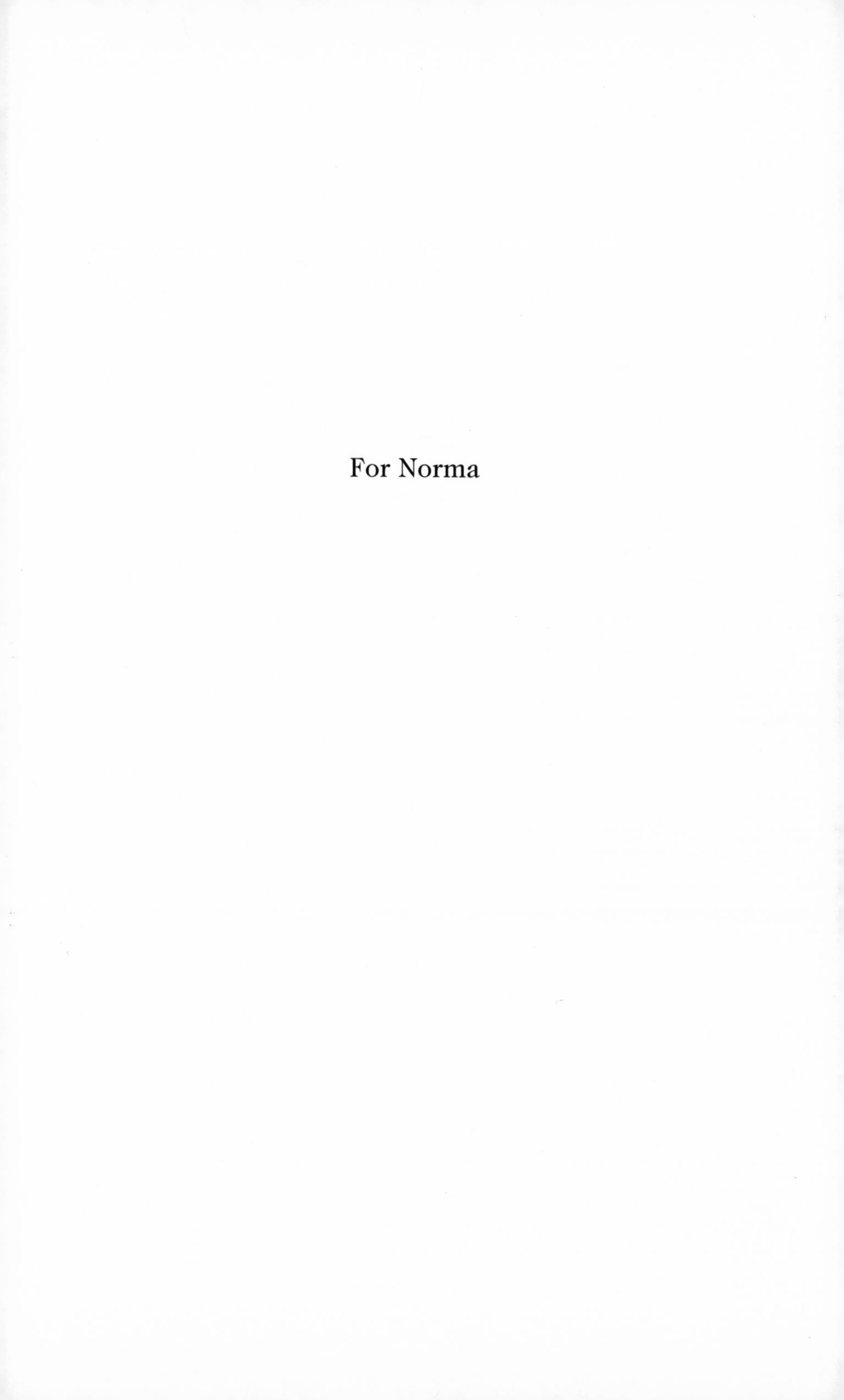

For Norma

Foreword

A.G. Lafley, former President and Chief Executive of The Procter & Gamble Company, once stated that "the best brands win two crucial moments of truth. The first moment occurs at the store shelf, when a consumer decides whether to buy one brand over another. The second moment occurs at home, when he or she uses the brand and is delighted or isn't."

I think there is a third moment of truth for most brands. In many cases it occurs before the store shelf or in-home use experience. It happens when a message is sent by an advertiser and received by a consumer. Sometimes it is used to introduce us to new products, sometimes to communicate improvements to existing brands. At other times to show us how certain brands can make our lives better. But in all cases, consistently great advertising must stop us and capture our attention, create the proper brand linkage, inform us, move us emotionally, persuade us to buy and in the end leave a positive impression of the brand. The challenge for marketers is to find valid and reliable ways to measure these components of effective advertising.

This handbook is for everyone from the most experienced researchers, brand managers and creatives to those learning about advertising research for the first time. It provides a comprehensive review of key metrics used by major pre-testing systems along with a glossary of terms, tips for branding Television commercials as well as advice on how to have a successful research meeting. It provokes everyone to think harder about how advertising works.

In short, this handbook is for those who want to know their craft better, stimulate their thinking and compete better in the marketplace.

Michael Robinson,
Demand Consulting/Omnicom

Introduction

For most people, a first-time visit to a new domain of knowledge is like a visit to a foreign country. The language is strange, the money is confusing, the proper names are peculiar, and while many things may look the same as they appear in their home country, the rules are subtly different. So different that, if a person is not careful, he may unexpectedly find himself driving on the wrong side of the road.

In terms of relative size, the domain of advertising research is like the very small Duchy of Grand Fenwick nestled somewhere between the much larger nations of Advertising and Finance, Hollywood and Business, Science and Art. Being at the crossroads of many disciplines, our small country attracts many tourists—account planners, brand managers, creative directors—though few are actual full time citizens as I am.

Much like a guide to Paris or Tokyo, I have written this book as a helpful guide for the tourist or occasional visitor who, upon passionately pursuing the dream of a powerful advertising campaign, finds him or herself stopped at a border checkpoint by one of our customs inspectors.

This book is intended to be neither a comprehensive nor an in-depth study of the subject. This is a topical reference piece with stand-alone chapters that can be read out-of-order, as needed. It's a survival guide to throw in your backpack and pull out now as you trek through the forest of advertising research concepts and over the mountain passes of test scores that you may encounter.

The book is divided into twenty chapters that represent four distinct and complementary views of the landscape.

The first six chapters in the book are about the practice of advertising research: the history, the models, and the measurement practices of different advertising research companies. This part of the book should provide a useful buyer's guide to the research practitioner.

The next six chapters shift to a more theoretical, psychological viewpoint, using some of the new findings of the exploding field of neuroscience and recent data from our own research practice to present new thinking about how the mind of the consumer processes the rational and emotional information in ads. These chapters are a deep dive into the reasons why ads score as they do on key measures such as attention, recall, branding, and motivation. Of necessity, the ideas presented in this part of the book should be viewed as a work-in-progress.

After that, six chapters shift to a creative development perspective, providing essays on a range of topics from the semantics of strategy refinement to suggestions on how to improve the branding in ad film to advice on the development of global advertising campaigns. These chapters include several creative topics that frequently come up in client/agency discussions, such as when to introduce the brand into the flow of a commercial, the value of 30-second versus 15-second commercials, and the usefulness of rehearsing advertising ideas in rough animatic form first before producing final film.

The final two chapters look at advertising research from the standpoint of a business process. One describes five different learning strategies that a company can use to improve the creative development process. The last chapter reveals the secrets of how to you can have a successful research meeting, so that what is learned by the ad researcher actually gets used by the ad team.

No one likes to feel like a Yokel on his first visit to New York, especially if you've come to attend your first presentation of research results on your advertising. So, the Glossary at the end of the book provides a handy dictionary that you can use to talk to the natives.

Charles Young, CEO
Albuquerque, 2008

The Advertising Research Handbook

I

A Short History of Television Copytesting

1

A Short History of Television Copytesting

In the late 1950s and early 1960s, television was just over a decade into its commercialization stage, about as far as the Internet is today. In those days there were just three networks. Programming was in black and white. A modern television viewer just might find the content tedious in terms of its visual pacing, and heavy on dialogue compared to the sophisticated cinematography of today.

Television advertising was different then, too. The basic unit of advertising was longer—the 60-second commercial. Many brands advertised in sole sponsor shows without commercial clutter. And there were fewer brands doing television advertising—but with more commercials surrounding the brand with a variety of messages.

To illustrate the last point: some years ago, an advertising agency undertook a bit of advertising archaeology, reviewing the ancient history of two Proctor & Gamble (P&G) brands, which they had handled from their very beginning. The agency was quite surprised to learn how much things had changed since the golden age of television. In 1959, P&G launched Mr. Clean household cleanser nationally and, during the first eighteen months of its introduction, aired 35 different 60-second executions. In 1961, when P&G launched Head & Shoulders shampoo, 27 distinct executions ran during the first eighteen months. Today, either brand would be lucky to produce two to three commercials in a given year and one would probably be a :15.

The reason for this profligate rate of commercial production was quite simple. According to historical records tracked down in the 4A's library in New York, in 1960 an average network-quality 60-second commercial would cost you $10,000 to produce—one fortieth the cost of today's production. An A-list director would cost you around $3,500, which is a tiny fraction of today's fees. Not surprisingly, given the low cost of commercial production, doing research on creative effectiveness was considered a relatively simple and straightforward filtering process.

In the years since, however, various methods of research have been developed to manage the risk associated with increasingly expensive media budgets. This category of research has historically been known as copytesting or, more correctly, pre-testing. Implicitly, all of these methods are intended to be predictive of commercial performance in some way. The other major form of quantitative advertising research that also developed over this time period involves tracking the effects of television advertising once it has actually aired and separating those effects from other variables in the marketing mix.

Much of the history of ad research resembles the fable of the three blind men describing the elephant with recall or persuasion replacing snake or tree trunk as the competing descriptions of the advertising animal. So, not surprisingly, clients have been much confused by the various pictures painted by the different copytesting systems to describe how advertising works. Yet most of the widely used approaches are probably valid up to a point. In the past twenty years, suppliers have produced an endless series of validation charts and regression lines with high r-squared statistics in support of their claim to having the best copytesting system. It should be noted that this wasn't always the case. As documented by Ostlund, Clancy, and Sapra, industry frustration with the lack of research hygiene among copytesting firms had reached a peak level shortly before the advent of the retail scanner revolution.[1]

So why do client and agency frustrations persist, despite the ongoing evolution of the "science" of copytesting? This frustration comes from overpromise and oversimplification of a complex subject—the question of how an endless variety of television commercials penetrate the human mind to motivate everyday behavior. Really, when you think about it, rocket science looks easy by comparison.

Because the U.S. was the dominant market for television advertising during this period, the story of how television copytesting evolved in the U.S. essentially highlights the various management debates over this time about how advertising is supposed to work—an issue that still holds our attention today with the emergence of global advertising campaigns and the proliferation of media choices. The current time, therefore, is a good vantage point for reviewing where we have been in our thinking. What follows is an attempt to provide a broad overview of the subject so that researchers currently in the field can move forward.

There are four general themes woven into the last half-century of copytesting. The first is the quest for a valid single-number statistic to capture the overall performance of the advertising creative. This is an attempt to summarize the various report card measures that are used to filter commercial executions and help management make the go/no go decision about which ads to air. The second theme is the development of diagnostic copytesting, whose main purpose is optimization, providing insights about and understanding of a commercial's performance on the report card measures with the hope of identifying creative opportunities to save and improve executions. The third theme is the development of non-verbal measures in response to the belief of many advertising professionals that much of a commercial's effects—the emotional impact—may be difficult for respondents to put into words or scale on verbal rating statements and may, in fact, be operating below the level of consciousness. The fourth theme, which is a variation on the previous two, is the development of moment-by-moment measures to describe the internal dynamic structure of the viewer's experience of the commercial, as a diagnostic counterpoint to the various gestalt measures of commercial performance or predicted impact.

THE RISE OF REPORT CARD MEASURES: FILTERING THE CREATIVE

Regardless of the issues of inspiration, risk-taking and creative freedom that are involved in the conceptualization of advertising executions, from a management perspective the creative development process is an expensive business process that outputs products—i.e., commercials—of highly variable quality. Like any industrial process, control is a function of our ability to measure it. For large firms, those for which advertising is mission-critical to their business, such as P&G, significant quantities of advertising executions are produced every year. Therefore, very simple metrics are needed to provide senior managers with a clear picture of how well the process is working and to provide a check on the quality of the decisions being made by the more junior brand managers and agency teams who are charged with the day-to-day business of making advertising. The key problem, of course, is one of validity—the relationship to sales.

The logic behind the first report card measure for testing television ads, the Day-After Recall (DAR) score, is quite simple. For advertising to be effective, it must surely leave some trace behind in the memory of the consumer. This memory effect metric was particularly credible given the traditional argument that advertising is superior to short-term promotions such as couponing only because of its long-term effect on sales. Recall testing, therefore, was interpreted to measure an ad's ability on-air to break through into the mind of the consumer to register a message from the brand in long-term memory.

According to Honomichl, DAR testing was first applied to the advertising measurement problem by George Gallup Sr., who built on R&D work done by a Naval Commander named Thompson who used it in the training of Navy pilots during the Second World War.[4] The Compton advertising agency then took up the development of the measure, evaluating an arbitrary range of forgetting periods such as 12, 24, 48 and 72 hours and exploring a range of variables operating in the on-air viewing environment. Compton soon began promoting it to their clients as proof of performance for their work. P&G conducted experiments of its own, became convinced of the usefulness of the measure, and subcontracted the fieldwork to a then small research company in Cincinnati called Burke. With P&G taking the lead, many other advertisers soon followed suit and Burke DAR scores became the dominant copytesting report card measure for the fifties and sixties.

In the seventies, however, some researchers began to question the relationship between recall and sales. According to some reports at the time, P&G reviewed a hundred split-cable test markets that had been conducted over ten years with ads that had been recall-tested and had been unable to find a significant relationship between recall scores and sales response. Not coincidentally, in a major validation study conducted at roughly the same time, Ross found that persuasion was a better predictor of sales response to advertising than was recall.[3] Much later, Lodish and his colleagues conducted an even more extensive review of test market results and also failed to find a relationship between recall and sales.[4]

During this period, therefore, the attention of advertising researchers shifted to the problem of measuring advertising persuasiveness. One of the researchers leading the way was Horace Schwerin, who pointed out "...the obvious truth is that a claim can be well remembered but completely unimportant to the prospective buyer of the product—if the solution the marketer offers is addressed to the wrong need."[5] Schwerin sold his company (and the pre-post shift approach to measuring persuasion that he developed) to ARS, which succeeded in getting it adopted by P&G as the new standard for measuring advertising effectiveness.

Recall continued to be collected as a companion measure, in part to ease the transition for the old-line researchers, with the caveat that recall is important up to some minimal threshold level, but persuasion is the more important measure. Again, with the imprimatur of P&G support, the ARS pre-post measure of persuasiveness became the category leader for much of the seventies and eighties.[6] Alternative post-exposure measures of motivation or persuasiveness were also developed at this time, such as the weighted five-point purchase intent scale—the industry gold standard for concept testing (which is currently used by the BASES simulated test market system as well as by several copytesting companies).

Meanwhile, other researchers during the late seventies began to question the validity of recall as a measure of breakthrough.[7] To some researchers, the construct of breakthrough is about the ability of the commercial execution to win the fight for attention and get noticed immediately, which is what many creatives assume is the first task that advertising must perform in creating a sale. Of course, this is not the same as measuring what happens to a commercial after it's been processed through long-term memory. An important distinction was made between the attention-getting power of the creative execution and how well branded the ad was. One of the reasons an ad may fail in a recall test, it was argued, even if it broke through the clutter and garnered a lot of attention, is that the memory of it might simply be filed away improperly in the messy filing cabinets of the mind so that it becomes difficult to retrieve with the standard verbal recall prompts.

This debate ran parallel to the ongoing debate of recall versus recognition as the best approach for tracking advertising awareness in-market. These two very different ways of tapping into memory for evidence of advertising awareness can produce very different measurements, usually substantially higher for recognition.[8]

For researchers on the recall side of the debate, the standard approach to measuring ad recall with telephone surveys provides consistency and comparability between the recall results of a pre-test and those of a post-test. Those on the recognition side of the debate remind us that memory is a complex subject, and that more than one memory system of the mind may be involved in determining advertising effectiveness.

Consider the difference between one's failure to recall the name yet ability to recognize the face of someone one has met before. For most people, the fact that one can recognize a face is taken as the more reliable "proof" that one has actually met a person before. In the last few years, the Internet created a practical research opportunity, unavailable in telephone surveys, to show consumers the "face" of an ad—i.e., a film clip or storyboard—in order to measure ad awareness with recognition-based questions.

Several companies, such as MSW Research, DRI, and Ameritest have developed alternative pre-testing approaches to recall testing as a measure of commercial breakthrough.[9] In these systems, attention and branding are measured separately. These approaches involve simulating a cluttered media environment off-air and measuring which ads win the fight for attention without the intervening variable of a day's worth of forgetting time. Recent research, jointly published by Unilever and Ameritest, has added substance to the debate by showing the findings from an analysis of a large database of commercials that had been tested with both approaches.[10] These results show that recall scores and attention scores are completely uncorrelated, suggesting that these two approaches to measuring breakthrough are in fact measuring completely different things. Moreover, recall scores for this set of ads had a strong negative correlation with commercial likability ratings, confirming what creative directors have been telling researchers about recall tests for many years.

Different approaches were also developed during this period to measure the well-brandedness of a commercial. Ipsos-ASI views brand linkage as the missing variable between recall and recognition and computes a measure of brandedness by looking at the ratio of a commercial's recall score to its recognition score. The Millward Brown approach to branding uses a five-point rating scale to measure how well a commercial execution is custom tailored to "fit" the brand. A third approach, used by Ameritest, measures branding by tracking a respondent's top-of-mind propensity to use the brand name as the "handle" to retrieve the memory of an advertising execution immediately after exposure in a cluttered media environment. Unfortunately, by using the same branding label to name three different measurement constructs, ad researchers continue to add to the confusion surrounding report card measures. Unilever reported an analysis of a database of commercials triple-tested with all three types of measures, showing that each of the three is measuring something uncorrelated with, and therefore different from, the other two.[11]

Finally, a very different approach was used by Millward Brown to create report card measures of commercial performance. In the late eighties, working with Unilever, they used a modeling approach to derive an overall effectiveness index from various component measures. Instead of starting with an a priori theoretical model of how the mind is supposed to interact with advertising, they reverse engineered the process by running a massive stepwise regression to identify pre-testing measures predictive of advertising tracking results from their continuous tracking program and then used a "black box" model to combine these component measures into an overall predictive score. This approach had the appeal of creating consistency between the two approaches, linking pre-testing to in-market tracking.

Over the last fifty years, category leadership in terms of market share for the commercial firms providing copytesting services has turned on the measure currently in vogue as the "magic number" predicting in-market performance. First, it was Burke's DAR score. Then it was ARS's measure of persuasion benchmarked against fair share. Currently in the U.S., it is

Ipsos-ASI's copy effect score, a composite measure integrating recall and persuasion. And, coming on strong in this highly competitive market, we have Millward Brown, the category leader outside the U.S., with its Effectiveness Index.

The Role of Diagnostics: Optimization

Accountability is always a tricky problem when it comes to marketing activities, since the real world where professionals operate has always been an exceedingly messy multivariate place in which to perform research. The mere fact that brands exist in the world is proof that marketing works at a general level. However, determining whether marketing resources have been allocated efficiently and effectively has always been a problem.

For that reason, providing marketers with improvements that result in an incremental sense of control over even part of the complex marketing process will be rewarded generously by the marketplace. One of the biggest innovations in market research over the past half century has been the availability of retail scanner data. According to advertising consultant Bill Moult, before the 1980s, the average marketing budget was divided so that 43 percent of every marketing dollar was spent on advertising, while 57 percent was spent on consumer and trade promotion.[12] By the early nineties, advertising's share of the marketing dollar had shrunk to only 25 percent, and promotion had grown to 75 percent. What had changed, in the meantime, was a shift in the balance of accountability. With huge amounts of accurate retail sales data coming out of stores, it became easy to measure the short-term return on promotion while the effect of the advertising spending in the longer term became relatively less predictable and therefore riskier to use.

The desire to harness the creative power of advertising more effectively so as to attract those vanished client dollars has motivated the industry to embrace advertising tracking studies—witness the continuous tracking and marketing mix modeling services offered by Millward Brown—to justify advertising budgets. This put a spotlight back on the renewed need for pre-testing measurements to predict the performance of advertising prior to airing.

But meeting the client's need for accountability has long been a source of conflict within advertising agencies. In particular, most creatives are skeptical of the value of copytesting. It is common for Creative Directors to caution us of the dangers inherent in "writing to the test," where advertising is created based on a formula for what tests well rather than truly original work that re-defines a marketplace. They express concern, also, at the inefficiency of throwing away good creative ideas that are designed to operate differently than the researchers' models imply—the role of emotion in advertising is an example of the debates that arise from this longstanding issue. From an agency perspective, pre-testing research provides value only if it delivers an understanding of why a commercial scores the way it does and insights into how to improve an ad's performance—how to clean and polish the creative idea to a shining brightness.

One of the earliest agencies to embrace diagnostic copytesting was Leo Burnett. In the sixties, ad researchers Bill Wells and Clark Leavitt, and, later on, Fred and Mary Jane Schlinger, developed a diagnostic pre-test for the agency called Communication Workshop.[13, 14] Extensive attitudinal rating statements were developed and factor-analyzed to provide a multidimensional profile of how a commercial was working in dimensions such as relevant news, believability, entertainment value and uniqueness. In addition, a series of open-ended questions were developed, based on the classic qualitative research funnel from general to specific, to provide insight into respondent reactions and message takeaway from the execution. A great deal of effort was also invested in developing complex coding schemes to better understand respondent reactions. For example, coding for spontaneous brand name playback became a key source of insight into brand linkage. Interestingly, this form of research was positioned within the agency as a learning tool, not a report card. For many years the research was done at agency expense and results were shared with clients only with the Creative Director's permission.

Following Burnett's lead, many other agencies developed their own custom approaches to testing their own work. Key to the agency approach to copytesting is the belief that advertising operates in more than one way and that the methods that are effective in reaching consumers at one point in time may become less relevant as the consumer becomes vaccinated against various styles of advertising. This makes agencies suspicious of report card measures since the lessons from such systems always seem to point to one particular type of advertising approach. For example, "show the brand early and often" is advice often given by copytest systems based on DAR. Agencies also typically question the validity of a one-number approach to capture the complex workings of an ad.

Agency research departments were downsized in the eighties as a result of advertising's shrinking share of the marketing dollar and client price resistance to media inflation and consequent pressure on agency margins. Since that time, most agencies have gotten out of the business of testing their own ads. To most clients, this smacked too much of the fox watching the henhouse, anyway. Nevertheless, agencies tended to push hard for softer, more qualitative approaches to understanding their work early in the creative development process and to opt for focus groups rather than quantitative research as a mechanism for injecting the voice of the consumer into the creative development process.

According to the 4A's, the cost of commercial production doubled during the 1990s, with the average cost to produce a network quality television commercial rising from $180,000 in 1989 to $358,000 in 2002 (see www.aaaa.org). This was twice the rate of inflation over the same period. At the same time, network audiences were shrinking. These factors all contributed to raising the risks associated with creating a television commercial but also shifted the interest of ad managers away from pure report-card testing systems like ARS and Ipsos-ASI and toward the hybrid systems combining validated performance measures with powerful diagnostics, systems like Millward Brown and Ameritest. The new need of the nineties was to squeeze every dollar's worth out of this increasingly expensive advertising film.

This shifted the value equation for the category away from simply filtering creative ideas on the basis of one report card measure or another, and put emphasis on gaining insights to improve the performance of individual executions. For some companies adopting this approach, the payback on research dollars has been considerable. In a recent review of the pre-testing work done by Ameritest over the course of a year by one of the major divisions of Unilever, it was found that roughly forty percent of all ads approved for airing had been revised or re-edited based on insights provided by quantitative diagnostic research.

Among copytesting suppliers, most diagnostic copytesting tended to follow the lead set by the ad agencies with some version of a test consisting of open-ended questions and attitudinal rating statements that bears more than a superficial resemblance to the Burnett model. But, for many practitioners, this purely verbal approach to describing the communication and response to advertising messaging seemed to leave important aspects of an ad's performance out of the picture. A clue to the

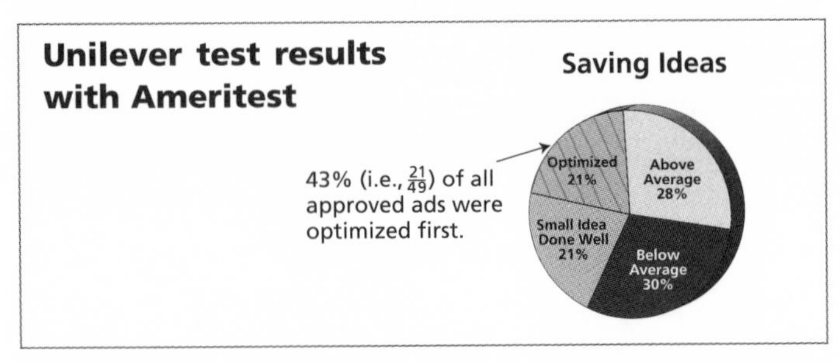

The new value proposition is filtering plus optimization.

limitations of the current research paradigm could be seen in the category descriptors: why call it *copy*testing when it's for tele*vision*?

The Search for the Unconscious Mind

It has long been a belief of advertising professionals that much of the way advertising works operates below the surface. Not that we believe in the subliminal advertising techniques popularized by Vance Packard's 1957 best seller The Hidden Persuaders. Nor do we believe in advertising magic. But our own day-to-day experience is that much of the way that we interpret the world is subtext; the mind is continuously engaged in the search for deeper meaning, understanding the important gaps between what we say and what we do.

For that reason, there has long been a strong interest in a range of nonverbal or physiological measures of advertising response. During the seventies, for example, Krugman published research on brain wave activity involved in viewing commercials.[15] Other researchers experimented with galvanic skin response, facial recognition, voice pitch analysis and pupil dilation methodology—all non-conscious measures of a biologic response that researchers tried to correlate with commercial performance. Many of these early efforts met with disappointing results, usually because of the limitations of the technology that was used at the time. Recently, with the development of better technology, there has been a resurgence of interest in these types of measures, such as using fMRI scanners to visualize brain activity during the commercial viewing experience.[16]

Theoretical developments in cognitive psychology have lead the evolution of advertising theory. Since the '50s, the standard model of how advertising works was called the AIDA model—the idea being that advertising first has to get Attention, then generate Interest and Desire before leading to a consumer Action. The mental processing was presumed to follow a linear "hierarchy of effects:" Learn-Feel-Do. This learning model supported the belief in recall testing since recall testing is the usual way in school of testing whether or not you've learned what you've been taught. Challenging this paradigm, however, was experimental data that frequently showed that attitude changes toward a brand were larger among respondents who could recognize an ad than respondents who recall an ad.

Scientific findings about the differences between the left side of the brain versus the right side of the brain attracted the attention of many ad researchers in the 1980s who felt that most quantitative advertising research was too left-brain focused. The processing of the left side of the brain is logical, analytical and verbal; the processing of the right side is nonlinear, synthetic and more closely tied to our visual and musical perceptions. The right side of the brain is generally considered the more creative half—and so many creatives and some researchers questioned whether verbal-based research methods such as recall provided a fair test of the emotional imagery of advertising.

Different ads work in different ways, depending on the job the ad has to do. Some ads are designed to make you think, for example about the advantages of a new product's features and benefits. Other ads are designed to make you feel, such as the high-image advertising of Coke or Pepsi. The hierarchy of effects model needed to be revised, it was argued, to include alternative paths for describing how the mind processes advertising. For example, the do-feel-do model suggests that high-image ads work by reinforcing consumption behavior through emotional association with the brand, without teaching anything new about the product.

Taking this one step further, some researchers argued that some brand categories are more *involving* than others. For example, automobile advertising is high involvement because of the amount of time and energy you would be willing to invest in researching different brands before buying a new car. Household products such as detergent would be low involvement because once you've had a successful brand experience you probably don't want to spend any more time or energy looking for something better—it's a category you simply don't want to think about. The kind of advertising needed to sell a car, therefore, is likely to be quite different from the kind of advertising needed to sell detergent—and, so it was argued, the kind of research needed to measure it.

At the end of the seventies Vaughn put together these ideas in the FCB planning model, which is a grid consisting of four different assumptions about the consumer's information processing. The two dimensions of the quadrant are thinking/feeling and high involvement/low involvement. The thinking-high involvement quadrant is the one representing the classical learn-feel-do of cognition—the kind of advertising most accessible to traditional, verbal based methods. The other three quadrants represent other kinds of advertising processing and called for the development of new research approaches.

Another theoretical approach to describing consumer information processing was represented by researchers like Rossiter and Percy who, in the 1990s, developed a different version of a planning grid. On their grid, one dimension was again high/low involvement, but the other was the kind of motivation that drives consumer purchases in different product categories—positive/approach motivations (e.g., to obtain good taste) versus negative/avoidance motivations (e.g., to avoid a headache.)

A related approach described by Hansen at about the same time posits two paths of information processing—central processing and peripheral processing. Central processing represents the traditional view of advertising and focuses on product-relevant information, recall, brand awareness, and brand preference. Peripheral processing concerns itself with how the commercial looks and sounds, the emotions generated by stories, and, in general, the aesthetics of the advertising. In this theoretical framework, a distinction between ad recall and ad recognition becomes important because recognition, not recall, is key to probing the peripheral path to advertising effectiveness.

Low involvement processing is largely below the level of consciousness. Many influential writers in the past decade, such as the neuroscientist Antonio Damasio, the journalist Malcolm Gladwell, and the Harvard Professor Gerald Zaltman, have taught ad researchers that emotions actually operate at an unconscious level, and are experienced indirectly through their mental representation as feelings, which may themselves be conscious or unconscious. Traditional word-based copytesting techniques can probe only those feelings that the consumer herself becomes aware of and can talk about—while much of the problem of how the mind of the consumer processes advertising remains to be explored with new tools and techniques.

Development of Moment-by-Moment Measures

One of the essential aspects of watching a television commercial is that it is a temporal experience—it's an unfolding of a sequence of ideas and emotions that takes place over time, in thirty seconds, or perhaps fifteen. From this research perspective, watching a television commercial is an event. Understanding the internal structure of that viewing event requires a very different approach to measurement.

The shift in analytic perspective from thinking of a commercial as the fundamental unit of measurement, a holistic and unified esthetic experience, to be rated in its entirety, to thinking of it in terms as a structured flow of experience gave rise to experimentation with moment-by-moment systems in the early eighties. As an analogy, this transition in thinking is similar in some respects to the ways in which quantum physicists struggled to define the nature of light: is it a particle or is it a wave? Effectiveness measures such as recall or persuasion take a particle view of advertising; the moment-by-moment diagnostics implied a wave view of the advertising experience. And like the theoretical resolution of modern physics, advertising researchers are now beginning to acknowledge the fundamentally dual nature of advertising.

In the 1980s, a number of firms commercialized moment-by-moment dial-a-meter response to television commercials. MSW and Millward Brown used a dial meter methodology to trace a one-dimensional response function of consumer liking or interest in different moments in the ad. While relatively little quantitative data has been published to validate the relationships between these dial meter systems and the general report card measures of attention, branding, or motivation, anecdotal evidence suggests this diagnostic technique can be a useful tool in the hands of a skilled interpreter.

A different approach to probing response to advertising film was developed more recently by Ameritest. The Ameritest Picture Sorts® uses a frame-by-frame recognition approach to deconstructing a viewer's dynamic response to the film on multiple levels. The Flow of Attention, one of three sorts, measures how the eye pre-consciously filters the visual information in an ad and serves both as a gate-keeper for human consciousness and as an interactive search engine involved in the co-creative process of constructing brand perceptions. The focus of analysis is on understanding the role of film structure and syntax in creating those powerful film experiences that can provide the basis for the consumer's emotional relationship with the brand. An example of a Flow of Attention for one particular ad is shown below.

Internet-friendly and therefore more mainstream than the biological measures, the Picture Sorts has been used around the world by major advertisers as diverse as IBM and Unilever in their standard pre-testing process. The strength of the diagnostic relationship between the different "flow" measures and all the major report card measures produced by other pre-testing systems has been validated in a series of publications in the last few years.[17–22]

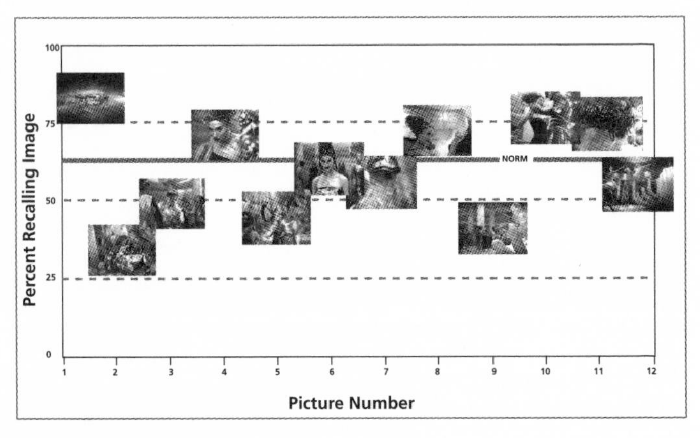

The Flow of Attention

FUTURE TRENDS

The state-of-the-art, circa the beginning of the twenty-first century, has been described. Looking backward for the past fifty years, we see that the art and science of measuring advertising has undergone a considerable amount of debate and change in our thinking and in our business practices. Looking around at the forces of change operating in our world today, there is no reason to think that the rate of change will slow down. The following are seven trends that will shape the way we do business in the future.

1. The emergence of global research standards for advertising global brands.

Increasingly, multi-nationals are focusing on the need to build global brands, and for their brands to speak with one voice around the world. This calls for global advertising campaigns that will be increasingly visual in style. Deploying global research systems to provide a standard way to measure advertising performance from one region to another, and for providing tools for making transparent how different cultural factors affect advertising response, will become an important management focus for managing ad spending in the global marketplace.

2. There will be more advertising measurement, not less.

Advertising is becoming more expensive and the range of executional options have become so diverse that more control over the process is being demanded by major advertisers. Procurement departments, in particular, under the banner of accountability, are challenging advertising agencies and research companies to provide more proof of value to justify ad budgets. This will drive growth in this important sector of advertising research.

3. Pre-testing will be Less Television-Centric

While the bulk of the advertising investment today continues to be in Television, clients are increasingly interested in optimizing the mix of different media, from print to outdoor to direct-response to the web. As a consequence more research will be conducted to measure the relative strengths and weaknesses of different creative elements—with an emphasis on understanding how the different parts of an integrated marketing campaign interact to create a total brand impression.

4. The new value proposition will be filtering plus optimization.

For the foreseeable future, the cost of advertising executions will continue to go up. To manage that cost, managers will be increasingly concerned to make sure not only that they air their strongest ideas, but that they don't spend half their advertising budgets on average ideas. Ad managers will be looking for every opportunity to make executions work harder and research systems will outperform this growing category if they can validate the power of their diagnostics, providing proof that they actually help make ads more effective.

5. Ad research will move beyond semantics, putting a new emphasis on non-verbal measurement.

Both the forces of globalization and the evolution of rich, multi-sensory media environments will continue to challenge researchers to think beyond the boundaries of language and semantics in understanding how advertising builds brand image. New learnings from neuroscientists over the last few years have challenged us to develop new methods and approaches to understanding the hidden responses of the mind.

6. New heuristic models will be built to help managers make ad decisions in a world increasingly confused by media fragmentation.

As the world of media becomes increasingly fragmented and media choices proliferate, the need for research is to simplify the decision-making process for advertising managers. This calls for new heuristics that describe how different media work, e.g., television versus print. These heuristics are necessary to provide a common measurement framework so that advertising managers trying to allocate budgets across television or print or the Internet can compare the relative strengths of the television execution to the print execution to the Internet ad.

7. New mathematical approaches will be developed to model advertising effects.

Currently, researchers working in the field of complexity and chaos theory have been revolutionizing approaches to studying complex, messy problems such as the seemingly random behavior of financial markets or the complex flows of industrial supply chains. A world center for this activity, the Santa Fe Institute in New Mexico, provides numerous examples of new dynamic, non-linear approaches to building computer models that move well beyond the predictive power of the traditional linear approach of regression modeling. (See www.santafe.edu.) Up to now, few efforts have been made by advertising researchers to apply these mathematical techniques to advertising measurement—the very definition of a non-linear problem. But it's only a matter of time.

II

Advertising Models

II

Advertising Models

A wise old researcher once explained that a market researcher has two jobs: first, to learn something useful that your clients didn't know before; and second, to teach them what you found out. Over time, researchers learn that the second job is the harder of the two. It is also the more important because it is the key to making sure that the research you do actually gets used.

This is particularly true of advertising pre-testing. No form of research is more fraught with barriers to learning. The issues raised by testing generate high anxiety for everyone around the conference room table having a vested interest in the advertising.

Confusion and anxiety do not, as a rule, form an ideal emotional climate for the learning process. Clarity and calmness are required.

How do we move beyond these limitations and become the teachers our clients need us to be? We must begin with a shared mental model.

To borrow from Peter Senge's well-known book on learning organizations, *The Fifth Discipline*: "The effectiveness of a leader is related to the continual improvement of the leader's mental models." In other words, the decisions your clients make based on pre-testing research are as much a function of the mental models they have about how advertising works as they are of the information that you provide them.

The next time you are in a meeting where a new piece of advertising is being discussed, sit back and ask yourself, "How much of this discussion is actually about the particular ad under consideration, and how much of this is a debate about how advertising works in general?" Much of the discussion will probably be about the various mental models everyone has about advertising. That's a barrier to learning and effective decision making.

TELEVISION

First, let's remember *why* so many professionals have different mental models of advertising.

Dating back to the early days of television, the first widely used pre-testing measure was Burke's Day After *Recall* Score. This model held that the key to effectiveness is that an ad should leave some kind of trace in the memory of the consumer.

Unfortunately, after many years of empirically trying to correlate recall scores with sales results, a number of advertisers, such as Proctor and Gamble, concluded that recall was missing something important. So, researchers searched for something else to predict sales. In the seventies, pre-testing research shifted its focus to measuring *motivation*, such as the Advertising Research Systems Corporation's (ARS) measure of persuasion.

In the eighties, another pre-testing company, ASI, found that recall could be better understood when its two component variables were separated: the *attention-getting* power of the commercial execution and the *linkage between the brand* and the commercial.

Meanwhile, other researchers argued that how well a commercial was liked was key—a result empirically confirmed by a famous Advertising Research Foundation validity study.

Most researchers also agreed that *communication* of a strategic selling proposition was the key to effective advertising, a point of view that continues to sell a great many focus groups to this day.

Creatives, who appear to have different mental models of advertising than Researchers, have always intuitively felt that the *entertainment* value of a television commercial is paramount; that it's important to be fresh and different in order to stand apart from the crowd.

What about *emotion*? Emotion sells. Advertising agencies, like the Leo Burnett agency, developed complex methods of coding and analyzing the verbatims from open-ended questions and constructed batteries of diagnostic ratings statements to profile viewer response to commercials on multiple dimensions of both rational and emotional response.

And finally, a number of researchers believe that pre-testing shouldn't just be *copy*-testing, which is what this type of research has historically been called. After all, we are attempting to describe the consumer's tele-*vision* experience. These researchers experiment with *non-verbal* techniques: brain waves, skin galvanic response, voice pitch analysis, and picture sorts.

So the debate goes on to this day. No wonder Clients are confused and creatives are skeptical!

A Model for Television Advertising Pre-testing

Is the real question, "Which of the above measurements is the correct one?" Consider this: many smart people have been working on this problem for years and each theory is probably right to some degree. From a learning standpoint, the real problem may be one of synthesis and interpretation.

If the goal is to make smarter decisions about advertising, so that the brand will become a leader in its business category, then ask yourself, "How do I fit these different ways of measuring the advertising experience together into a more *complete* and *intuitive* description of the advertising?"

Our answer to this question is the following advertising model.

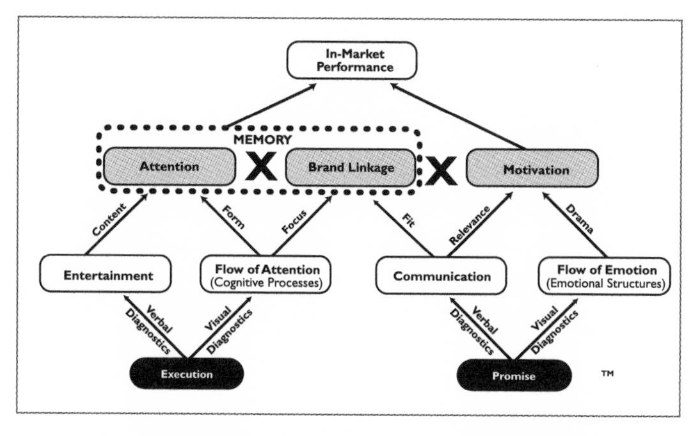

Ameritest's heuristic Television Advertising Model.

This is a *heuristic* model or teaching model. The purpose of the model is to focus attention on learning *how* and *why* an ad is working, with the goal of improving understanding and aiding judgment. The model organizes all the questions asked by earlier theories in order to provide us with a complete picture of how to fit together all the different dimensions of performance that modern ad researchers usually attempt to measure.

In the model, information is arranged in a hierarchy that bridges the divide of report card systems provided by some ad researchers and the diagnostic systems provided by others.

At the top is what pre-testing is supposed to predict: in-market results.

One level down are the *evaluative* measures that provide the "report card" portion of the research. These are the measures that are used to make the go/no go decision. Taken together, they answer the question, "Is this advertising good enough to put on air?"

Two levels down are the "diagnostic" measures that are correlated with, and therefore *explain*, the evaluative measures above. These are the measures that can be used to optimize the advertising. They answer the question, "How could I improve this ad?"

The arrows in the model highlight the primary relationships between the different variables measured. This is a road map for interpreting the data.

Essentially, the model says that for any commercial to be effective it must accomplish three things:

1. It must get noticed and attract an audience.
2. The audience must know who is sending the advertising message.
3. Once the commercial has the audience's attention; it must "sell" them something—i.e., drive sales in the short run or at least create a positive predisposition for sales in the long run.

Other variables are important only insofar as they help to explain the variables of Attention, Brand Linkage and Motivation. For example, entertainment value or the originality of the

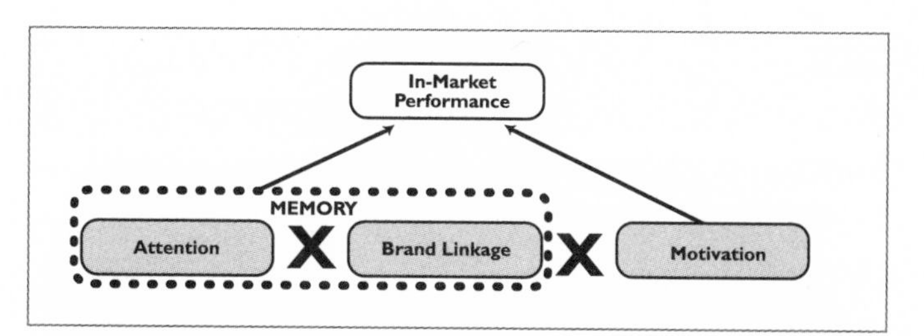

Evaluative variables are at the top of the heuristic ad model.

execution is not important in and of itself but because it is a predictor of Attention.

The same is true of liking. On the face of it, it may be possible for a commercial to be not well liked and still be effective. Wisk's famously irritating classic, "Ring Around the Collar" campaign is a widely mentioned example. Getting into the conscious mind of the consumer and selling the brand is always the bottom line for advertising!

Diagnostics

The model shows us that Attention is a function of two primary aspects of the execution:

1. Entertainment: Does the execution entertain or reward viewers with an enjoyable or engaging and unique experience in return for the 15 or 30 seconds that they are asked to spend with your client's message?

2. Flow of Attention is the execution a well-edited piece of film in terms of structure and syntax that captures and maintains the

viewer's attention over time, focusing her thoughts and feelings on the important ideas and images in the commercial at a pace she can easily keep up with?

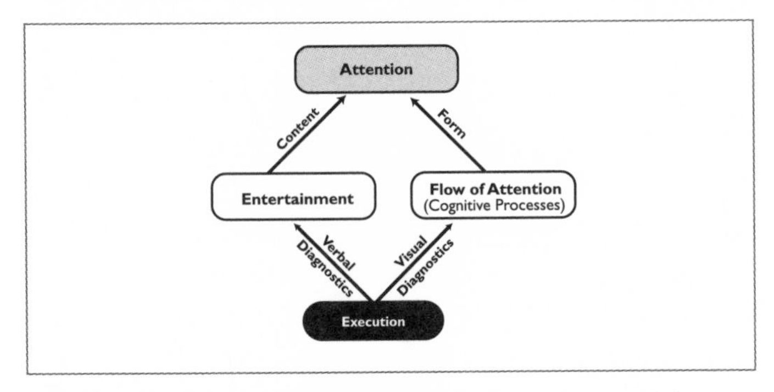

The Attention component of the heuristic model is about form and content.

Branding is a function of two other constructs:

1. Focus: At some point in the film does the execution focus your attention on the brand being advertised?
2. Fit: How well does the execution fit the

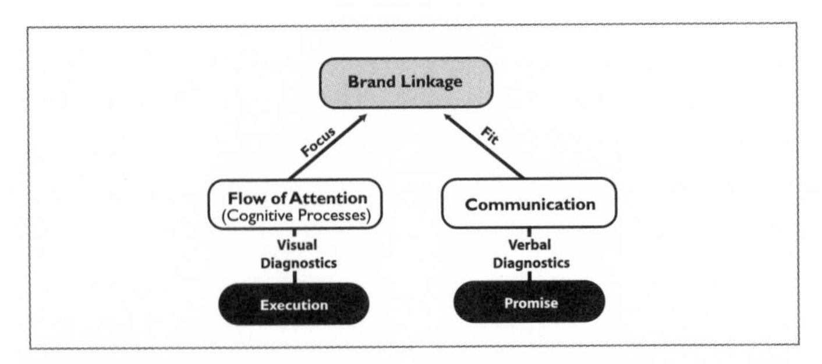

The Brand Linkage component of the heuristic model is about focus and fit.

perception of the brand that the consumer already has?

Motivation is also a function of two separate constructs:

1. Communication: How relevant, believable and brand differentiating is the strategic promise you are communicating to your customer?

2. Flow of Emotion: How much emotion have you tapped into with the power of film to make your brand's promise seem "larger than life" and even more compelling?

In short, the key to Motivation is communicating a relevant idea in a dramatic way.

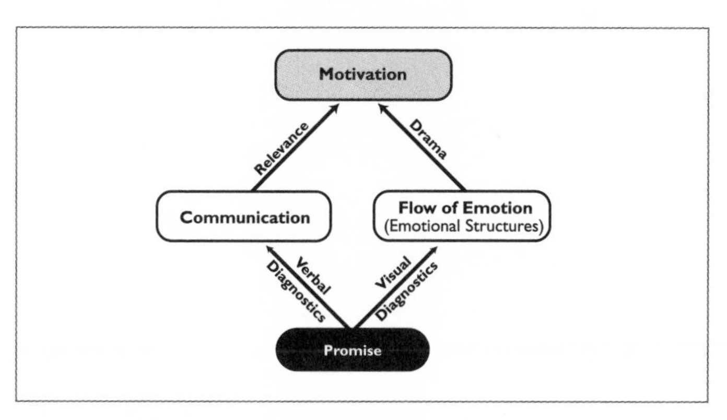

The Motivation component of the heuristic model is about relevance and drama.

Print/Outdoor/Newspaper

While there are no formulas for effective advertising, there are general principles that need to be taken into account when trying to penetrate the mind with effective selling ideas.

It's important not to think of print ads as static simply because they don't have temporal dimensions like TV commercials. Although a print ad doesn't move, the consumer's mind must move through the ad to create an effective advertising experience. Researchers need to help clients think of print in a more dynamic way.

Just as with television advertising, remember that the human eye is not a camera, or a passive recorder of stimuli. Instead, think of the eye as an intelligent search engine, an active gate-keeper for the mind. A large part of the human brain is devoted to creating what we call *visual perception*. That is why a measurement of what the eye sees is an incomplete understanding of what the conscious mind of the reader *constructs* from the images and ideas in the ad. So, from a diagnostic standpoint, you need a dynamic way of measuring how the mind is processing an advertisement.

Metaphors help us think clearly about complex subjects. A useful metaphor is to think of a print ad as kind of a virtual store, where the consumer is "shopping information."

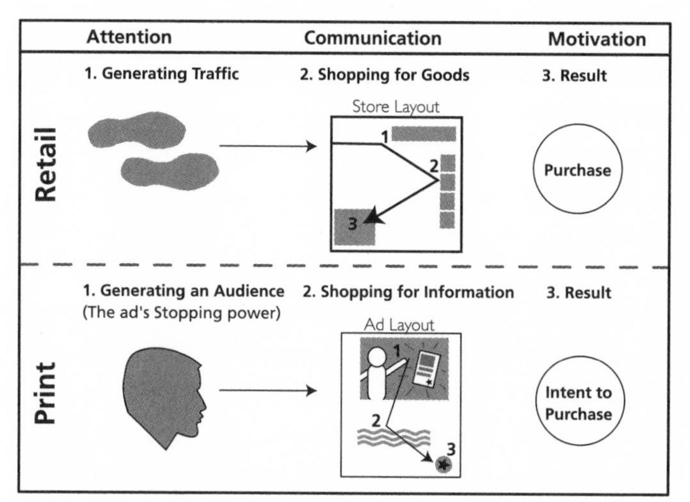

The Retail Metaphor: Parallels between print advertising and the retail in-store environment.

If you were the manager of a store, there would be three things you would try to do to build your business:

1. Get customers through the door by using attention-getting devices to generate traffic to the store;

2. Plan the layout of your store very carefully so customers can find what they are looking for and discover something while browsing;

3. Make sure you have closed the sale and motivate them to buy something before leaving.

These same general principles apply when you analyze a print ad. Ask yourself:

1. Is there a clear entry point to the ad where the majority of readers start their journey?

2. Is the path through the ideas and images

clear and easy to follow in a continuous sequence so the reader has a cohesive advertising experience?

3. Does the reader have a unique selling idea or clear brand image in their mental shopping basket before they get to your brand "checkout counter," i.e., your logo?

Print is a more active medium than TV in the sense that more work is required from the audience in processing the information in the ad. Because of this potentially higher level of involvement from readers of print ads, it is possible to transmit more complex messages in a print ad than a TV ad. However, we also know that readers are quite frugal with the time they will spend with advertising messages.

Importantly, most of what we need to measure about print advertising is very similar to what needs to be measured for a TV commercial. Attention-getting power is important for both kinds of advertising. Both print and TV ads need to be well branded to be effective. And both must motivate a sale. Indeed, we only need to change one variable in our TV model to have a model for print—the cognitive measure of the Flow of Attention.

Television and print are different in two important ways: First, the order in which readers process the ideas and images and second, the amount of time readers spend with the ad are both under the control of the audi-

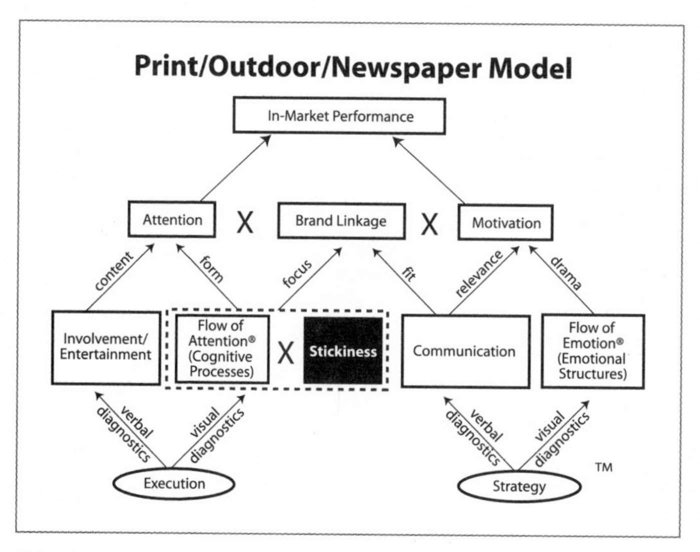

The Print/Outdoor/Newspaper Model.

ence for print, but not for TV. For example, one reader may start with the headline, while another starts with the main visual. And one reader may spend ten seconds looking at the ad, while another flips the page after a half-second glance. To reflect these differences between the two mediums, the print model needs a different measurement of Flow of Attention, and a measure of "stickiness" which tells us how much time the reader would spend with the ad in the real world environment.

For print, the construct of Flow of Attention introduces "time into space;" the inverse operation of the technique used in TV which "freezes time" so that we can study the level of audience attention at different moments in the ad.

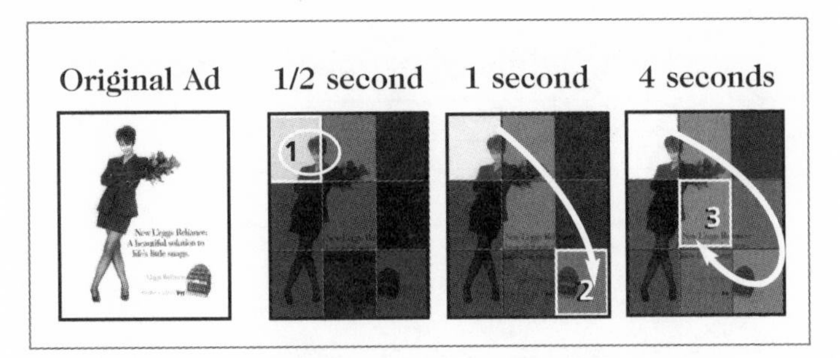

Print Flow of Attention. The trajectory of the mind through this ad is from her face (1) to the product (2) to the headline (3).

From an integrated marketing standpoint, the use of a similar model for TV and print leads to considerable efficiencies. By using a common measurement framework, researchers can compare TV test results with print test results in the same report.

DIRECT RESPONSE

By reputation, direct response is the most accountable of the advertising forms because you can accurately measure the response rate after an ad has run. By comparing the response rates for different executions, it is relatively straightforward to create a closed feedback loop for continuously improving direct response campaigns over time. For that reason, unlike TV or print advertisers, direct response marketers have historically made little use of pre-testing research.

However, this has begun to change. More

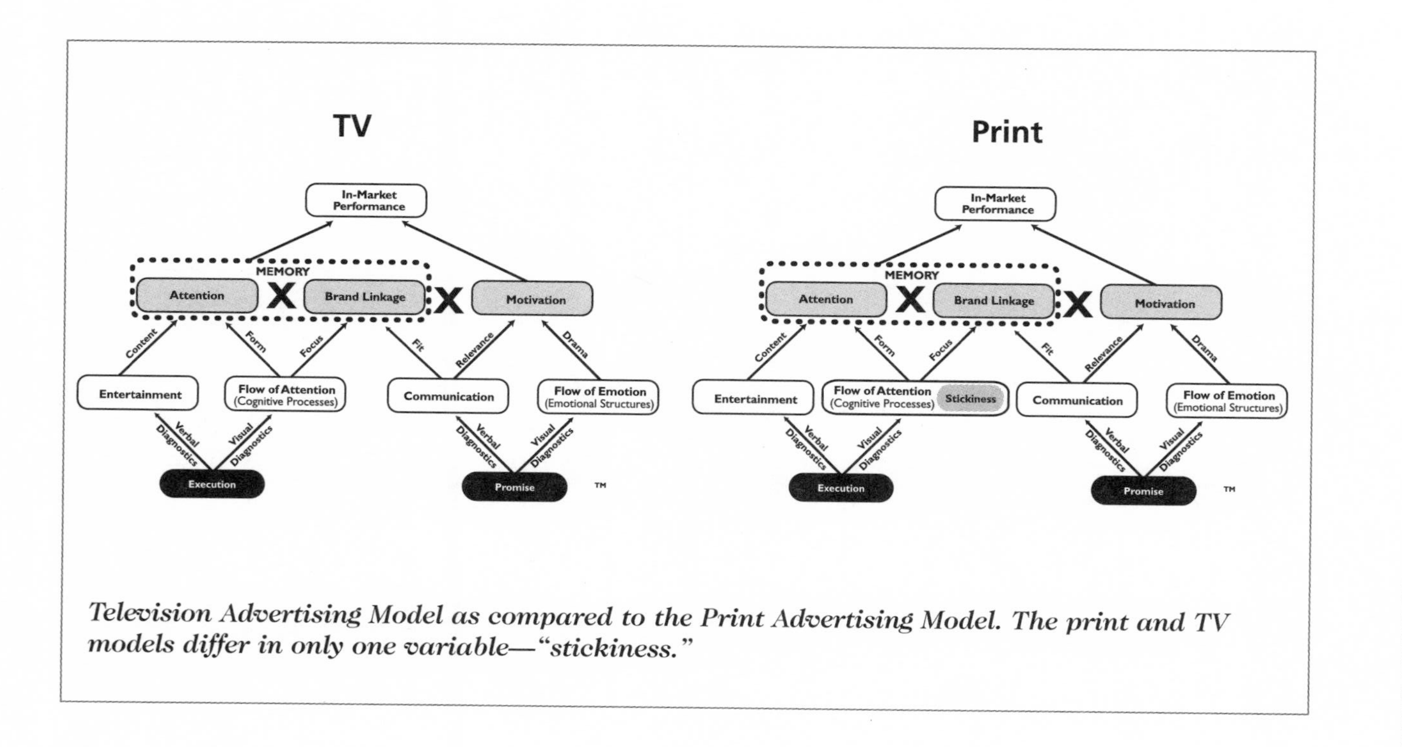

Television Advertising Model as compared to the Print Advertising Model. The print and TV models differ in only one variable—"stickiness."

sophisticated advertisers have realized the value of obtaining diagnostic research in advance, for the purpose of optimizing executions before the budget is spent. Research has shown it is important to know not only which of two mailings has the greater selling power, but to know the reasons why.

In addition, pre-testing research can provide value by helping the advertising manager synchronize the creative elements of direct response with the other elements of an integrated ad campaign.

Direct response, whether it be television or print based, is different from the more general type of advertising in one important respect. It is expected to trigger a behavioral response from the consumer right away (or at least within a very short period of time) rather than be stored in the consumer's memory in order to enhance sales of the brand at some point in the future.

Indeed, the consumer's behavioral response may be engaged from the very beginning of the interaction with one type of direct response—direct mail. When you sort through your mail, what is it that causes you to open one unsolicited piece of mail, while you toss others unopened into the trash? Is it the gold lettering, the high quality of the paper? Is it the personalized address? Are you more, or less, likely to open an envelope addressed to "resident?" Or is it the brand logo on the envelope? Are you more likely to open a piece you receive from American Express than one you receive from the Acme Loan Company? In any event, attention-getting power and branding are still relevant constructs of interest to the direct response researcher.

But from a pre-testing standpoint, the essential difference that describes direct response advertising can be captured by our basic ad model by adding a qualifying variable to Motivation: the *call to action*. Call to Action defines the specific response that the advertising is designed to evoke. For example, calling an 800 number is usually a higher level of commitment on the part of the consumer than is elicited by most advertising in general.

To achieve this commitment, direct response is usually very promotional in its communications, e.g., "We are making a special offer!" In addition, direct response ads are frequently designed to define a time period for action, e.g., "The special offer ends Sunday!" The purpose of these messaging strategies is to impact consumer emotions in a particular way by creating a *sense of urgency* that drives the call to action. Of course, more sophisticated users of direct response can deploy emotion in negative as well as positive ways to create the sense of urgency. One way is to raise the level of concern about some problem, e.g., "Do you have these symptoms…?" which creates stressful emotional anxiety that is resolved when the consumer responds by taking the prescribed action.

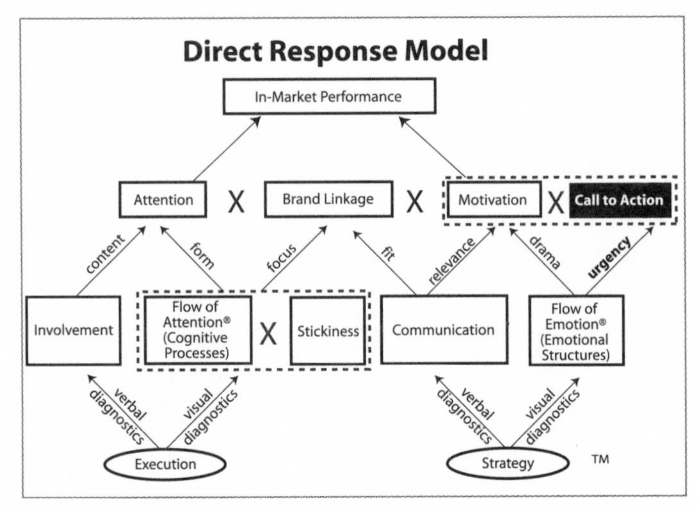

The Direct Response Model. A call to action is an important variable.

Web

Web advertising, with all the degrees of creative freedom the Internet provides, is chameleon-like in that it is able to emulate any of the other types of media. Like TV commercials, Web ads use moving images and visual novelty to attract attention. Like print, Web ads try to engage consumer interest while consumers are reading. Like direct response ads, Web ads call for an immediate action—just click on the image!

A Web ad is a barker who stands by the entrance to the carnival tent and solicits customers with loud, colorful sales talk. The first click-through is actually part of the attention-getting function of advertising. It is the first hesitant decision the consumer makes to engage with the advertiser, which is really no different than the decision to open unsolicited mail.

Once the consumer clicks through the door of the ad to the advertiser's video or website, the consumer finds he is in another ad or a virtual store. Here, the friendly, sticky salesman must keep communicating to keep the consumer engaged, inviting the consumer to browse through information until he finds something he likes and motivates him to go to

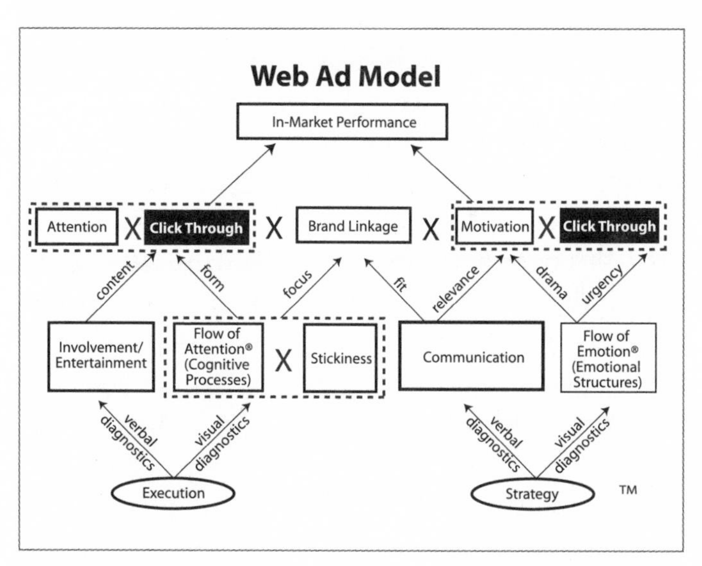

The Web Model. Click through is a new variable for Web ads.

the virtual check-out counter to click again, either to a destination website or perhaps on the "purchase now" button.

With the Internet, the boundary between advertising and in-store or point-of-purchase communication has dissolved. The ad model above provides a road-map of all the variables the researcher needs to take into account in order to plot the path of the consumer's mind from attention all the way through to the second click.

To describe that path from a diagnostic standpoint, the Internet ad researcher may need to use all the tools in the toolkits developed for other media. The exhibit below shows you some parallel techniques Ameritest has developed to measure how the attention of the consumer flows: first, through moving images, second, through lines of copy and third, through graphic layouts. What these three techniques have in common is an appreciation for the cognitive processes of the mind. In particular, the consumer is not—and never has been—a passive receiver of brand communications, but is always actively engaged in googling the ideas and information in advertising.

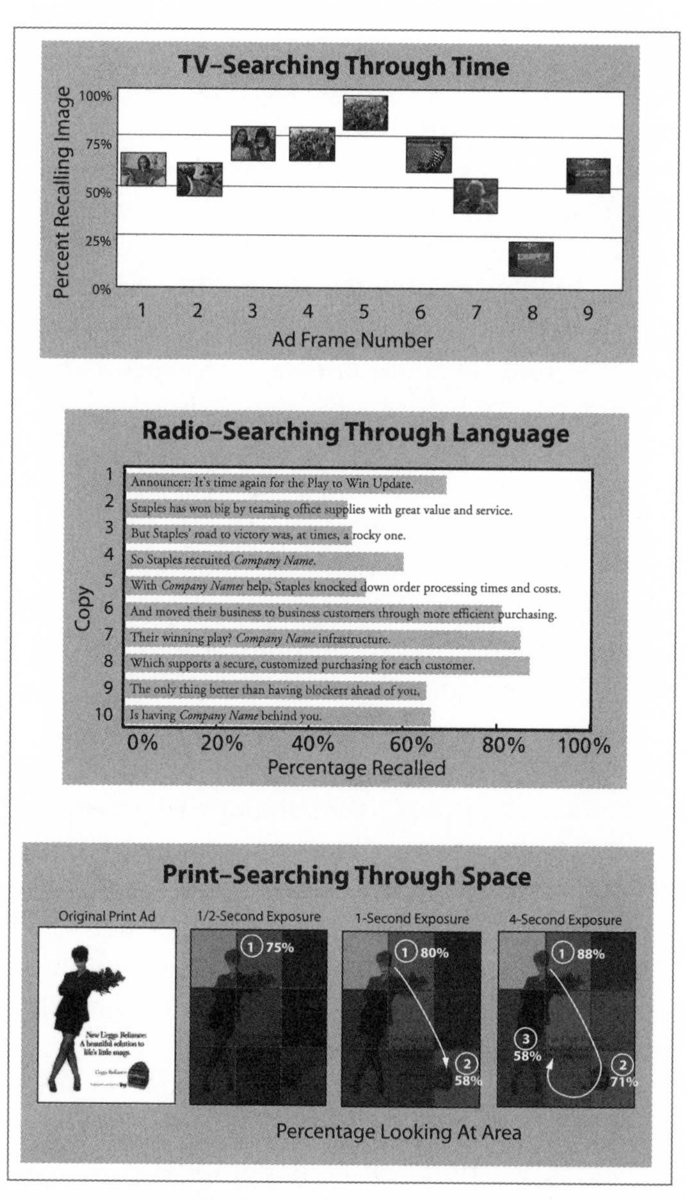

Three parallel techniques for measuring Flow of Attention through film, copy and images.

Packaging

There is an old saying in the packaged goods business that "the package is the last ad the consumer sees before buying the product." Unfortunately, most ad researchers seem to consider packaging research to be almost a separate, highly specialized discipline. Yet all of the constructs we have been talking about apply equally well to effective package design as they do other forms of advertising.

In terms of risk, getting the package wrong can be extremely costly. The reason for this speaks to the essence of what is special about the package-as-advertising. Unlike other forms of advertising that may simply create an enhanced intention to purchase the brand, the package must actually close the sale!

From a communication standpoint, a package needs to systematically remove all the barriers to purchase that make the consumer hesitate. It must provide a point-by-point argument about why it's better than the competitor's product that is sitting beside it on the shelf. And it must do this in the most emotionally appealing way in order to drive home the impulse to purchase.

Because of the media constraints of other forms of advertising such as TV—what you can reasonably hope to accomplish in 30 seconds—a tight focus on one clear idea may be the best practice. But when the consumer is holding the package in her hands, trying to decide between your brand and a competitor, it's best to cover your bets. The package needs to communicate all the advantages of the product.

The need for multiple points of communication does not mean package designs should be cluttered or confusing. Quite the opposite. The information on a package should be easy to find. That means the order in which the consumer "sees" the information on the package should match the order of importance in order to help make the sale, with the most important information standing out first in the consumer's perceptions.

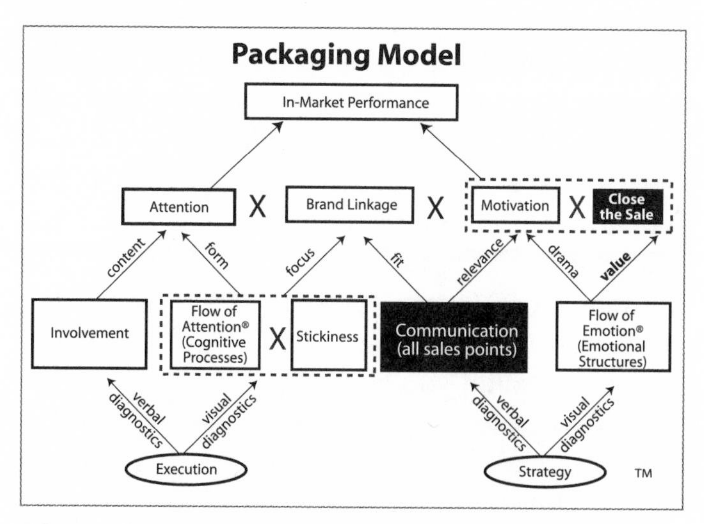

The Packaging Model. The package must communicate all relevant sales points to close the sale.

MODELING AN INTEGRATED CAMPAIGN: BREADTH AND DEPTH

The traditional way of making media allocation decisions is to trade off reach versus frequency in the media buy. This is still the standard approach to thinking about programming advertising exposures. It also provides us with a useful conceptual framework for thinking about how consumers are engaged by different creative executions across an integrated advertising campaign.

Even though the different elements in a campaign are designed to work together, that does not mean that all the creative executions will work equally well. Consider the scenario shown below where the motivation scores (using standard top box purchase-intent scores) for creative elements from two alternate campaigns are being compared. In this hypothetical example, the TV commercial from Campaign 1 is significantly more motivating than the TV from Campaign 2; on the other hand, the print and outdoor from Campaign 2 is more motivating than the creative from Campaign 1. Which campaign would you choose?

A key question to ask when testing creative elements across media platforms is whether or not the different pieces of creative are motivating to the same consumer segments. In this example, we might ask the question, "How many consumers were motivated by at least

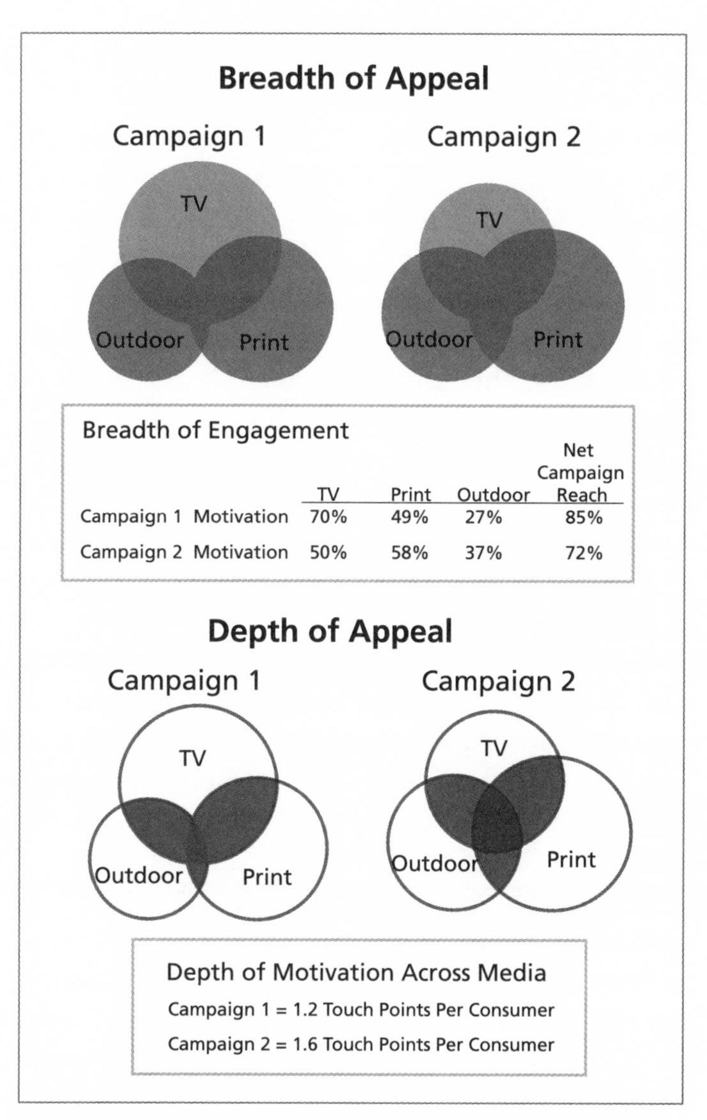

The media concepts of "reach" and "frequency" can be modified to fit motivation scores.

one execution in the campaign?" The answer is the union of the sets of consumers motivated by different elements in the campaign. We see that Campaign 1 has more "breadth" of appeal, 85% to 72%. What if, on the other hand, we were to ask the question, "On average, how many different executions impact a given target consumer in a motivating way?" The answer is the intersection of the sets of consumers motivated by different elements of the campaign. Now we see that Campaign 2 wins, with an average of 1.6 versus 1.2, of what we call "motivational touchpoints" or motivating ads per consumer. So we can say that Campaign 2 has greater "depth" of appeal.

This example makes several important points about campaign testing. First, it points out the importance of using standard measures of key performance across different media, so that the relative impact of the creative can be compared. This is one reason the adoption of an integrated set of media models is so useful. Second, it underscores the importance of diagnostics. In this case, either campaign choice is like a wobbly stool—one of the media legs supporting each of the campaign ideas was suboptimal. From a diagnostic standpoint, the question for Campaign 1 is, "Can I fix the print and outdoor to make them work harder in support of the TV?" The question for Campaign 2 is, "Can I re-edit the TV film to make it work harder with the print and outdoor idea?" Hence, we see the importance of diagnostic measures for different media creative elements.

Finally, it reminds us that in this new age of exploding media choices there is the fundamental need to view advertising holistically. And if this is to happen, advertising research needs an integrated testing approach.

III

Pre-testing: A Review of Report Card Measures from Different Systems

III
Pre-testing: A Review of Report Card Measures from Different Systems

While most of the major research providers today agree that attention-getting power, branding, and motivation are all critical components of advertising effectiveness, each approaches the problem of how to measure these theoretical constructs somewhat differently.

In this chapter we will provide an overview of the various methods used to measure each of these constructs. We have attempted to summarize the major differences between methods. At the end of this book we also provide a list of journal articles providing quantitative evidence in support of the various arguments different suppliers make in favor of each of the different approaches. While we have a preference for our own approach, we also believe that other approaches have merit and may represent a piece of the total "truth" of advertising. Consequently, we have attempted to be as fair as possible in our description of the objective differences between systems.

We cannot, of course, describe every pre-testing system available in the market since there are so many. Those reviewed here were selected because they represent the leaders in the industry, and together account for perhaps as much as 70% of the television pre-testing category.

Unfortunately, while the medium is older, the theory of testing print advertising is much more fragmented and less well-developed. Unlike television, there is no dominant approach to testing print, though various approaches to eye-tracking—Perception Research offline, or the Ameritest online approach—are among the most favored. For that reason we have chosen to omit a review of the print testing systems and instead simply focus on television.

Advertising research is a continually evolving business, particularly when everyone is attempting to adjust their methods to new media technology. Moreover, as the other research suppliers we reference here are our competitors, we may simply not be aware of the latest developments in their systems. We assume, therefore, that as potential buyers of pre-testing research, anyone reading this book would do their homework in contacting these companies for additional details and updates.

We leave the conclusion to the reader as to which is the best approach to measuring each dimension of advertising performance.

ATTENTION AND RECALL

Most pre-testing systems report some kind of measure of "breakthrough," either recall or attention, as an indicator of how efficiently a commercial execution will leverage a given level of media weight to capture a wide audience for the advertiser's message.

Even though they are both considered measures of breakthrough by users of the different systems, published research confirms that recall and attention measure fundamentally different aspects of commercial performance. Our own research suggests that recall is a measure of teaching—how effective a commercial is if you simply view it as a sales presentation of product information or product "news." Attention, even when measured in a variety of different ways, is a better measure of intrusiveness or breakthrough, rewarding executions that are interesting, involving, and unique—critical dimensions of performance in this new age of permission-based marketing.

Undoubtedly, recall is an appropriate measure for certain advertising applications. However, it appears to reward only one kind of advertising; ads where the brand is cued early and often and the focus is on communicating rational product features and benefits—i.e., ads that have a linear, rational structure.

Our experience is that advertising can work in more than one way and some of these other ways may be more appropriate when you are attempting to differentiate your brand based on emotional, rather than rational, consumer benefits.

Moreover, the various systems measure even the same constructs differently. In measuring recall, for example, different systems employ different periods of forgetting time: the original Burke, and later, the Ipsos-ASI systems give the consumer 24 hours to forget the advertising before calling them back, while ARS allows 72 hours of forgetting time. The original Burke system exposed the test ad "on air" to obtain results as close to the real world as possible, while for a variety of reasons Ipsos-ASI mails respondents a videotape which they can watch at home. ARS exposes ads in a theater setting with a large group of respondents at a time. These kinds of practical differences can affect the direct comparability of measures from different systems even if they all claim to be measuring recall.

One of the main philosophical differences between systems is whether or not the test ad should be embedded in a program environment so that the ad has to compete for attention against other advertising during breaks within a simulated television show.

The chief argument in favor of this approach is that context affects communication, and by simulating the programming context the test is more like the real world. Interestingly, the argument against this approach is that context is such a powerful and unpredictable variable that we should be cautious about introducing it into the measurement. A given commercial may be strongly helped by appearing in the context of a comedy show, while it may by penalized by appearing in the context of a drama. Another commercial may do well in a drama, but not in a comedy. By not simulating all possible programming effects in some randomized order, systems that use program environments run the risk of introducing a bias into the measurement that affects the test ad in an unpredictable way, favoring some while penalizing others. Since a pre-test should be a test of the strength of the creative idea and not the media buy, some testing systems prefer taking the standard scientific approach of controlling or eliminating those variables that are not the subject of the measurement.

Another important difference between testing systems is the size of the database of norms that would be available for interpreting test results. Most clients would agree that the most relevant benchmarks for a test ad would be those that are "closest" to the work—either the client's own most recent advertising that has been successful in the marketplace or, perhaps, the current advertising campaign that the competition is running. Norms, however, provide a useful frame of reference for interpreting "how high is up," putting the test data in the context of the best and worst advertising that has been tested over the years.

Most systems will provide norms according to the characteristics of the test execution—for example, providing different norms (and clutter reels) for animatics than for finished film. Commercial length (e.g., :15 vs. :30 vs. :60) is a variable that also appears to affect both recall and attention scores in most—but not all—systems. Typically the longer, more expensive formats are rewarded with higher breakthrough scores.

Obviously, the older the system, the larger the norm base will be. However, the emergence of the Internet as a primary channel of data collection changed the game somewhat, since on-line measurements are not directly comparable to off-line measurement.

Attention (Ameritest)

This is a direct measure of a commercial's ability to win in the street fight for audience attention. The test ad is shown with control ads in a clutter reel environment designed to simulate a commercial "pod" on television. The test ad is embedded in clutter made up of either directly competitive advertising, or ads from non-competing product categories, depending on client preference. After watching the reel, respondents are asked the question, "Which of these ads did you find *interesting*?" If the test ad is spontaneously mentioned as one of the ads the respondent found interesting, that is counted toward the attention score. The same approach is used on-line as well as offline. While this measure is not a memory test of advertising, when combined with the measure of brand linkage it has been found to correlate well with awareness measures from recognition-based in-market tracking studies.

Attention (MSW)

This is a measure of the audience's ability to remember the test ad on an unaided basis after viewing it in a simulated program environment which also contains other control and test ads. While this breakthrough measure is based on a form of memory retrieval, published research suggests that the MSW is not correlated with day after recall scores and therefore is measuring something different. From the published literature, it is not yet known how it correlates with the other measures of attention described here.

Attention (Millward Brown)

This is a derived measure of an ad's ability to gain attention based in equal parts on two variables: 1) how enjoyable the ad is to watch (a rating scale) and 2) how actively the viewer is engaged by the execution (measured from three multiple choice questions). In the offline version, these questions are asked after a "warm-up" clutter reel; in the online version the clutter reel has been dropped. This measure was modeled from MB's extensive database of in-market continuous advertising tracking and generally produces a good fit—hence the name "Link"—with MB measures of advertising awareness.

Attention (Ipsos-ASI)

This measure is collected after an audience has been exposed to test and control commercials embedded in a simulated program environment played in their homes on a videotape. Twenty four hours later, respondents are read de-branded verbal descriptions of the commercials over the telephone and those who remember having seen the commercial are counted toward the Attention score. As a rule of thumb, the Attention score obtained from this form of verbal recognition will be roughly twice the level of the Recall score obtained from the same interview. Because verbal prompts are used for this "recognition" score, this measure generally correlates well with telephone-based measures of advertising awareness from in-market tracking studies.

Recall (Ipsos-ASI)

In this form of recall testing, respondents are sent a videotape containing a simulated program and various control and test commercials and asked to watch it in their home. Respondents are then contacted 24 hours later and asked to recall all the advertising they remember seeing from a series of category and brand prompts. This measure also appears to correlate well with telephone-based measures of ad awareness, though the correlation with actual in-market sales has been debated vigorously over the years.

Recall (ARS)

In this form of recall testing, respondents are invited to a theater, ostensibly to watch a pilot television program, which contains various control and test commercials. Respondents are then contacted 72 hours later and are asked to recall all the advertising they remember seeing from a series of category and brand prompts. (Note: the 72 hour period was selected for this test to calibrate the different levels of recall obtained from theater testing versus the original Burke on-air test which used a 24 hour "day after" forgetting time.) This measure also appears to correlate well with telephone based measures of ad awareness.

Branding

Most pre-testing systems report measures of "branding" or "brand linkage." Not surprisingly, each system defines their "branding" construct using their own proprietary procedures, measures, or operations. And sometimes the measures that are created don't map tightly enough onto the theoretical constructs. For example, the Ipsos-ASI approach described below may be limited by their use of a verbal rather than a visual cue to commercial recognition, a primary component of their branding measure.

We must be careful to recognize that although the same "surface" label is being used, the "deep" constructs being measured are not necessarily equivalent.

In fact, published research suggests that the three approaches used to measure branding are uncorrelated, and therefore different from each other. Each might, in fact, be measuring some important facet of the complex problem of constructing well-branded advertising. The models that have been built to understand each of these branding measures suggest different approaches to achieving a good branding score. The Ipsos ASI approach, for example, suggests an "early and often rule"—showing the brand in the first few seconds of the ad to frame the communication and using brand name repetition to achieve a good branding score. In contrast, the Ameritest approach suggests that only a "single minded branding moment" is required: a peak visual moment somewhere in the commercial—it could be either at the beginning, the middle or even the end—where the attention of the audience is focused clearly on the identity of the brand. The Millward Brown approach suggests the importance of the audio component in achieving well branded advertising. Philosophically, all three approaches to measuring branding appear to have merit.

Brand Linkage (Ameritest)

This measure of branding is also similar to the unaided, or top-of-mind brand awareness measure generated by a traditional advertising tracking study. At the beginning of the interview, respondents are shown a clutter reel of five commercials, including the test commercial. Then the respondent is asked the question "Which of these ads did you find interesting?" If he mentions the test ad as one of the interesting ads, the open-ended response to this question is coded for whether or not the respondent used the brand name. Brand Linkage, then, is the ratio of respondents spontaneously referencing the brand to the total number of respondents who found the ad interesting.

Since the respondent only has to retrieve the brand name from short-term memory, this measure is not really a memory test but rather is a measure of brand salience or how top-of-mind the brand is in being associated with the memory of the ad. Consequently, an appropriate metaphor for understanding this branding construct is that of a *handle* which the consumer uses to hold on to the experience created by well-branded advertising.

Brand Linkage (Ipsos-ASI)

Of the three pre-testing firms represented here, the Ipsos-ASI measure of brand linkage is the only derived measure, calculated from two other primary measures rather than measured directly. It is of particular theoretical interest because the two primary measures are Recall and Recognition. The Ipsos-ASI measure of Brand Linkage is the ratio of Recall to Recognition.

On a conceptual level, the Ipsos-ASI measure attempts to quantify the strength of the connection between two different memory systems where advertising content might be stored. Recall uses category and brand cues to retrieve memories from the semantic memory system. Recognition, by contrast, uses verbal descriptions of the ad to elicit the memory of the advertising from the episodic memory system which is then reported as an Attention score. In metaphorical terms, we might think of this measurement construct as the *bridge* between two memory systems.

Branding (Millward Brown)

This measure of branding is of major interest since it was specifically designed to line up with continuous advertising tracking data. Specifically, Millward Brown uses the mean of a five-point verbal scale ranging from "You couldn't help but remember this commercial is for (brand)" all the way to "It could be a commercial for almost anything."

The idea here is that advertising should avoid being generic. A poor ad is one in which you could substitute any brand in the category and it would remain the same. In contrast, a key diagnostic for this measure is that a well-branded ad is one in which, in open-ended playback, it is impossible for consumers to talk about the ad without talking about the brand. This measure of branding, therefore, is characterized by strong product/narrative integration. In metaphorical terms, we might think of this measurement construct as *tailor-made*. Advertising is like a suit that a brand wears; the well-dressed brand should wear a custom-tailored, "bespoke" suit rather than one ready-made right off the rack.

Motivation and Persuasion

The difference between advertising film and entertainment film is that advertising has to *sell* something. For that reason, almost all pre-testing systems provide some measure of motivation or persuasiveness.

The role of motivation is not to be confused with the role of reason versus emotion in advertising, though it sometimes is. Motivation is not just a function of rational argument or persuasive selling propositions. Football coaches do not usually motivate their players with rational arguments.

Thought and emotion have a role to play in all pieces of advertising. One of the sources of confusion is that the balance between the two changes as the brand evolves over its lifestage.

For that reason, the benchmarks or norms used to interpret motivation scores usually take into account the lifestage of the brand. Most systems, for example, will provide a different normative comparison for new product advertising than for established brand advertising, since new product ads are seen as operating in a different way than established brand ads. New product ads, for example, perform much more of a teaching role, showing the consumer what the brand looks like, how it fits into her world and how it differs from other alternatives in the category. Established brands, in contrast, are more focused on strengthening the loyalty of the relationship with the consumer, typically through emotional appeals rather than rational argument.

As an extension of the lifestage argument, a few companies also posit a third category for normative comparisons, the "power brand." These are brands that are so dominant in their market share—brands like IBM or Intel—that they play the role of leader in their category, trying to hold their category empire together rather than differentiating themselves on the basis of the secondary performance dimensions advertised by niche players.

Motivation (Ameritest)

Ameritest employs standard five-point rating of consumer *intentions* toward the brand after viewing the ad, ranging from "definitely will" to "definitely will not." The wording of the question varies slightly depending on the advertised category: for consumer package goods, the question is purchase intent; for the automotive category, it is purchase consideration; for retail, it is intended store visits; for a media entertainment brand it is intention to view, etc. The motivation score gives the strongest weight to the top box or "definitely will" score. This measure is quite similar to that used by various concept tests or simulated test market systems, like the widely used BASES concept testing system. Because of the placement or location of the motivation question in the Ameritest interview immediately after forced exposure to the test ad, this measure is designed to respond to both the rational and emotional components of advertising. Norms are provided based on the lifestage of the brand—e.g., new products, established brands, "power" brands—as well as the category.

Motivation (Ipsos-ASI)

Similar to Ameritest's measure, the ASI Motivation measure is usually a rating of consumer intentions to consider/visit/buy, depending on the category. Frequently, the ratings collected in the ad test are benchmarked against a "control" where the sample ratings are collected from a demographically matched sample of consumers who were not exposed to any advertising. By comparing the two ratings, it is possible to see how much the advertising has shifted the probability that consumers will purchase the brand.

Persuasion (Millward Brown)

This is one of two primary measures that gauge the consumer response to the advertising message. Persuasion is divided into a three-part question, with slight differences in wording, depending on whether the respondent is a regular user of the brand, someone who has tried the brand but does not use it regularly, or a non-trier of the brand. Because of the placement or location of the persuasion question in the MB interview, this measure is designed to capture the "rational" response to the advertising, with the emotional response being captured by the enjoyment rating, so that the two measures when added together capture the total "effect" of the advertising.

Persuasion (ARS)

This is a "pre-post" measure of how the advertising shifts consumer intentions to purchase the brand. Before viewing the program in the theater, respondents are given envelopes containing a "photoshelf" of the brands in the test category and asked to indicate which brand they would prefer to win in a prize drawing. After viewing the program and advertising, respondents are given the photoshelf again and asked their preferences once more. Persuasion is calculated by subtracting the pre-exposure brand preference from their post-exposure preference. The benchmark against which this measure is compared is known as the Fair Share™ score—a modeled norm which takes into account factors such as how fragmented or competitive the category is and the brand's market share.

Persuasion (MSW)

Similar to ARS, the MSW measure of persuasion is based on a pre-exposure to post-exposure shift in consumer intentions to select the advertised brand from a "photo shelf" of competing alternatives.

COMPOSITE MEASURES

Composite measures exist as a matter of convenience. These "single" number measures are designed to make it easy for senior managers of an organization to keep track of the many ads for which they are responsible, possibly in many different countries, and to communicate to other non-research oriented senior managers the performance of that advertising.

Composite measures are not designed to provide insights into or understanding of an ad's performance, but simply to provide a headline for the ad's performance in an elevator conversation.

The various composite measures that different systems provide, therefore, do not represent new measurement and are subject to the same criticisms and limitations of the component measures.

Ameritest Performance Index [API] (Ameritest)

This is calculated by combining Branded Attention (which is itself the product of Brand Linkage and Attention) with Weighted Motivation, then indexing it against the average of the relevant distribution of API scores (e.g., all :30 ads, all :15 ads, etc.). Like an IQ score, the Ameritest API is frequently used to rank an ad versus current competitive advertising. Conceptually, this means that an effective ad must break through the clutter, be well-branded and motivate the consumer to purchase the product or use the service.

Awareness Index [AI] (Millward Brown)

A measure designed to predict the incremental impact of a TV commercial on advertising awareness—as measured in the marketplace by one of Millward Brown's continuous trackers.

For example, an Awareness Index of 1 should generate 1 additional point of ad awareness per 100 GRP's, if the base level is zero. (When base level is non-zero, the predicted gain is less than 1 point per 100 GRP's.) The AI score is derived from a combination of pre-test measures of enjoyment, involvement (memorability) and Branding. The AI is a component of Millward Brown's Effectiveness Index (EI), which also takes the ad's persuasiveness into account.

Copy Effect Index (Ipsos-ASI)

This is calculated by combining measures of Recall and Persuasion that have been previously indexed to their respective norms. Conceptually, this means that effective advertising must be both memorable and persuasive.

Effectiveness Index [EI] (Millward Brown)

This is calculated by summing a weighted combination of Attention, Branding and Communication Effect (a measure that in itself includes Persuasion and Enjoyment). Conceptually, this means that an effective ad must break through the clutter, be well-branded and must motivate the consumer either rationally or on an emotional level.

LIKING

Liking is strongly correlated with both Attention and Motivation, and therefore is related to the sales effectiveness of advertising. The relationship between Liking and Recall is more problematic, with some studies showing a negative relationship between Liking and Recall and others showing little or no correlation.

Commercials that are liked tend to be entertaining and also tend to convey relevant, believable, brand differentiating messages. But knowing that you have a well-liked execution does not tell you, by itself, what it is about the commercial that is liked: the commercial execution or the advertising message.

IV

Pre-testing: A Review of Diagnostic Techniques from Different Systems

IV

Pre-testing: A Review of Diagnostic Techniques from Different Systems

Diagnostic questions in a pretest are used to provide insights into how advertising executions are working. Unlike report card measures, which can be used by management as a filtering process to make a go/no go decision about airing a particular ad or to choose between two or more campaign alternatives, diagnostic research is generally used in a more qualitative way. Results of diagnostic research inform creative judgment with consumer feedback on a host of creative issues the advertising team might be debating.

One major objective of diagnostics, usually obtained in open-ended measures of communication, is to confirm that an execution is "on strategy." From a brand management perspective it is essential to understand how the message communicated by an ad is going to position the brand for long term competitiveness. Report card measures generally focus on short-term effects, e.g., will the ad drive sales within the first few weeks or months of an ad airing?—

rather than the longer term effects of advertising—a brand's positioning within its competitive set and a brand's image within contemporary culture. A narrow-minded focus only on report card measures can lead to the production of advertising that might, in the short term, drive sales, but be damaging to the long-term health of the brand.

A second important objective of diagnostic questioning is to provide an explanation of the "reasons why" an ad is performing well or poorly on the various report card measures used in the system in order to suggest opportunities for optimization. When confronted with a mediocre performance on a key performance metric, the first question the advertising manager should ask is, "Is this advertising idea a small idea that's been well-executed, or is this idea a diamond-in-the-rough, an execution that still needs some polishing and editing to release its full potential?"

For example, a commercial that generates only an average score on attention but that gets above-average ratings on entertainment value or uniqueness or involvement is probably a potentially bigger idea than the attention score indicates; it just needs additional work. In that case, you might look to diagnostics such as the Flow of Attention that identify structural weaknesses in the syntax or grammar of the film in order to pinpoint opportunities to improve the breakthrough performance of the film.

In general, because advertising works in the mind of the consumer in complex, non-linear ways, relatively small edits to advertising film can frequently lead to large improvements in an ad's overall performance scores. In contrast to pre-testing with a report card testing system—which creatives tend to view negatively as a threat to their beloved creations—diagnostic research's chief goal might be defined as the saving of creative ideas. From a business process perspective, it is because of its potential contribution to the salvaging and optimization of very expensive advertising executions that diagnostic pre-testing can be justified as adding a great deal of value to the creative development process.

Even when ads score well on report card measures diagnostics add value by making sure that management draws the right conclusions from success. Sometimes an ad generates a good score for different reasons than its creators expected. Diagnostics can provide insights into what's really working in an ad, so that you can distinguish between what is essential to the core idea and what is incidental to the particular execution. This can be a great source of creative freedom. Otherwise a successful score on the report card can be a trap. For many years Proctor and Gamble was known for producing "cookie cutter" advertising, because once a commercial got a good report card, management was afraid to change anything in the successful ad "formula" because they didn't really understand the reasons for their success. A third objective of diagnostics, therefore, is to provide an empirical foundation of learning for evolving a successful ad campaign in fresh directions.

Other important objectives for diagnostic research would be to address ad hoc issues that are specific to a particular execution. An example would be to determine the appropriateness of a particular celebrity spokesperson for a given brand. Or, in test cells where multiple ads from the same campaign are shown to the same sample of respondents, diagnostic questions might be used to assess the coherence of an integrated marketing campaign.

Over the years different research companies have developed a wide variety of diagnostic approaches, some of which are proprietary to their developers. But in general there are four broad classes of diagnostic techniques. First, almost all tests include open-ended probes that are designed to collect consumer verbatims which are then coded to produce thematic tables of consumer comments about an ad. Second, most tests contain standardized lists of closed-ended statements that consumers use to rate an ad, which are then interpreted by comparing scores to a normative database of other ad tests. Third, some tests include moment-by-moment measures designed to get inside the ad in order to analyze its structure and to identify its executional strengths and weaknesses. And newer research companies are introducing a fourth class of diagnostics, strongly related to the third, based on the emerging field of advertising biometrics, which uses the new tools of modern neuroscience to explore how consumers process advertising on an emotional and unconscious level.

What follows is a brief summary of some of the major diagnostic pre-testing techniques in use today.

Communication: Open-Ended Questions

Communication open-ended questions are designed to get respondents talking freely about an ad so that you can see if the respondent plays back the intended communication points of the ad spontaneously, without prompting. These questions are usually asked very early in the interview to get initial reactions to the ad unbiased by thoughts that might be contained in the probing interview itself.

Typical communication questions might include:

Q: What thoughts or feelings did you have as you watched the ad?

Q: Please tell me in your own words what you saw and heard.

Q: What do you think the main message of the ad was?

Note that this particular sequence of questions follows a qualitative "funnel design" where the respondent is first invited to share whatever thoughts come to mind, without "leading" them to any particular idea, but at the end converges on the question which asks them to make a judgment about what they thought the main point of the ad was.

Likes/Dislikes

These open-ends are designed to elicit, in their own words, what respondents liked and disliked about the particular ad being tested:

Q: What, if anything, did you like about the ad you just saw?

Q: What, if anything, did you dislike about the ad you just saw?

Such questions can be useful, though in general the comments tend to be superficial—a result that historically gave rise to the more nuanced diagnostics described below. If the length of the interview is an issue, it should be noted that the comments generated by these questions are usually redundant with the communication questions described previously. Usually likes/dislikes are mixed together with the sales messages played back in the communication questions—and spontaneous positive and negative comments that a respondent plays back immediately after seeing an ad will provide a more reliable indicator of her true feelings about the ad.

RATING STATEMENTS

There are two broad categories of rating statements to be found in a typical diagnostic pretest. The first is rating statements that describe a respondent's reactions to the advertising execution being tested. Second is rating statements of brand perceptions following exposure to the ad.

Executional Rating Statements

The first kind of rating statement is exemplified by the Viewer Response Profile, pioneered by the Leo Burnett advertising agency in the 1960s and still widely used today in one form or another. With this approach, a list of rating statements were developed. The list was then factor-analyzed in order to group them into a standardized battery of statements, each according to the underlying dimension of response being measured, e.g., entertainment value, empathy, relevant news, credibility, confusion, etc.

An alternate method of grouping statements reflects their purpose in explaining a commercial's score on report card measures. With this method, statements are grouped according to how strongly they correlate with measures of attention, branding or motivation. Here are some examples:

Drivers of Attention
The commercial is entertaining.
The commercial is involving.
The commercial is unique.
I like the music in the commercial.

Barriers to Attention
The commercial is ordinary.
The commercial is boring.
The commercial is confusing.

Different companies use different scales—one to five or one to six or one to ten—according to preference. No definitive research exists to support the superiority of one scale over another. In designing pre-testing research, therefore, the operative principle is simple consistency in the application of scales from one test to another or within the flow of a single interview.

Scores can be reported out as means, or as "top box" scores (the highest rating) or "top two box" scores (the two highest ratings.) Tests of statistical significance, e.g., "at the 90% confidence level," are used to classify an ad as significantly stronger or weaker than another test ad or as above norm, at norm, or below norm on a particular dimension of response.

The usefulness of diagnostic ratings of ad executions is highly dependent on the quality of the normative database. Quality is determined by such factors as the size or number of ads in the database, the freshness of the database—were the ads tested recently or twenty years ago?—and the comparability of ads in the database—are you comparing a new product test ad to other new product ads?—are you comparing a food commercial to other food commercials?

Emotion Ratings

Because the subject of emotion and advertising has received a lot of attention lately, a recent variation on the execution ratings approach is to use a list of "feeling words," or visual icons to capture the emotions being evoked by the advertising. For example, Millward Brown uses an emotional palette of sixteen feeling words to describe the range of emotions being conveyed by an ad. In contrast, Ipsos-ASI argues that using words to describe the non-verbal, emotional component of advertising communication is just another game of semantics and instead uses their proprietary Emoticons®

technique, a battery of around forty cartoon facial expressions, which respondents use to identify the emotions being conveyed by an ad.

Because the intent of these closed-end approaches to measuring emotion is to interpret ad performance relative to a normative database, the lists of emotional descriptors are of necessity designed to be a short and fixed list of feeling words or icons. One criticism of emotion ratings, therefore, is that they lack subtlety and nuance to express the specific emotions being expressed in an ad.

A more important criticism of emotional ratings is that the emotional response of an audience to an ad is not only non-verbal, but may in fact be unconscious, and therefore not accessible through self-consciously derived rating statements.

Brand Rating Statements

With brand ratings, respondents are asked to rate their perceptions of the brand, not the execution, based on the advertising they just saw. In a sense, this is a closed-ended way to check whether or not the communication is on strategy, as either a supplement or an alternative to coding the verbatims from open ends as described above.

Brand rating statements generally consist of ten to twenty phrases or sentences that can be used to describe the different features and benefits provided by competitive offerings in the category, e.g., product is made with premium ingredients, tastes good, is healthy, is a good value etc. Since brand rating lists are customized to fit individual product categories, with items frequently added to individual tests to reflect the nuances of specific advertising strategies, brand ratings are not interpreted with reference to a normative database. Instead, brand ratings may be used to assess advertising performance across different test executions for the same brand, against a historical database for the brand, or against a baseline provided by a control cell.

A control cell is a separate sample of consumers, matched in terms of key demographic and brand usage variables, in which respondents who are *not* exposed to any advertising are also asked to rate the brand with the identical list of rating statements. A lower cost alternative to a control cell, also known as "pre/post" ratings, is to collect brand ratings both before and after exposure to the advertising stimulus. A criticism of the latter approach is that it sensitizes respondents to the messages the advertising is designed to convey.

Brand Image Ratings

For high image categories such as cars or cosmetics, a list of brand personality attributes might be collected in a checklist to develop a profile of the brand's persona—sexy, smart, contemporary, confident, down-to-earth, authentic, etc. A second approach would be to develop an image profile of the brand user. An interesting variation on this theme, which is related to the projective techniques used in focus groups, is to use scrap art, rather than verbal descriptors, to portray various user types.

MOMENT-BY-MOMENT MEASURES

Dial Meters

Dial meters have been around for a long time and have been used on a variety of research problems, from measuring voter response to presidential debates in a focus group, to rating audience response to movie endings in a theater setting. Examples of dial meters in pretesting include the Interest Trace® provided by Millward Brown and by MSW.

In a dial meter test, a respondent is asked to rate his responses to different moments in film by turning a dial as he watches the film. In the online version, the dial meter has been translated into movements of a mouse.

When dial meters are used to measure responses to an ad on the first exposure—as they are typically used in focus groups—some researchers have raised the concern that dial meters make respondents artificially introspective while they're watching the ad, creating an unnatural self-awareness which could distort the normal viewing experience, essentially changing an advertising experience into a research experience.

Typically dial meters measure only one dimension of audience response to the film—such as "liking" or "interest." This can be a problem for interpretation since the multi-dimensional report card measures in pre-tests are generally designed to be independent variables. How do you know whether a specific moment in the ad identified by a dial meter explains the attention score, brand linkage, or the measure of persuasiveness?

In practice, dial meters seem to provide only a coarse-grained level of information about an ad—that is, many dial meter trace curves tend to be flat and fairly featureless, with only a few bumps or changes in the direction of the curve. As a result only one or two key moments in an ad tend to be highlighted.

One reason for this may be the differences in reaction times across respondents. For example, the physical reaction times of younger respondents used to playing video games is faster than the reaction times of older respondents. Averaged across all the respondents in a sample, this tends to smooth out the fine detail in the curve.

From an information theory perspective, a second reason that dial meter curves change direction slowly, is that with dial meters, self-aware respondents tend to provide feedback at a much slower rate of signaling than the actual pace of information flowing through the commercial, and much slower than the rapid rate at which their unconscious mind is processing it. For example, the average thirty-second commercial contains over thirteen cuts, representing thirteen distinct decisions by the director in the editing room regarding the cutting and timing of the film, all of which represents important "visual bytes" of information embedded in the film. Yet, it would be extremely rare to see a respondent use a dial meter to cast thirteen distinct "votes" about the different shots in one thirty-second commercial.

For a number of reasons, therefore, when experiments have been conducted to compare dial meter results with other moment-by-moment techniques, such as Picture Sorts or biometric measurements, there is almost no correlation. Moreover, little quantitative validation work has been published to show how the patterns produced by dial meters systematically correlate with traditional measures of ad performance, such as attention, recall or persuasion. As a result, dial meters tend to be most useful as a qualitative tool for generating group discussion and insights into key moments in film.

Flow of Attention®

This is the first of three proprietary Picture Sorts® techniques offered by Ameritest.

Following the multi-dimensional logic of report card measures—that the advertising job of getting attention is different from the job of persuading the consumer—the suite of three Picture Sorts provides a moment-by-moment analysis of different cognitive processes that come into play as an audience watches film.

The Flow of Attention® measures how the mind performs as a search engine, actively googling the ideas and emotional imagery in an ad in order to find the most meaningful content. Importantly, the search processes of the mind are largely pre-conscious, with unconscious emotions driving the selective attention of an audience.

The rapidly fluctuating flow of audience attention through an ad is measured by asking respondents to sort through a randomized deck of still photos from the film—or, in the companion Copy Sort, verbal excerpts or lines of copy from the ad. The sorting criteria is a simple binary question—do you remember seeing this image in the ad or not? Because it doesn't make sense to ask a consumer to turn a dial or verbalize what he didn't see in an ad that was in fact there, this frame-by-frame and line-by-line recognition test provides a fundamentally different kind of diagnostic information about an ad than that provided by dial meters.

The number of pictures used to deconstruct an ad varies as a function of the visual complexity of an ad, with a typical sorting deck containing from 15 to 30 images representing a thirty-second commercial. Pictures are frame-grabbed from the video on the basis of whether or not, in the judgment of a trained analyst, the additional image represents a meaningful change in the esthetic information content on the screen from the preceding image in the sorting deck. As a result, the picture sorting measurement tool is calibrated to the rate of information flowing through an ad.

One potential criticism of the technique is that different analysts might choose different pictures to represent the ad—though in practice inter-coder reliability tests confirm that properly trained analysts will choose the same pictures over ninety percent of the time. Depending on the level of detail needed, however, fewer pictures might be used to describe longer pieces of film. For example, while thirty pictures might be used to describe a thirty-second commercial where every second counts, a two-hour movie might be sorted with only a deck of a hundred pictures because the analyst isn't interested in fine-grained detail but rather has chosen to "zoom out" to graph the overall arc of audience attention through the longer story.

The wave-like patterns of Flow of Attention curves tend to stabilize very quickly, after only about twenty respondents. As a result, analysis of sub-segments of an audience—e.g., younger versus older viewers—can be performed easily.

Diagnostic analysis of Flow of Attention curves focuses on the shape and content of the curve. (Interestingly, the overall height of the attention curve is not predictive of the overall attention-getting power of the ad.) Four parameters are important for analysis:

1. Opening frames—a rising opening is characteristic of attention-getting ads.
2. Overall trend-line—an effective ad holds attention from the beginning to the end of the ad.
3. Continuity in the flow—ads with discontinuities or turbulence in the flow suggest the audience has gotten "off track" and is confused by some transitions or sections in the ad.
4. Focal points of attention—more attention-getting ads have more peak moments of attention where the audience is focused on the content that is most important for the advertiser to communicate.

A number of papers have been published to validate the usefulness of the Flow of Attention in explaining the breakthrough measures of various pre-testing systems, including the attention scores of Millward Brown and Ameritest and the recall scores of Ipsos-ASI and ARS. The technique also provides an important input (the Focus variable) to mathematical models of various measures of brand linkage. The Flow of Attention does not, however, explain motivation or persuasion—for that, another picture sort is needed.

Flow of Emotion®

The Flow of Emotion is designed to measure the level of conscious feelings evoked in the audience and to determine the emotional valence of those feelings: are they positive or negative?

The picture sorting data are usually collected after the first attention sort and the same sorting deck of pictures is used. With this sort, respondents are asked to sort pictures on a 5-point scale, from very positive to very negative. In graphing the data, only the positive and negative ends of the scale are plotted in order to visualize the dramatic emotional tension produced by the ad.

A key concept in analyzing the flow data is that negative emotions are sometimes important in an ad for dramatic storytelling, a point discussed more fully in chapter XI. Therefore, an important consideration for interpreting the data correctly is determining whether the negative emotions are there by creative design or are unintended negatives or flaws in the execution.

In terms of validation, a number of journal articles have been published that demonstrate the area under the Flow of Emotion curve—the volume of emotion being pumped through an ad—is highly correlated with motivation and persuasion, but is not correlated with attention or recall.

Flow of Meaning

One of the principal jobs of advertising is to create brand loyalty by imparting meaning to a product or service, so that the consumer adopts the brand as an important part of her life. The third picture sort is designed to capture the meaning conveyed by each image in an ad in order to understand its contribution to the overall communication.

Using the same deck of photos used in the other two sorts, the respondent this time sorts images into one of several categories of meaning designed to reflect the strategic communication objective of the advertising. For some ads, the relevant set of meanings might describe functional features and benefits, the semantic goals of the communication: When you saw this image in the ad were you thinking about...healthy, good tasting, convenient, good value? For other ads, meaning might be probed on an emotional level: When you saw this image in the ad were you feeling...joy, love, excitement, surprise? And for other ads, it might even be useful to probe the meaning on a more primitive, sensory level: When you saw this image in the ad did you get a feeling of sweetness, of refreshment, of crunchiness?

Like brand ratings, different categories of semantic or emotional meanings may be relevant depending on the goals of a particular ad campaign. As a result, the third picture sort is based on a flexible, open-system approach to describing the meanings of advertising imagery rather than using a standardized list of predetermined meanings.

Millward Brown's Emotion Trace®

This is a new variation on the dial meter approach that is specifically designed to describe the emotions that are being produced at different moments in an ad.

With this technique, the respondent first identifies the primary and secondary emotions he felt while watching the ad from a standardized list of sixteen feeling words. Next he watches the ad again and use a dial meter to mark the moments in the ad when he feels the primary emotion and then he watch the ad a third time and uses the dial meter to mark the moments when he feels the secondary emotion.

This approach offers several advantages over the conventional Interest Trace. First, because the list of sixteen emotions is standardized, commercial scores on these emotions can be kept in a norm base for comparison to other ads. Second, because the dial meter portion uses the spectrum of sixteen emotions, it's multi-dimensional, as compared to the one dimensional interest curve. Third, because two passes of the dial ratings are done, the resulting curves tend to be bumpier and more fruitful to analyze than the single pass dial meter curves. Finally, this approach to measuring emotions recognizes a fundamental truth in film storytelling that what matters most about emotions is how they move or change as the story unfolds.

One criticism of this approach is that since different respondents might pick different words to describe their feelings towards the commercial, the dial meter ratings for any given emotion word is not based on the whole sample but rather is limited to the subset of respondents who chose that particular word.

Another criticism is that the closed-system approach of using a fixed list of 16 words is lacking in nuance to describe the full palette of human emotions—comparable to a computer screen capable of displaying only 16 colors rather than millions of hues.

Because the technique is new, little validation work has been published yet to demonstrate how the Emotion Trace relates to Millward Brown's report card measures.

BIOMETRICS

Recent advances in the field of neuroscience have produced a variety of tools to test advertising using the physiological response of viewers to an advertising stimulus. There appear to be several factors creating interest in this area. First, there is the commonly held belief that much of the work of advertising is done at the non-verbal or unconscious level and hence is inaccessible to the "self-report" methods used in standard pre-testing. Second, biometrics hold out the promise that at some future date, less intrusive, more passive, and more direct means of measuring advertising's effects can be built into future technology, much as the simple measure of click-through rates drove the early adoption of the Internet as an advertising medium. Third, there is a certain trendiness to the subject since the industry went through a similar fascination with this topic in the 1970s and '80s.

At this time, however, the techniques described below are highly experimental, expensive, and cumbersome to use in the field. Much work remains to be done in terms of relating biometric measures to theories of how advertising works and to validating particular biometrics to standard measures of advertising performance or to in-market sales results.

A wide variety of approaches are under development and what follows is necessarily an incomplete list. It also appears that different approaches are likely to be accessing different dimensions of advertising performance. To put these techniques in some perspective, a recent study by the ARF (Advertising Research Foundation) on the subject of emotion in advertising positioned some of the biometric techniques along with some of the more standardized diagnostic approaches as follows:

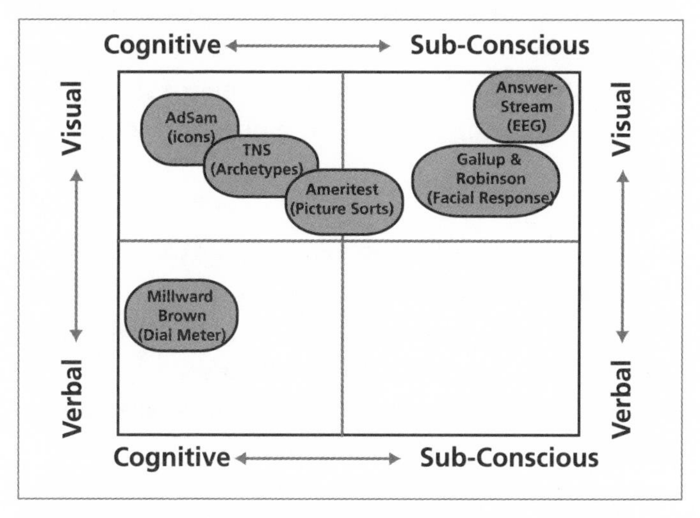

An ARF map of diagnostic tools.

Brain Waves

With this approach, the researcher measures changes in the electrical activity of the brain with an EEG machine (a kind of cap you wear on your head with a lot of wires coming out of it) while the respondent is exposed to advertising.

The technology that is used today is much more accurate than that available to earlier generations of researchers, and the demonstrated usefulness of this approach in the field of neuroscience suggests that this is an area of great promise.

One of the big advantages of EEG measurement is that it is extremely accurate in time, down to milliseconds, in terms of measuring the arousal of the brain's neural circuits. As a result, it is likely to lead to new insights into the processes of rapid cognition, or how our unconscious minds filter our perceptions.

Brain Imaging

With this approach, the researcher uses a brain imaging machine, like a CAT scanner, to take pictures of the different parts of the brain that light up as a respondent watches an ad.

While these imaging machines are very expensive, the growth of the field of neuroscience is making them more accessible to market researchers. The per hour cost of using the machines is high, but fortunately relatively small samples of consumers—as few as twenty respondents per test—are needed to produce stable measurement results.

The advantage of imaging machines is that, unlike EEG, they are extremely accurate spatially—they can tell you to the cubic centimeter what part of the brain is being aroused by an ad. Unfortunately, because they usually rely on some physical phenomenon to occur such as increased blood flow to some part of the brain, they are much less accurate than

EEG machines in terms of timing. As a result, synchronizing events in a fast paced commercial to the brain's response is more problematic.

Nevertheless, this approach holds great promise for uncovering new insights into how advertising creates memories—e.g., determining how the rational, semantic memory system of the brain interacts with the emotional, episodic memory system of the brain.

Eye-Tracking

Eye-tracking has been around since the late sixties as a standard tool for measuring print ads and packaging. It is most commonly offered by niche research companies such as Perception Research or The PreTesting Company that have the specialized equipment in the field to perform it.

The advantage of eye-tracking is that it is very precise in terms of telling you where on a page or a package the respondent is looking and how much time a respondent spends looking at it. The disadvantage is that while eye-tracking tells you precisely where the eyeball is pointing, it doesn't tell you what the brain is thinking or feeling as it looks.

Like most research techniques that require special equipment, eye-tracking tends to be relatively expensive. As more and more advertising research moves onto the Internet, resulting in lower per-test costs, eye-trackers are increasingly challenged to also import their technique to the online universe. The increasing penetration of cameras built into computers suggests that the future of online measurement of physiological response to advertising, such as eye movement, pupil dilation, or facial recognition, may not be far off.

Reaction Time

One diagnostic approach to studying consumer response to advertising is to measure respondent reaction times to a stimulus. For example, measuring how long it takes someone to respond to a question—e.g., before hitting a key on a computer—can be correlated with how certain she is about her answer to that question.

Before the advent of eye-tracking, a standard psychological approach for diagnosing the impact of a print ad or a package was to measure the brain's reaction times with a tachistoscope (t-scope). With a t-scope an ad was flashed on a screen for brief controlled periods of time and afterwards respondents were asked what they thought they saw. This was a simple method for determining what a respondent looked at first or second or third in an ad. It also provided a simple way of measuring things like familiarity—how long did it take to recognize that celebrity?—and confusion—which brand was that?

The Internet has brought the t-scope back in a new form with Ameritest's proprietary Flash Test for testing print ads and packaging. Because every computer has to have a highly accurate clock inside the processor in order to work, it is easy to expose a print ad or a package on a computer screen for brief, highly controlled periods of time.

With the Ameritest print diagnostic, an ad is exposed three times—for half a second, one second, and four seconds. After each exposure, the ad disappears, replaced by a grid matching the shape of the ad that was on screen. The respondent clicks on a cell or cells of the grid to indicate where she was looking. Then the respondent answers an open-end question about what she thought she saw. The data is then graphed to look very much like an eye-tracking analysis of the path of the eye and the verbatims are coded to measure short-term communication.

One advantage of this approach is that it can be done on the Internet, without specialized equipment. A second advantage is that the verbatims that accompany each exposure allow the researcher to interpret what the consumer was thinking as she looked at different parts of the ad. A disadvantage is that the technique is not as spatially accurate as eye-tracking, so that while you can tell whether a respondent was looking at a headline or not, you can't tell which particular word in the headline he was looking at.

One of the key benefits of the many of the diagnostic techniques described, is that they provide rich new data for evolving our theories about how advertising works in the mind. Collectively, they provide new insights into how the brain processes and filters information, how quickly the brain forms thoughts in response to an ad, how it responds emotionally, and how those thoughts and emotions are turned into long-term brand memories. Just as advertising continuously evolves to reach the consumer with new ideas in new ways, research has to evolve new ways to measure it. Consequently, the techniques described above represent an incomplete list and a work-in-progress.

V

Tracking: Measuring Ad Awareness In-Market

V

Tracking: Measuring Ad Awareness In-Market

The measurements provided by in-market tracking studies are key performance indicators used by senior management to assess the success or failure of advertising campaigns. Consequently, the size of the advertising budget, and even job performance reviews, are tied to these numbers. The accuracy of these advertising measurements therefore, is of critical concern to both advertising and brand managers as well as their agencies.

Typical measures in an in-market tracking study might include the following mix of brand health and advertising impact measurements: Top-of-mind brand awareness, aided brand awareness, unaided ad awareness, aided ad awareness, advertising message recall, brand trial, brand repeat purchase, brand frequency of use, brand purchase intent, price perceptions, brand image ratings, media usage, and demographics.

Many companies provide ad-tracking services including Arbor, Ameritest, Communicus, Ipsos-ASI, Millward Brown, OTX, TNS and others. In the past ten years the data collection channel for most tracking studies has moved from the telephone to the Internet for several reasons; lower cost, higher respondent cooperation rates, and to shift from a recall to a recognition-based measurement of ad awareness. Consistency is key to the design of tracking studies. Once a questionnaire design is settled on it is executed in exactly the same way over time so that changes in the advertising and brand metrics can be attributed to changes in the market and not changes in methodology. As a result, this kind of research tends to be executed in high volume production mode, which makes it very expensive and thus very attractive to large research companies. Usually, tracking research is one of the most expensive line items in the research budget.

CONTINUOUS TRACKING VERSUS DIPSTICK MEASUREMENT

There are two basic approaches to tracking studies, each based on the timing of the interviews.

A very expensive approach, pioneered by the Millward Brown company, is to collect data continuously, with a small number of interviews each week. The data is then aggregated into monthly or quarterly rolling averages that smooth out the random bumps in the weekly data and scroll out like the rising and falling patterns of a stock market track. There are three advantages to this approach.

First, with all the time series data points available it is easy to model the wear-in and wear-out effects of new advertising campaigns. Second, if some unexpected event occurs in the marketplace that has the potential to affect a brand's sales—a product recall, the launch of a major competitive effort, a natural disaster of some kind—then the research is already in place to measure the before and after effects of that event. Third, once a continuous tracker is in place it requires little management attention and can pretty much run on auto pilot.

The alternative approach to tracking is to collect data in waves, or flights, of interviews spaced several months apart. With this "dip-stick" approach, there are usually two or three waves of interviewing.

Because advertising spending to advertising awareness is a non-linear relationship, and since it takes at least three points to describe a curve, three waves of interviewing are preferred.

Typically there is a *pre-wave* conducted shortly before the launch of new advertising. This provides a benchmark for interpreting the changes in the market caused by the new advertising that is then measured in one or two *post waves*.

The first post wave is usually conducted early on (during the wear-in phase) to provide an early warning system for management. The second wave would be conducted some months later, after the bulk of the media has been spent, to measure the full awareness generated by the campaign.

A more expensive but more powerful variation on the discrete wave approach to ad tracking is provided by Communicus, which measures awareness and perceptions among the *same respondents* before and after advertising has run—that is, the same group of consumers would be interviewed at different points in time. The value of this approach is that changes in purchasing behavior among consumers who became aware of the new advertising can be measured directly. This provides a straightforward means of estimating the return on the advertising investment and for determining the relative contribution that different media—TV, print, outdoor, web—make to the total campaign effort.

The more extensive respondent sample is needed for this type of analysis in order to avoid the chicken-or-egg-first causality conundrum: is brand consumption higher because of the new advertising or does higher brand consumption make it more likely that those consumers will pay attention to their brand's new advertising?

RECALL VERSUS RECOGNITION

There has been a long running debate in advertising research circles regarding the relative merits of recall versus recognition. Which is the best way of tapping into consumer memories of advertising?

Recall was the first report card measure used in commercial pre-testing. and it is still widely used today. Those who favor a recall approach use the common sense argument that for advertising to be effective it must first lodge itself in memory—a necessary, if not sufficient, condition for advertising to work. This is particularly relevant given the standard argument that the real payout for the advertising investment, as compared to short-term promotions, is to be found in its long-term effects on the brand.

Those who favor recognition argue that a consumer's inability to recall or actively retrieve the memory of a television commercial based on verbal cues it is not a valid indicator of whether or not the consumer has in fact seen the ad or whether that ad has indeed made a lasting impact on their stored impressions of the brand.

Imagine you are at a party and someone approaches you who you're sure you recognize—but you can't recall their name! What do you conclude? That you really have not met this person before because you don't know their name? Or maybe you're simply bad at remembering names? The problem with memory, which was not well understood by early ad researchers, is that there is more than one kind of memory system in the brain.

These days, cognitive psychologists make many distinctions about the different memory systems in the brain. For example, long-term memory is different than the short term memory that makes up our experience of the here and now—the present moment in which the mind is continuously engaged. At an unconscious level, the mind is sorting out those experiences that are unimportant and can be discarded like so much spam from other memories that are deemed worthy to be stored in one or several of the multiple long term memory systems of the brain.

Long-term memory can be divided into several categories. First is the distinction between explicit memory and implicit memory. Explicit memories are those memories you have conscious control of, such as recalling the date of your birthday. An example of implicit memory is your ability to recognize the meaning of an unusual word in a book that you would not consciously think of when you are writing.

Memories tend to be encoded in a hierarchy, reflecting their importance or salience. (*See below.*) This is why measures of awareness, such as top-of-mind awareness or first mentions of brand names, are important predictors of in-market ad effectiveness. Another example

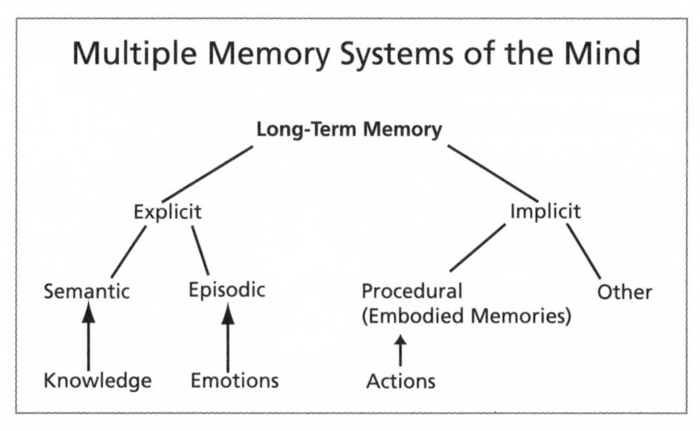

Memory Types.

would be peaks of the picture sort graphs of audience attention flowing through a commercial. The peak moments of the ad are, in the eyes of the viewing audience, the most salient parts of the ad that should be stored away in long-term memory—the essence or gist of the ad. Conversely, the lower recalled images from the ad represent a map of forgetting, or how quickly different parts of an ad fade from conscious memory within a few minutes of exposure to it.

At another level we can describe three different long term memory banks in the brain that may be important for the brand building process. First, the semantic memory system, where facts and concepts are stored; second, the episodic memory system, where auto-biographical memories and emotions are stored; and third, the procedural memory system, where physical memories and sensations are stored, such as the memory of how it feels to drive a car, or what clean hair feels like—which is related to what cognitive psychologists call "embodied cognition." For marketing purposes, we call these Knowledge memories, Emotion memories, and Action memories and will discuss them in greater detail in chapter X.

Recall, using verbal cuing, taps only into explicit, semantic memory. While that is important, for example in learning whether or not a brand has clearly positioned itself in the marketplace, it misses the other ways that an ad campaign can touch the consumer. The emotions generated by an ad are also important, but words are limited in their ability to evoke emotions from the episodic memory system. One of the early problems with recall was discovered by trackers who noticed that attitudes towards a brand were frequently higher among those who could recognize an ad with a visual cue than among those who recalled it verbally. This is not evidence of the unconscious effects of advertising, hidden persuasion, but rather points out the fact that many of the images and emotions associated with a brand in the consumer's long term memory cannot be accessed with words.

To cue ad recognition, therefore, telephone-based trackers historically used verbal descriptions of an ad. A criticism of this approach, however, is that verbally cued measures do not reliably evoke memories of the visual experience of an ad. To think about the difference between a verbal cue and a visual cue, imagine you had to find someone in a crowd that you had never met before. Which would be easier and more accurate: (1) you had a written paragraph describing the face of the person you're looking for, or (2) you had a picture of the person's face? The part of an ad that you can't easily put into words is sometimes the more important part of an ad.

Another reason to use visual recognition measurement is that it allows you to measure awareness of individual ad executions and not just awareness of the campaign as a whole. This ability to measure ad awareness by individual execution can be quite useful in our age of fragmented media and integrated marketing. Advertising managers want to know more than simply, "How many consumers have seen the ad campaign?" Increasingly, they ask more precise questions such as, "Which of my ads has the consumer seen?" In other words, which are the strong performers in my advertising mix, and which are the weak performers? These are questions that recognition-based measurement, not recall-based measurement, can address.

Optimizing the Recognition Stimulus

Most research companies now tracking advertising over the Internet use a visual stimulus to measure advertising awareness. For television commercials, or online video, the most common method is to use a storyboard of key frames from the ad to stimulate recognition. A thirty-second commercial, for example, would use a storyboard comprised of between four to six de-branded still photos taken from the commercial.

Early adopters of Internet tracking used storyboards rather than playing full video due to bandwidth restrictions. But now the main rationale for storyboards as the preferred approach is based on interview length. You can gather more data on more advertising executions using still photographs, which the respondent might spend a few seconds looking at, than you can if the respondent has to spend the time to watch full ad films.

But, you can get a very different impression of the commercial depending on your choice of visuals. The storyboard samples below show two versions constructed from the same commercial. While there is some overlap, it looks like the storyboards are describing two different commercials.

One of the two storyboards was constructed by an ad hoc panel of twenty experienced researchers The other storyboard shown was constructed using consumer feedback from a Flow of Attention graph.

If this was your advertising being tracked in the marketplace—and next year's ad budget depends on how well it performs—which of these two storyboards would you use to cue recognition of your ad?

In constructing ad-tracking storyboards these "peak" moments of attention identified in pre-testing are particularly useful. By definition, these are the images the consumers remember best after their experience of the ad has been transferred from short term to long term memory—so it should not be surprising that these images are related to the long term memory effects of the advertising.

In a recent experiment Ameritest tried to understand how well researchers could predict in advance which visual moments in the advertising the consumer was likely to focus on. We looked at ten commercials representing a range of categories from packaged goods to high tech. We asked the panel of researchers to predict which ones would be the peak images of the commercial from the consumer's viewpoint. We then compared the results to actual consumer data from pre-testing.

What we found was that even experienced researchers were not very good at predicting what consumers would focus on in the ad. Using judgment, researchers were correct only

44% of the time in predicting what the peak visuals in the commercial would be for the target audience consumer. And yet, most research companies rely on the research analysts' judgment to select the frames that will represent the commercial in a tracking study.

Of course, it's likely that creatives might be better at this prediction business, but our experience in meetings to report pre-test results, suggests that creatives are also frequently surprised by what the consumer focuses on as well. More to the point, creatives are rarely asked to provide input on which visuals to include in tracking studies.

Does the choice of pictures used in the storyboard stimulus really matter? To answer this question, we recently performed a separate experiment with one of our major clients. (*See below.*) Using two cells of matched samples, each consisting of 100 target consumers, for one of their successful personal care brands. We took visual samples from eight commercials and measured ad awareness using a recognition approach with two different sets of storyboards.

One set of storyboards consisted exclusively of recognition stimuli identified as peak images from the pre-test Flow of Attention. The second cell used stimuli that were entirely non-peak visuals. For the very same set of commercials, advertising awareness was **40% higher** for the stimulus using peak visuals compared to the

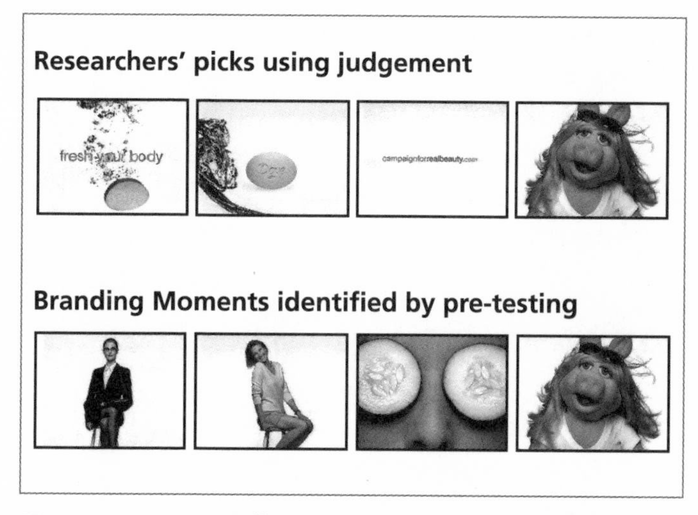

You can get two different impressions of an ad depending on which frames you pick.

one using non-peak visuals!

This magnitude of difference would be sufficient for researchers to reach entirely different conclusions about the success or failure of the advertising campaign.

Of course, this is the extreme case. In the real world a storyboard constructed using judgment is likely to contain a mix of both peak and non-peak visuals, as demonstrated by our first experiment. Nonetheless, the results underscore the importance of identifying the right images to use in recognition-based Internet ad tracking in order to narrow the range and improve the accuracy of awareness measurement.

The key to good measurement is to build a

bridge between two critical pieces of advertising research, pre-testing and tracking. By feeding consumer input from pre-testing into the tracking system, you can achieve a critical methodological improvement in the accuracy of in-market ad awareness measurements.

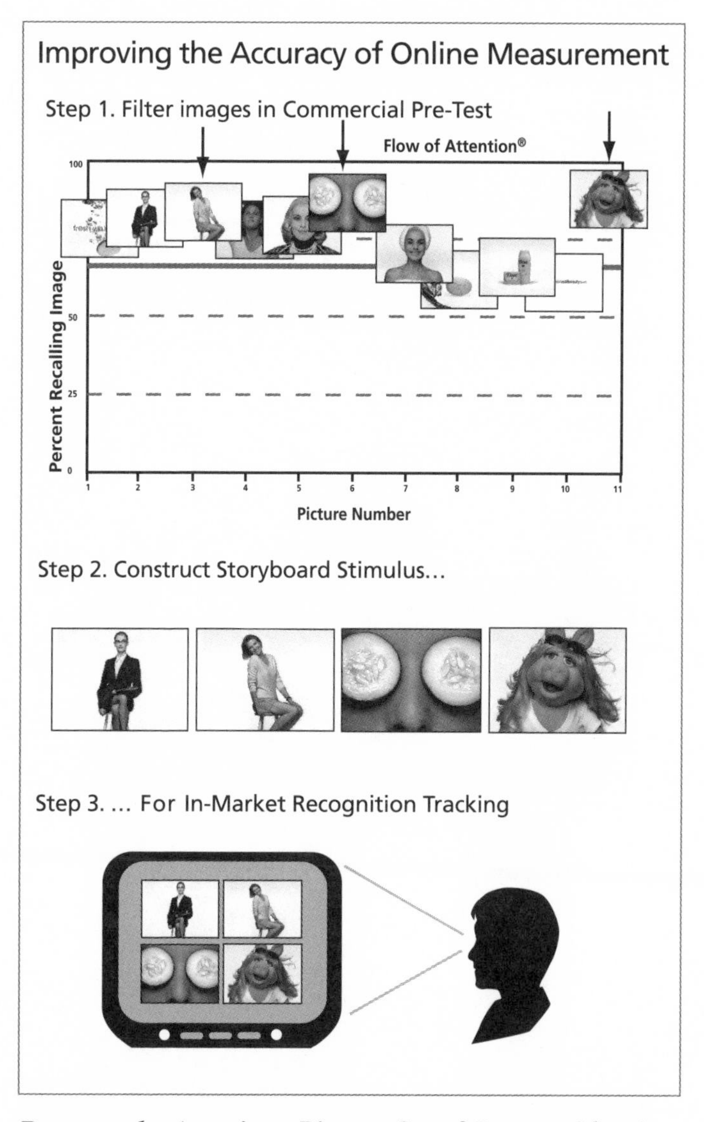

Because the Ameritest Picture Sorts® Pre-test identifies the commercial images that stick in long-term memory, it provides critical input for improving the accuracy and reliability of Post-test/Ad Tracking.

VI

Creative Tracking: Benchmarking Performance to Competitive Ads

VI

Creative Tracking: Benchmarking Performance to Competitive Ads

Change is a new constant in twenty-first century advertising. For many businesses the Internet is certainly changing how companies do advertising today and, as we will see, the Internet continues to change how advertising creative can be tracked. Yet traditional advertising forms are not going away. For many industries such as the Quick Service Restaurant business—fast food—television is likely to continue to be the main channel for driving customers through the door. Nothing beats television for its ability to create top-of-mind brand awareness and to romance the appetite appeal of food. According to the U.S. monitoring service Competitrack, over thirty new commercials for QSR restaurants debut on national television every month.

In this industry, spending on TV advertising is likely to increase. A decade ago in the QSR category, there were 14 companies with over a billion dollars in annual sales. Today there are 24. Advertising is a mission-critical function for every one of these franchise organizations competing for their share of the enormous amount of money Americans spend eating away from home. Many of the ads are for new product offerings, as these companies continuously reinvent their menus to attract fickle customers.

These highly efficient operators can tell you to the second how long it takes to cook the perfect french fry; they can tell you the sales rates of new product offerings within a few days. But the creative battlefield that their advertising has to compete in is shrouded in fog. For example, few QSR operators pre-test their commercials before airing them. A typical reason given for not doing this kind of research is that they are moving too quickly for the research step. As a corollary, it's almost unheard of to test competitive ads.

Many companies use tracking studies to evaluate the performance of their advertising in-market. While traditional tracking studies are effective at monitoring certain advertising effects over time with brand metrics, such as awareness and preference—they are severely limited in their ability to pinpoint the particular advertising executions which are driving them. In a typical twenty to thirty minute tracking interview there is simply not enough time to collect more than a few recall or recognition metrics about four or five commercial executions. In a cluttered marketplace where many new ads are coming out each month, this creates a considerable gap in knowledge about what is really going on from a creative standpoint.

Some of the more sophisticated firms use marketing mix modeling in an attempt to get a handle on advertising ROI. But statistical modelers rarely include a variable in their models to explicitly represent the creative quality of the advertising, and instead focus on the amount and timing of media spend. The reason for this is, of course, the paucity of quantitative data, e.g., copytesting metrics, profiling the strength of individual creative executions. This has the potential to cause management to undervalue the contribution that brilliant creative can make in terms of leveraging the media investment.

Here's a question: Would Man o'War have beaten Seabiscuit? The answer: It doesn't matter because these horses never ran in the same race. One of the limitations of conventional copytesting, as it evolved in the pre-Internet era, is that it's norm-based. Scoring an ad based on how it performs versus a database of commercials that have been tested at some time in the past, perhaps five, ten or more years ago, could give a false sense of security in the quickly changing world of QSR advertising.

Imagine that you are the ad manager for a major fast food brand. How would you feel if your research gives your commercial a grade of "B"? How would you feel if I tell you your major competitor's latest commercial got a score of "C"? Now, how would you feel if your competitor's commercial got an "A"? Businessmen intuitively understand that the job of advertising isn't to beat some abstract historical norm—it's to beat the other guy's advertising, right now.

Until recently real time competitive intelligence about advertising performance in very dynamic categories like fast food has not been available, largely because of the prohibitive cost of such research. The Internet provides a fast and inexpensive channel for data collection, and has begun to drive the development of automated tools for interviewing, analysis and reporting. As a result, a number of research companies have begun to develop new systems for producing a continuous stream of data on traditional media such as television and print advertising.

One such company is IAG (a part of Nielsen) which uses a traditional recall methodology to track all of the ads in a wide variety of categories in order to provide rankings of advertising on a few simple metrics such as recall, recognition (from a verbal cue), brand linkage and liking.

Another approach, developed by Ameritest, is designed both to provide real-time rankings of advertising performance, using standard metrics of creative quality, and in-depth diagnostics into the reasons why the winners are winning and the losers are losing. So far, this new approach to tracking the creative landscape has been applied successfully in a variety of fast moving categories, from retail to financial services, and for print as well as television media. Most of these studies, however, are proprietary—but in the case of QSR our data source is syndicated and thus can be reported here.

Compared with older methods of tracking, creative tracking provides a more complete dataset of all the commercials currently airing in a highly competitive category. This greatly expands the scope of analyses that can be undertaken on the dynamics of advertising performance. Using the QSR category as an example, we will see how this kind of data can be used to validate management assumptions about how advertising is supposed to work to drive short term sales results, as well as to provide new insights into how consumers process fast food commercials into long term brand images.

CREATIVE TRACKING: REAL TIME RANKINGS OF CREATIVE QUALITY

The Ameritest Ad Appraiser system is a syndicated information service that provides in-depth information about the creative quality of television commercials currently airing in the QSR category. Every new television commercial in the category is tested while it is fresh, within a couple days of its appearance on national television, and results are uploaded to a web portal within two weeks of airing. As such the data that is reported is based on a census, not a sampling, of the television advertising in the QSR category, which allows users to analyze the entire body of creative work that competing brands are putting on air over any given time frame.

Each commercial is tested monadically, with a twenty-five minute interview based on a standardized Ameritest pre-test. The performance metrics collected include attention-getting power (in a clutter of current QSR ads competing for the consumer's attention), branding, motivation to visit the restaurant, motivation to buy the featured product and brand attribute ratings.

The primary measures of Attention, Branding and Motivation are combined into a single summary statistic called the Ameritest Performance Index (API), which is indexed to a rolling past year database of QSR ads tested.

Diagnostic measures that are collected include open-end communication, verbal diagnostic ratings of the ad, three Picture Sorts and two copy sorts. From the screening interview, the fast-moving brand metrics from traditional tracking studies—such as top of mind brand awareness and brand preference—are also collected.

Respondents are recruited nationally to be past 30 day fast food consumers, with quotas for age, gender, and brand usage. Respondents are also screened to live or work near a restaurant of the brand whose advertising is being tested. For the case history described below, approximately a year's worth of QSR advertising was analyzed, therefore, the size of the total respondent database is slightly more than 30,000 interviews.

CASE HISTORY: PREDICTING MCDONALD'S SALES FROM STUDYING THE CREATIVE LANDSCAPE

During the past few years McDonald's has enjoyed one of the most positive stories of any QSR brand in terms of growth in same store sales versus a year ago in the U.S. Publicly available monthly sales data for the period January '07 to Feb '08 is shown in the chart below. During this same period McDonald's aired 42 new TV commercials nationally.

Media spend data for this period is not publicly available. To approximate a monthly share-of-voice, a surrogate measure can be easily constructed from the creative tracker data by dividing the number of new McDonald's ads in a given month by the total number of

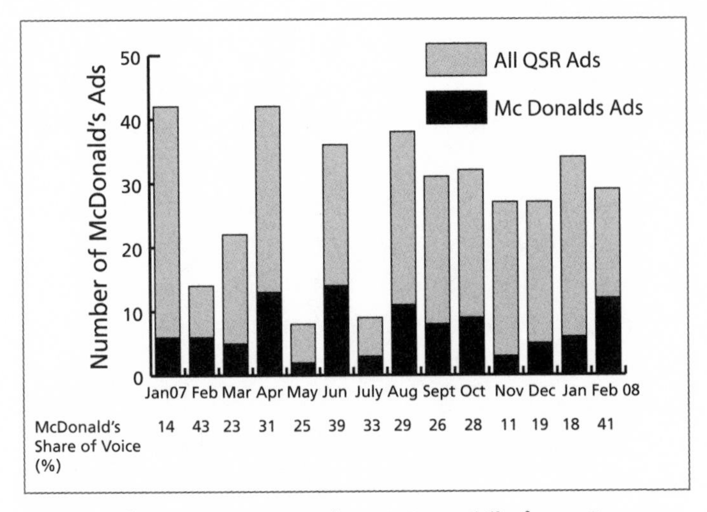

Share of Creative Voice for McDonald's from January 2007 to February 2008.

new QSR ads for that month. Measured in this way, we find that McDonald's "share-of-creative-voice" varies considerably across the time period of this analysis, from a low of 11% to a high of 43%.

The quality of McDonald's television creative also varies considerably. The percentage of McDonald's commercials scoring above versus below average for each month is shown in the following graph. Again, the measure of creative quality used here is the Ameritest Performance Index, which is a weighted combination of branded attention and motivation, with each carrying roughly equal weight in the performance index.

Finally, the focus of McDonald's messaging

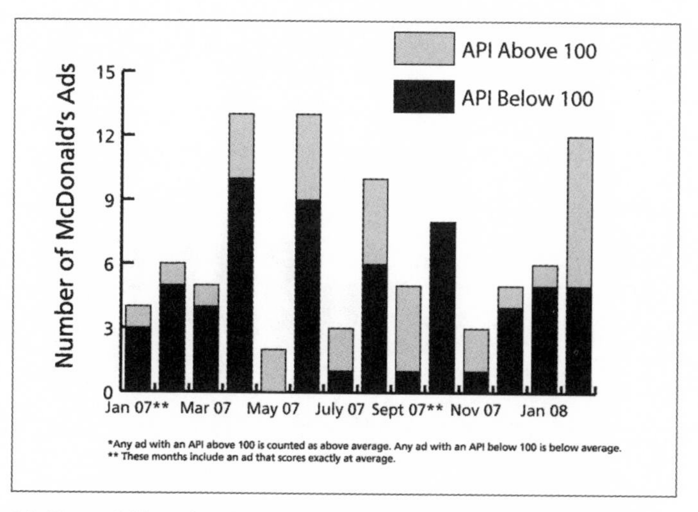

McDonald's ads: Creative quality varies widely from month to month.

varies from ad to ad. Taking as a measure of the brand value being communicated an index score greater than 110 (category = 100), "convenience" and "for the whole family" are the most common messages conveyed by McDonald's commercials, shown below.

Using these inputs we built a regression model to explain McDonald's sales growth over this fourteen month time period. The most important predictive variable in the model was the Ameritest Performance Index, which by itself explained 43% of the variation in sales growth. Adding the variable share-of-creative-voice improved the R-square to 52%; and adding the communication of the "for the whole family" brand positioning further

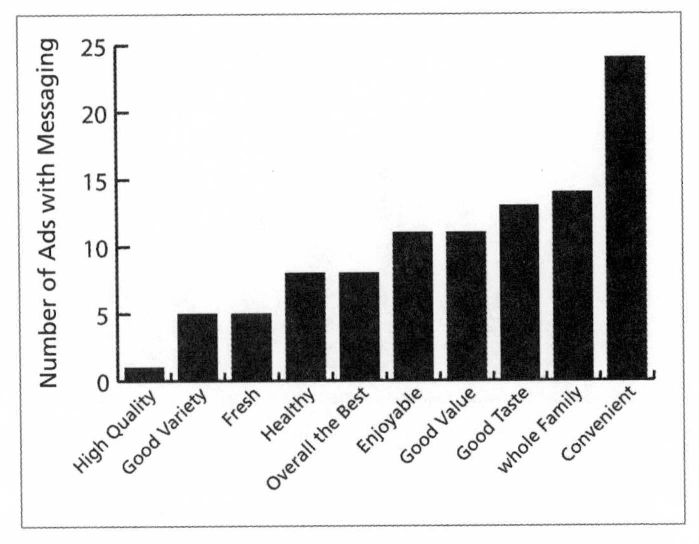

Messages communicated by 42 of McDonald's Ads.

increased the R-square to 62%. In other words, using only three variables from the data self-contained in the creative tracking system, we can explain approximately two-thirds of growth in same store sales for McDonald's over this time period.

As an additional point, we also note that midway through this time period a new item—"fresh ingredients"—was added to the set of brand value ratings collected by the creative tracker, reflecting emerging communication strategies in the category. Looking at the set of new commercials from August '07 through February '08, we found that the correlation with same store sales growth is highest for this new message of fresh ingredients, at 63%,

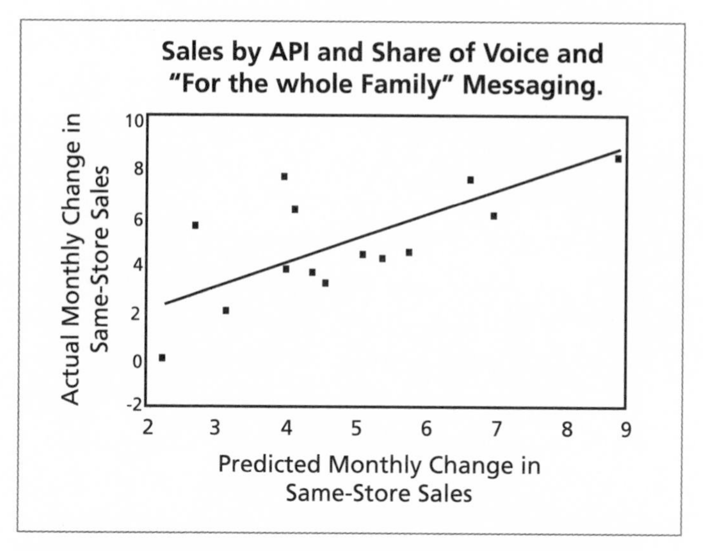

Three variables together explain two-thirds of the growth in McDonald's same-store sales over a 14 month period.

which is significantly higher than the 40% correlation found for the whole family. This suggests that in adapting to the rapidly changing realities of fast food advertising, McDonald's was also successful in finding a fresh, new communication strategy for their advertising.

McDonald's Model of Success

The simple regression model for McDonald's recent sales success story over this time period is thus: Sales Growth = Ad Quality + Share of Voice + Communication of Brand Positioning. This three variable model explaining advertising's impact on sales should have face validity for advertising practitioners for the following reasons.

First, advertising professionals understand that the quality of the creative, and not just the amount of spend, is essential for generating a good return on the advertising investment. This belief drives the specialized research category of commercial pre-testing.

Second, share-of-voice has long been known to be a predictor of sales based on work done by Michael Moroney and, independently, James Peckham. While the share-of-voice estimate used here, which is derived from a count of commercial executions, may not be as accurate as a figure calculated from actual spend data (or even better GRPs,) it's a reasonable surrogate for a company as prolific in its creative as McDonald's. One source of error in this estimate, however, is that it does not include commercials which are no longer new but which McDonald's chose to air again or update with minor re-edits.

Third, this model shows that a consistent communication strategy over time is also important. The clear communication of a relevant message is an important driver of motivation—the cumulative effect of reinforcing the same message again and again across executions is important for maintaining a stable market positioning for the brand. For any given execution, however, tactical considerations may call for a different communication objective, as evidenced by the variety of messages that McDonald's has been broadcasting and in particular, by their increasing use of the fresh ingredients message.

VII

Leading Audience Attention

VII

Leading Audience Attention

Two books share a core metaphor and provide important lessons for advertising practitioners: *Blink*, by Malcolm Gladwell, and *In the Blink of an Eye*, by Walter Murch. These books provide valuable insights into how an audience experiences advertising film—and ultimately, in how brand images get built.

Gladwell is a best-selling science journalist who writes about the new science of rapid cognition, the role of the unconscious mind in decision making. Murch is an award winning Hollywood film editor who has worked on such movies as *American Graffiti*, *The Godfather Part II, Apocalypse Now, Ghost* and *The English Patient*. As one of the leading craftsmen of the cinematic art form, Murch describes his work habits and esthetic theories.

Rapid Cognition and the Attentional Blink

Gladwell created quite a stir in advertising circles because of his science based defense of the role of the "gut" in effective decision making. He writes about the theory of the "adaptive unconscious." This is the notion that up to 95% of the decisions we make everyday are outside of our conscious field of attention. The mind is thought of as a kind of giant computer that quickly and quietly processes a lot of the data behind the scenes while we focus on a few icons on our cerebral desktop.

A blink is a particularly apt metaphor for this theory because of its reference to the eye. It is what modern neuroscientists call the "attention blink" or "spotlighting."

As we watch television, the eye actively filters film images—on a pre-conscious level—deciding what to let into the conscious mind, and into long term memory, to form those images associated with a brand. It's a snap-decision process, like the way you sort through junk mail, when and decide in a fraction of a second to toss a piece of advertising, unopened, into the trash or set aside the letter from the IRS to look at later. As a defense mechanism, the eye has evolved efficient anti-spam filters to avoid sensory overload.

If you stop to think about it, without such pre-conscious filtering you wouldn't be able to drive a car. At even a moderate speed, as you look through the windshield at the road, thousands of pieces of information from the outside world are competing for your attention: the oncoming traffic, the bicyclist, the pedestrian about to cross the street, the signal light up ahead about to change color, the car getting ready to make the left turn, the voice over from the passenger in the seat next to yours, the number on the house you're searching for, and so on. Without the ability to filter and focus on the street scene ahead of you, you'd quickly have an accident.

According to Gladwell, the reason we can do this is because of how our minds "thin-slice" the information that we take in. Gladwell says,

> *"'Thin-slicing' refers to the ability of our unconscious to find patterns in situations and behavior based on very narrow slices of experience."*

THE PSYCHOLOGY OF EDITING FILM

In terms of film, we as an audience are using the same pre-conscious ability of thin slicing as we participate in the process of making meaning. Gladwell tells a story in *Blink* of how the scientist Paul Ekman, an expert in reading faces, deconstructed a film of Kato Kaelin's testimony in the O.J. Simpson trial and demonstrated thin slicing in action. By taking apart the film down to a single frame, one moment stood out from the others. During hostile questioning by the attorney Marcia Clark, Kato's face was utterly transformed. His otherwise passive face was caught in that "slice" of film with teeth bared, eyebrows lowered. Ekman described him as "a snarling dog."

As all editors and filmmakers know, this deconstruction is vital to the process of storytelling through film. From a filmmaking perspective, the art of editing lies in determining how to cut the visual information in film into meaningful slices of experience.

Walter Murch considers the discovery that our visual experience could be thin-sliced as the defining moment in the history of film. He states,

> *"The discovery early in the century that certain kinds of cutting 'worked' led almost immediately to the discovery that films could be shot discontinuously, which was the cinematic equivalent of the discovery of flight."*

Anyone who has watched an unedited home movie can see why editing is so important to the success of movies. Yet it was not obvious to early film-makers that slicing up visual experience and rejoining them in a way that violates the continuity of "real life" would be anything but confusing. After all, if the "wholeness" of experience was divided, wouldn't something of the essence be lost? Murch continues,

> *"The mysterious part of it, though, is that the joining of those pieces—the 'cut' in American terminology—actually does seem to work, even though it represents a total and instantaneous displacement of one field of vision with another, a displacement that sometimes also entails a jump forward or backward in time as well as space."*

While their business is making movies and

not writing books about the psychology behind the movies, experienced film artists must operate with at least implicit psychological theories about why they do what they do. One of the greatest film directors of all time, John Huston, gave this down-to-earth description of the psychological nature of the cut in an interview, which Murch quotes in his book:

> *"Look at that lamp across the room. Now look back at me. Look back at that lamp. Now look back at me again. Do you see what you did? You blinked. Those are the cuts. After the first look, you know that there's no reason to pan continuously from me to the lamp because you know what's in between. Your mind cut the scene. First you behold the lamp. Cut. Then you behold me."*

Indeed, much of the art of editing film lies in controlling the discontinuities of thin slices of film experience. As Murch explains,

> *"We must render visual reality discontinuous; otherwise perceived reality would resemble an almost incomprehensible string of letters without word separation or punctuation."*

The cut in film is comparable to the essential role of the gutter in a comic strip. It is into that infinitely thin space between two adjacent but distinct slices of experience that the audience's imagination enters in order to close the gap in continuity. It is here that audience's imagination participates, on equal terms with the filmmaker, in co-creating the meaning of the film.

Together, the filmmaker and the audience are engaged in a creative dance. The job of the filmmaker is to "lead" his dance partner from one idea or emotion to the next. As Murch points out,

> *"Your job is partly to anticipate, partly to control the thought processes of the audience. To give them what they want and/or what they need just before they have to 'ask' for it—to be surprising yet self-evident at the same time."*

All together, Murch describes six criteria for what makes a good cut as follows,

> *"An ideal cut (for me) is the one that satisfies all of the following six criteria at once: 1) it is true to the emotion of the moment; 2) it advances the story; 3) it occurs at a moment that is rhythmically interesting and 'right'; 4) it acknowledges what you might call 'eye-trace'—the concern with the location and movement of the audience's focus of interest within the frame; 5) it respects 'planarity'—the grammar of three dimensions transposed by photography to two (the question of stage-line, etc); 6) and it respects the three-dimensional continuity of the actual space."*

Emotion is the most important of these to Murch by far. And for that reason it is interesting to describe the work habits he has developed over time for keeping track of the emotions he is trying to create in the film.

As part of his preparation for a project he creates a visual vocabulary for the emotional language of the film he is working on. He does this by taking still photographs from the raw film that has been shot. Murch states,

> *"But in addition to the usual procedures, I also would select at least one representative frame from every setup and take a still photograph of it off the workprint. ...and they were put onto panels arranged according to scene..."*

The reason he does this is that he understands intuitively the limitations of language. Words, while they are important, cannot capture all of the esthetic information contained in a picture. Murch continues,

> *"...the most interesting asset of the photos for me was that they provided the hieroglyphs for a language of emotions. What word expresses the concept of ironic anger tinged with melancholy? There isn't a word for it, in English anyway, but you can see that specific emotion represented in this photograph."*

Murch's purpose in using still photographs is "to embody the nameless but familiar emotion I see in that photograph." The still photographs provide a set of keys to the emotions flowing through the film experience he is constructing. Murch explains,

> *"In choosing a representative frame, what you're looking for is an image that distills the essence of the thousands of frames that make up the shot in question, what Cartier-Bresson—referring to still photography—called the 'decisive moment.' So I think, more often than not, the image that I chose wound up in the film. And also, more often than not, quite close to the cut point."*

The heart of the art of editing lies in developing an intuitive feel for the "right" time to make the cut. That requires a feel for the response of the filmmaker's creative partner, the audience.

Early film theorists suggested that a cut should be made at the peak of the "content curve," which is the point in the shot at which the audience has been able to absorb most of its information. Cut too soon and the audience gets confused; wait too long and the film begins to drag and gets boring. According to Murch, the blink is tied to the audience's comprehension,

> *"I believe you will find that your listener will blink at the precise moment he or she 'gets' the idea of what you are saying, not an instant earlier or later."*

Blinks occur at focal points of audience attention. They correspond to the idea of the "beat" in music; in acting, the beat is also used to describe the emotional transactions between two actors performing the dialogue in a scene. An actor who is fully engaged in a scene can react to unpredictable events "without missing a beat." Similarly, in film the visual "beat" is the emotional or informational transaction between the filmmaker and the audience. A sequence of such peak moments of audience attention gives rise to structure in the flow of experience.

The importance of rhythmic structure in communication extends beyond film.Cognitive researchers, for example, have commented on the importance of rhythm and beat in language to help us organize the information in a conversation to avoid cognitive overload by focusing on predictable, strategic moments to pay attention. In spoken language, for instance, the words you stress are the important ones, and you automatically speed up or slow down on the words in between so that the major points of stress form a regular chain of beats. The beat is when speakers often convey key information and bring up new topics.

In advertising film, the visual beat of the film is strongly related to the attention-getting power and the recall score of a television commercial. Research published by Ameritest shows that the number of peak moments, or visual beats, is the single best predictor of a TV commercial's ability to break through clutter. The number of visual beats is tied to narrative structure, how the film is edited to involve the audience. For example, good stories are generally characterized by more beats.

The same research shows that the difference between attention and recall is the type of information content of the visual beats of the ad film.

Ads that do well on day-after recall tests will focus the audience attention on product-related information, such as visualizations of the consumer need, product attributes, product demos, the package or the brand name. This is not surprising, since recall testing is based on the theory that advertising works by "teaching" you something about the product. In fact, that's where recall tests came from originally—your teacher taught you a lesson on Wednesday and gave you a recall test on Friday to see if you learned anything.

In contrast to recall, attention scores are driven by the esthetic or emotional content of the ad. The images in the visual beat of the film may not show the product, but by engaging the attention and emotions of the audience they can still make a profitable contribution to the brand's image. Indeed, recent research on a successful ad campaign has shown that the images that occur in those visual beats—and not any of the other images from the commercial—can still be found in the memories of consumers up to five years after the commercial has gone off air. So, it appears that those peak moments are where the long term work of advertising is being done: creating brands.

Using the same techniques we use for advertising film, we thin-sliced the film experience of a classic silent film, *The Tramp,* (See the exhibit at the end of this chapter). Looking at the Flow of Attention, you can see the editing rhythm of the film through the eyes of the audience. In this thirty seven minute movie there are twelve major peaks of audience interest that stand out above all the other images in the film. And what, do you suppose, is the irresistible magnet for the eye of the audience? The brand: Charlie Chaplin.

Many in the advertising community who have embraced Gladwell's book on the grounds that you should "trust your instincts" have overlooked one of the important lessons of the book. Gladwell says,

> *"Our unconscious is a powerful force. But it's fallible. It's not the case that our internal computer always shines through, instantly decoding the 'truth' of a situation. It can be thrown off, distracted, and disabled."*

For researchers the story about how it was possible for ordinary people to obtain insights into the operations of the subconscious is particularly salient. *Blink* tells the story of a researcher who developed a complex model to predict whether or not couples would get divorced over time by analyzing videotapes of them having conversations. As a training exercise, the researcher took a number of couples' videos and showed them to non-experts. The researcher thin-sliced the videos into very short sections, and gave them a simple list of emotions to look for. What happened? The non-experts predicted with 80% accuracy which marriages were going to make it.

The potential contribution of research to the creative process appears to be a belief shared by Walter Murch as follows,

> *"Toward the end of the editing process on Julia, Fred Zimmerman observed that he felt the director and the editor, alone with the film for months and months, could only go ninety percent of the way toward the finished film—that what was needed for the last ten percent was 'the participation of the audience', who he saw as his final collaborators. Not in the sense that he would respond to them blindly, but that he felt their presence was helpful as a corrective, to keep certain obsessions from becoming corrosive and to point out blind spots that may have developed through over-familiarity with the material."*

Toward this end, Murch urges a certain kind of "virginity"—the ability to see the movie as if for the first time. He states,

"The editor, on the other hand, should try to see only what's on the screen, as the audience will."

Gladwell and Murch have contributed valuable insights into exactly how rapid cognition and film work. Expertise in making advertising films, and in-depth knowledge about a brand—these give individuals the expertise Gladwell talks about, the kind that can often enable reliable and extraordinarily fast decisions. Yet, it is the product of that expertise that must thrive away from home and out in the world. In the final analysis, it is the audience whose advertising experience matters and who will, or will not, create a vigorous brand.

If researchers have one thing to add above all else, it's audience experience. The analysis of thousands of commercials have demonstrated without ambiguity that audiences, taught from childhood how to watch films, have an expertise of their own to add, and they do it in the blink of an eye.

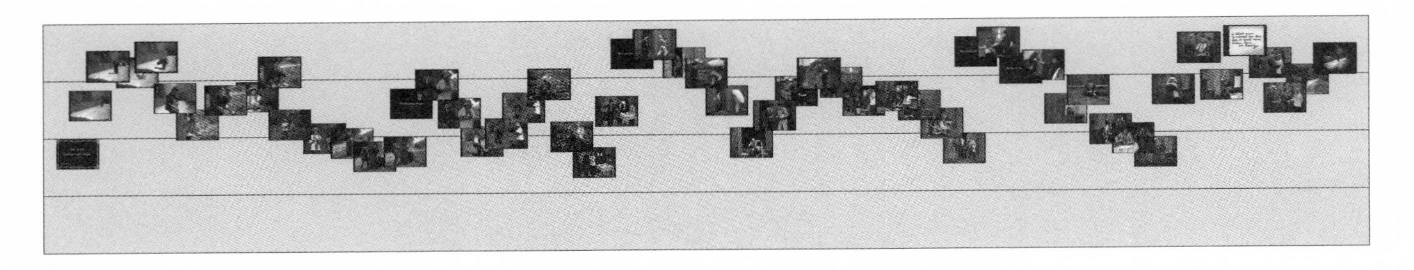

The Ameritest Flow of Attention graph makes visible the rhythms of visual storytelling. This is an audience analysis of the 37-minute film classic, "The Tramp." *On this graph, the height of each picture tells you the percentage of the audience that is paying attention to a particular image. Notice how the star, Charlie Chaplin, is the focus of audience attention—his image occurs in most of the memorable storytelling peaks. Peak moments are key to understanding how the structure and drama of film creates an emotional experience. In TV advertising, the same creative process is used to make products famous and build brand image.*

VIII

How Attention Drives Recall

VIII

How Attention Drives Recall

All major copytesting systems report "Recall" or "Attention" as a measure of "breakthrough"—a commercial's ability to leverage a given level of media weight to capture the attention of a wide audience and thus deliver its intended message.

Some years ago Unilever reported on the analysis of sixty television commercials that had each been tested separately by three different major pre-testing systems. The correlation between recall and various attention measures is shown in the table below. You will observe that they are in fact uncorrelated measures.

Thus, we arrive at an important insight: recall and attention cannot both be measuring "break-through" power—they are actually measuring fundamentally different aspects of a commercial's performance.

In order to see clearly past the labels with which we name things, we need to examine diagnostic variables that help to explain what it is we really are measuring when we talk about attention and recall. An analysis of structure and content in communication can provide important insights into the measurement constructs of attention and recall.

Breakthrough Measures

	Ipsos ASI Recall
Ipsos ASI Attention	0.67**
Ameritest Attention	0.09
Millward Brown Attention	-0.28*

*Note: * > 95% confidence ** > 99% confidence*

Correlation between recall and attention measures of the three pre-testing systems.

THE IMPORTANCE OF RHYTHMIC STRUCTURE

The importance of rhythmic structure in communication has been studied by a number of social researchers. Rhythm and beat in language help us organize the information in a conversation to avoid cognitive overload by focusing on predictable, strategic moments to pay attention. In spoken language, the words you stress are the important ones, and you automatically speed up or slow down on the words in between so that major points of stress form a regular chain of beats. Researchers have found that the beat often occurs when speakers convey key information or introduce new topics.

In video, a sense of rhythm and pace are just as important. In terms of making a cut from one shot to another, Raymond Spotiswoode, an early film theorist, suggested that a cut should be made at the peak of the "content curve," which is the point within a single shot at which the audience has been able to absorb most of its information.

Content is in the eye of the consumer as well as under the control of a commercial director. Frame-by-frame viewer attention to the visuals in television advertising can vary widely even during a 'forced' viewing of an ad. This is due not only to the effects of film editing but also to the operation of selective perception.

Video communication can be thought of as having a structure that reflects a complex dance between a commercial director and their audience—one partner might lead but the other certainly must follow. In operational terms, the rhythms of that interaction can be described with a visual processing curve known as a Flow of Attention® as illustrated below.

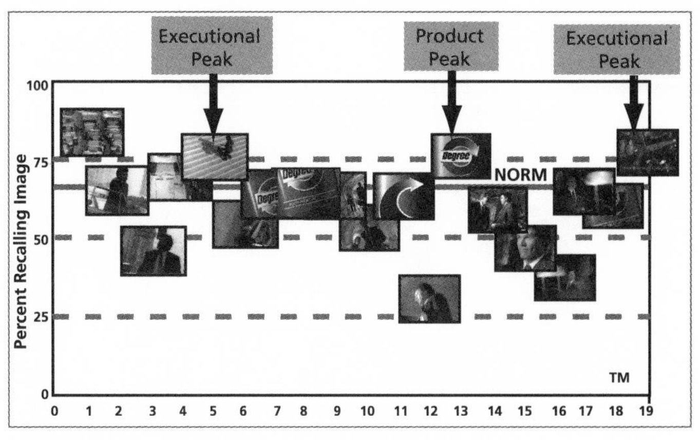

Flow of Attention for Degree Ad.

This measure of attention is based on the insight that the human eye should not be thought of as a recording device like a camera, but rather should be thought of as a search engine. The intelligent eye is a gatekeeper of perception that pre-consciously filters visual stimuli as part of the complex mental process of first deconstructing and then reconstructing visual perception.

In analysis, this wavelike structure can be characterized using three parameters.

First, we have found that the opening frames of attention should either start at a high level or rise rapidly in the first three or four frames, indicating that the commercial has done a good job of "hooking" the viewer into the ad. The presence or absence of category or brand cues in these early frames may also be important for understanding how well an ad "sets up" the viewer for the message that is to follow.

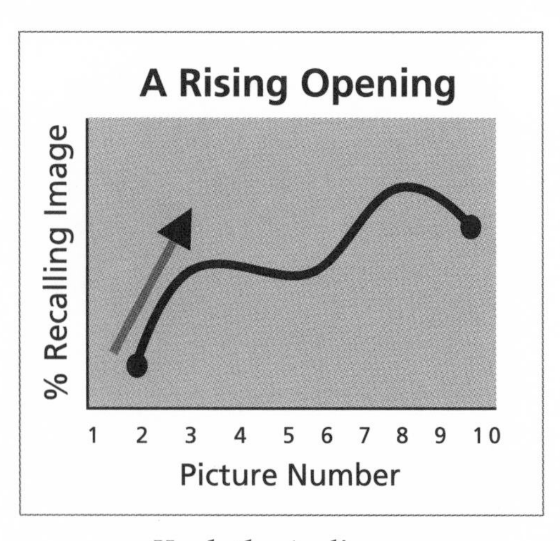

Hook the Audience.

Second, well-structured commercials will exhibit a positive, or at least level, trend line for the entire time series of image recall data. This indicates that the commercial has held attention from the beginning to the end of the ad, or, even better, built curiosity and involvement over time.

Third, and most importantly, the peaks of the wave represent the "beats" of the video rhythm curve. Another way to think about these peaks is that they are focal points of viewer attention as it varies over time. In general, the greater number of beats in a given execution—which indicates that visual information is being focused on and assimilated at a faster rate—the higher the attention or recall score of the ad.

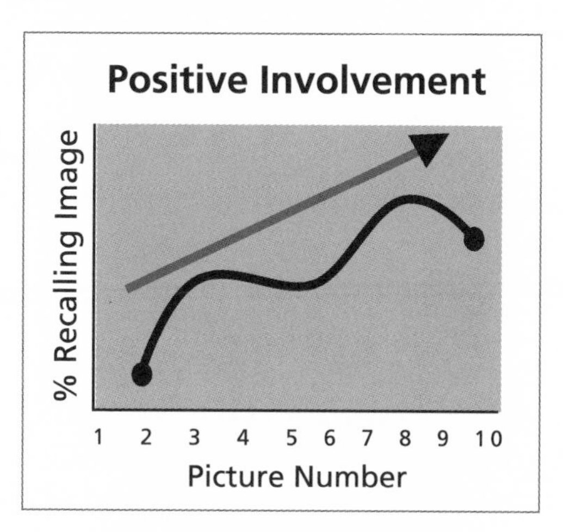

Hold Attention over time.

Peak moments are defined as local maxima in the flow curve. These are images in the graph that are relatively higher than adjacent images in the neighborhood of that moment in time and are not defined relative to a norm or some absolute level of recognition. Also, by conven-

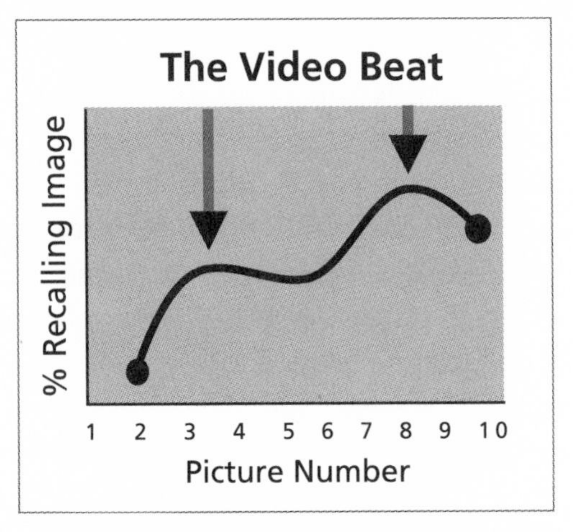

More beats generate higher Attention and Recall scores.

tion, the first image in a flow graph is not counted as a peak.

Peaks of attention in a commercial may be classified into different categories based on the type of visual information contained in the peak. One simple classification scheme for packaged goods advertising is to look at product-related versus executional (or non-product) content. By product-related we mean package shots, product demos, product-in-use shots, specific product claims, or information about support points such as ingredients, or simply the brand name. All other peaks would, by default, be classified as executional—these are frequently the key visuals that convey the emotional content of the ad. More generally, executional content might be thought of in terms of the idea of "esthetic information" as described in Abraham Moles' classic work, *Information Theory and Esthetic Perception.*

Semantic Content Drives Recall Scores

If your goal is to diagnose or predict a recall score, such as those provided by Ipsos-ASI, it turns out that counting the number of *peaks containing product-related information* is the most important variable to focus on. More product peaks are associated with higher recall scores. On the other hand, if your goal is to diagnose or predict an attention score, such as those provided by the Millward-Brown or Ameritest pre-testing systems, you need to focus on the *total number of peaks*, including the executional or non-product peaks containing emotional content. The more peak moments in an ad, the higher the attention scores in either system.

Looking at our Degree deodorant example again, we note that there are three peaks in the Flow of Attention®—one product peak and two executional peaks. The product peak contains a brand mnemonic which summarizes Degree's functional product positioning—the idea that when your body heat rises, Degree kicks in to work harder. The two executional peaks contain dramatizations of that idea. The first executional peak shows a man running up a flight of stairs to give a speech before a large audience. The need for the brand is conveyed in the symbolism of the rising stairs—his body heat is rising as he runs, late for his presentation. The second visual contains dramatic proof that the brand works—he looks cool and collected on the platform as he begins his speech.

A fourth pattern to look for in analyzing the flow of audience attention through a commercial is to look for evidence of turbulence, or discontinuities, in the flow of attention curve. This would usually be a series of images that fall out of the smooth flow of the curve, with attention abruptly dropping by a significant amount, say twenty

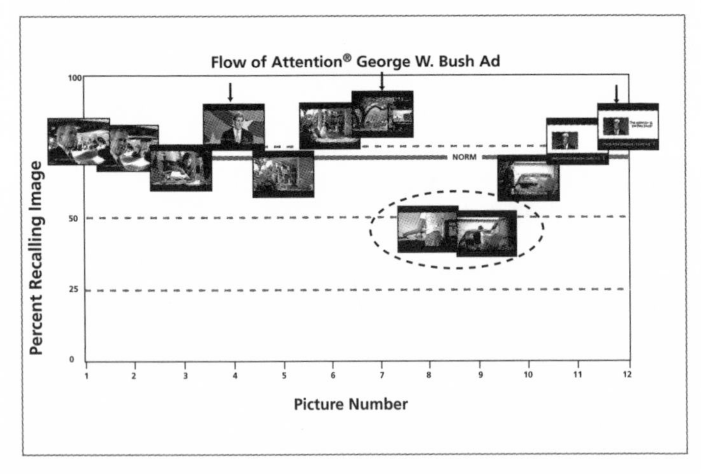

Evidence of turbulence in the Flow of Attention graph for a political ad.

or thirty percentage points, indicating that a significant fraction of the audience got off track and missed this part of the film. A single image falling out is usually discounted as a transitional image and is not considered important—unless inspection of the image reveals that it contained key information that the commercial was intended to convey.

Such a break in the continuity of audience attention is direct evidence of audience confusion, even if the audience does not admit to being confused by the ad (they rarely do). Confusion or the interruptions in our train of thought can undermine both attention and recall scores.

This kind of confusion is usually caused by flaws in how the film is edited together—the film equivalent of violating the rules of grammar and syntax when writing a sentence. From an attention standpoint, the director took an unexpected right turn in transitioning from one idea or image to another and the audience didn't follow. Fortunately, these kinds of problems with attention are usually an easy fix in the editing room.

Finally, we should also keep in mind that attention varies and flows through the copy or audio-track accompanying the film, and not just the visuals. Audience attention to verbal thoughts can be measured with a Flow of Attention graph of the copy, measured by a copy sort that is similar to the picture sort.

Words and pictures interact to create thoughts and meaning in the mind of the audience and this interaction is strongly affected by timing, sequencing and synchronicity. For example, recall scores are strongly affected by the early introduction of audio brand cues, while attention scores are not. Failures in communication or weaknesses in brand linkage can frequently be traced to a poor synchronization of what is being shown with what is being said.

To sum up, the ability of a commercial to attract the attention of an audience, and the ability of the audience to recall the commercial later on, is a function of both the structure and content of the ad. In terms of structure, both types of performance measures benefit from a strong opening, strong and frequent focal points of visual attention, and an overall build in visual interest over time. Both types of commercial metrics suffer when there are breaks in the train of consumer thought or when confusion enters to interrupt the smooth flow of audience attention. Where the two types of performance metrics differ is in content: recall reflects the rational, verbal, semantic content of the ad, and attention responds more to the esthetic or emotional content of advertising. Depending on the strategic objective of the advertising, which may differ as a function of such variables as the lifestage of a brand, or the news you have to talk about, both metrics can be useful measures of advertising performance.

IX

Three Measures of Branding

IX

Three Measures of Branding

What is the role of the brand in the little movie that is a television commercial? Is it the star of the movie driving the plot forward and occupying the center spotlight of consumer thoughts whether on screen or off? Is it a supporting actor carrying a scene or two in the service of the action and providing essential information to move the story along? Or perhaps it's more like a director or producer, only appearing in the credits at the beginning or end of the film?

Many commercial pre-testing systems report metrics with such labels as "branding" or "brand linkage." Not surprisingly, each system defines this "branding" construct using its own measurement approach. But we must be careful not to assume that just because the same "surface" label is being used, that the "deep" constructs being measured are equivalent. As you will see, the branding measures provided by three major pre-testing systems are each measuring something completely different.

Not too long ago Unilever, which produces hundreds of commercials a year in support of over a thousand brands, performed some research-on-research to study the measures that were being produced by the three different research pre-testing suppliers that they were using: Ameritest®, Ipsos-ASI and Millward-Brown.

The database was 60 television commercials that were tested in all three systems. The sample of commercials were all taken from the home and personal care product division, but represented a considerable range of creative work from over a half dozen ad agencies. Half the ads tested were for new products, and half were for established brands. Half were final film, and half were animatic rough productions. The conclusions we drew from each of these types of ads were similar.

This research focused on one of the key "report card" measure that is used to evaluate creative work—"brand linkage" or "branding".

IPSOS-ASI'S "BRIDGE" BETWEEN RECALL AND RECOGNITION

Of the three pre-testing firms, the Ipsos-ASI measure of Brand Linkage is the only measure derived from two primary measures rather than measured directly. It is of particular theoretical interest because it tries to combine the two fundamentally different approaches that we have for tapping into memory—recall and recognition.

On a conceptual level, the Ipsos-ASI measure is quite attractive. It attempts to quantify the strength of the connection between two different memory systems where advertising content might be stored. Recall uses category and brand cues to retrieve memories from the semantic memory system. Recognition, by contrast, uses a verbal description of an ad to elicit the memory of the advertising from the episodic memory system that is then reported as an attention score. In metaphorical terms, therefore, we might think of this measurement construct as the bridge between two memory systems.

Millward Brown's "Fit" Between Brand and Execution

Millward Brown's measure of Branding is of major interest since it was specifically designed to help predict incremental gains in advertising awareness measured by their continuous tracking studies. Specifically, Millward Brown uses the mean of a five-point verbal scale ranging from "You couldn't help but remember this commercial is for (brand)" all the way to "It could be a commercial for almost anything."

The idea here is that advertising should avoid being generic. A poorly branded ad is one where both structure and/or style fail to direct the viewer beyond broad category cues; there is no unmistakable signpost for the viewer to identify the specific brand being advertised. In contrast, for a well-branded commercial, it is difficult for consumers to talk about the ad without also talking about the brand. This measure of branding, therefore, is characterized by strong product/narrative integration.

In metaphorical terms, we might think of this measurement construct as *tailor-made.* Advertising is like a suit that a brand wears; the well-dressed brand should wear a custom-tailored, "bespoke" suit rather than buying one ready-made right off the rack.

AMERITEST'S "TOP-OF-MIND" LINKAGE

Ameritest's measurement of Brand Linkage uses a method different from the other two systems. This measure of branding is similar to the unaided or top-of-mind brand awareness measure generated by a traditional advertising tracking study. At the beginning of the test interview respondents are shown a clutter reel of five commercials—a test ad preceded and followed by two control ads—and are then asked the question, "Which of these ads did you find interesting?" If they mention the test ad as one of the interesting ads, the open-ended response to this question is coded for whether or not the respondent used the brand name. Brand Linkage, then, is the ratio of respondents spontaneously referencing the brand to the total number of respondents who found the ad interesting (not the total test sample).

Since the respondent only has to retrieve the

brand name from short-term memory, this measure is not really a memory test but a measure of brand salience. Consequently, an appropriate metaphor for understanding this branding construct is that of a *handle* that the consumer uses to hold on to the experience created by well-branded advertising.

RELATIONSHIPS AMONG THE BRANDING MEASURES

In analyzing our database, the first thing we looked at was the correlations between the three measures of branding. Even though each system is approaching the problem differently, perhaps these measures are all tapping into the same thing in the mind?

As you can see in the table below, the Ipsos-ASI measure of Brand Linkage is uncorrelated with the Millward Brown measure of Branding and has only a small positive correlation with the Ameritest measure of Branding. The

	Branding Measures	
	ASI	**Ameritest**
Millward Brown Branding	.14	-.02
Ameritest Brand Linkage	.32*	1.0

** Significant > 99%* *n=60 commercials*

Branding Measures for three major pre-testing systems are all uncorrelated.

Millward Brown and Ameritest measures of Branding are also uncorrelated. In short, each of these three measures of branding appear to represent three unrelated views of how well-branded an ad is.

Next we examined the correlations between these three measures of branding and measures of breakthrough—recall and attention—produced by the three systems. As you can see in in the table below, for this particular dataset Ipsos-ASI branding measure is highly correlated with recall and is only nominally correlated with the Ipsos-ASI measure of attention. The Ipsos-ASI branding measure is also uncorrelated with the Ameritest measure of attention, but negatively correlated with the Millward Brown measure of attention at a significant level.

One reason the Ipsos-ASI measure is correlated with recall is that the particular measure of attention used in the test is a verbal descrip-

	Branding Measures		
	ASI	Millward Brown	Ameritest
ASI Recall	.82*	.14	.19
ASI Attention	.15	.16	-.04
Ameritest Attention	-.02	.20	.06
Millward Brown Attention	-.47*	.16	-.26*

** Significant > 99%*

Branding and breakthrough measures are also uncorrelated.

tion of the advertising—a verbal cue for the semantic memory system which may unfairly penalize visually interesting television commercials that are hard to describe in words but which might have been recognized with a visual cue. If this is true, then the apparent flaw in the Ipsos-ASI measure of branding may be in its operational definition of attention rather than in the underlying construct of recall divided by attention.

THREE MODELS OF BRANDING

To gain further insight into these measures of branding, we built three regression models to explain understand the conceptual basis of commercial well-brandedness using such executional variables as the timing and occurrence of audio category and brand cues, total audio brand name mentions, as well as visual diagnostics produced by the Ameritest Flow of Attention. All three models showed a good fit with actual commercial performance on the branding measures, with each explaining over half of the variance in actual scores.

Five variables did the best job of explaining the Ipsos-ASI branding score. Liking enters the model with a negative beta, which is consistent with published research on this particular dataset which showed a negative relationship between liking and recall—a finding that was used to argue that recall testing penalizes emotional advertising. The Ameritest brand linkage measure also enters the ASI model, which is not surprising given the small positive correlation reported above. Two audio variables also carry significant weight in the model. The first is the presence of an early audio category cue and the second is total number of brand name mentions in the commercial. Both of these variables have frequently been commented on by Ipsos-ASI in their recommended list "best practices" for advertising. Finally, a visual variable representing a focus on the rational information or product-related content in the commercial adds to the predictive power of the ASI model.

Five variables do a good job of explaining the Millward Brown measure of branding. The first is purchase intent while the second is the entertainment value of an execution. Here, we found that the Millward Brown measure also implicitly performs some of the "bridging" function between strategy and execution claimed for the Ipsos-ASI measure.

Next, we find two audio variables entering the model: the presence of an early brand cue and the total number of audio brand name mentions. Finally, the presence of an early brand visual in an attention peak also leads to higher Millward Brown branding scores.

The Ameritest measure of branding can be explained in large part by four variables. The first is brand fit, which is the same question used in the Millward Brown branding measure, but weighted somewhat differently.

The next two variables pertain to the level of viewer involvement in processing the visuals in the commercial: the overall average level of attention to the visuals and presence of a strong opening or visual hooks to the ad. The fourth variable is the presence of a "single-minded branding moment" in an attention peak. A single-minded branding moment is an image in the commercial in which the identity of the brand is the focus of audience attention and, within-the-frames, does not have to compete for viewer attention with other executional elements within the frame.

Importantly, this last variable makes no reference to where in the overall flow of the ad—i.e., beginning, middle, or end—that the peak might be located. Of the three branding measures, therefore, this is the one most likely to respond to commercials that withhold the brand identity until the end of the ad.

The multiple regression results suggest that two of the three models of branding, i.e., those for Ipsos-ASI and Millward Brown, appear to be weighted somewhat more heavily toward the audio or verbal components of commercial executions while the Ameritest model is driven more by the visuals. This suggests that these measures may in some sense be complementary, balancing out both verbal and visual ways of branding television commercials. None of the three, therefore, could be considered a complete measure of brand linkage.

X

Four Types of Memories

X

Four Types of Memories

The Naming of Cats is a difficult matter,
It isn't just one of your holiday games;
You may think at first I'm as mad as a hatter
When I tell you, a cat must have THREE DIFFERENT NAMES.
—T.S. Eliot

How advertising creates memories has long been a principle subject of advertising research. After all, it is only through the processes of memory that advertising can create the long-term value which sets it apart from other forms of marketing such as promotion or price competition. Indeed, the "equity" of a brand can be thought of as the sum total of the ideas, images and emotions that we associate with a given product or service and store in our long term memories.

Not surprisingly, therefore, the first standard for measuring TV ad performance was day-after-recall. This metric is still widely used today and generates much controversy among research practitioners and agency creatives because of the counter-intuitive results it regularly produces; highly emotional ads, for instance, frequently do not generate good recall scores. The reason for this conflict is the underlying assumption of recall testing that memory works in only one way. In fact, the current science of cognitive psychology suggests that traditional recall research has it only one-third right.

The grandfather of modern memory research, Endel Tulving, actually described three different memory systems in his book *The Elements of Episodic Memory:* (1) the semantic memory system, where the brain stores facts, concepts and language, (2) the episodic memory system, where the brain stores sensations, emotions and personalized memories—i.e., the private memories that define the self, and (3) the procedural memory system where the brain stores learned behaviors and sensations of bodily movement, such as how to tie your shoelaces, drive a car, or play a violin.

The memory systems of the brain are highly organized, not simply "junk drawers" of the mind into which the traces of our experience are dropped at random. As modern researchers in cognitive neuroscience have pointed out, this organization of our memories is necessary for the brain to form internal "models" or "representations" of the external world. These models or representations such as ideas, concepts, brands, etc., determine the functional usefulness of our memories of past experience in guiding our future behaviors. Critical to understanding how our memories are organized, is knowing how the perceptions of our experiences are "tagged" for future retrieval.

In his book *Hidden Order* John Holland points out that "tags" are fundamental building blocks that make up complex dynamic systems of all kinds, from biology to the stock market. Tags are essential for creating order out of chaos. At a higher level of description, brands themselves are tags for the marketplace. To understand how advertising forms memories, we ad researchers need to better understand the different types of tags that form the basis of long term brand building.

The French musicologist Abraham Moles wrote about the different types of information that plug into the different memory systems of the mind. He makes a key distinction between semantic and esthetic information, and the "non-literal" kind of information contained in works of art such as music, poetry and film. Semantic information is the part of a message that can be translated from one channel of communication to another, e.g., the part of a picture you can describe in words. The "esthetic" information is the part of message that is lost when you change channels—the part of the picture that you cannot put into words. For commercials the primary channel for semantic information can be thought of as the copy (minus the poetry of the words), while the primary channel for esthetic information in Television is the visual.

The way various types of information enter the brain is also different. Semantic information is processed in a linear, "logical" sequence, while the esthetic information is acquired through a non-linear, right-brain "scanning and sorting" process. One of the reasons the Picture Sorts methods work so well in explaining advertising performance is that pictures from the ad itself provide an ideal "visual vocabulary" to reverse engineer the "scanning and sorting processes" the brain uses to acquire esthetic information from moving pictures.

Let's look at some examples from advertising of how the three different memory systems might come into play.

KNOWLEDGE TAGS

Knowledge memory tags are the card catalog to the library of the mind. They are the key words, the author or title that you use to search through Amazon.com to find the book you want. Word-tags are important, which is why good domain names can be so valuable on the Internet. Marketers spend a fortune just to put their names on the sides of sports stadiums.

Knowledge tags are critical at the beginning of a brand's lifestage; when advertising a new product, semantic information content is high.

That's why new product commercials need to be "introductory" in tone, heavy with semantic baggage, because they have the job of introducing the baby brand to the consumer, teaching her who the baby is and how it fits into her world.

Knowledge tags are the most familiar form of tags studied by advertising researchers since they're the basis of recall testing, with the brand name being used to retrieve advertising memories. Because the semantic system deals with language, these tags can be identified by researchers through the study of verbatim responses to open-ended recall questions or closed-ended rating statements.

Emotion Tags

The creation of easy-to-use tags by YouTube for ordinary people to search through the creative landscape of a hundred million home made videos is one secret of their success. Hallmark built a fortune by marketing emotion tags for human relationships in the form of greeting cards.

In an Advertising Research Foundation study conducted by Ameritest on two of the famous seven-minute online movies the Fallon advertising agency made for BMW, incorrect tagging of emotional memories made all the differences in how this new form of branded entertainment performed. One of the movies was a good ad for

BMW, but the other—actually the more emotional of the two movies—was a good ad for cameras and film, but not for BMW car. Incorrect tagging, in this second case, lead to the creation of a brand vampire movie.

One of the longest on-going debates among ad researchers concerns the correct types of cues—or tags—to retrieve long term memories of advertising: recall versus recognition. Both methods are valid since ad memories reside in all the memory systems of the mind. But emotional memories are more likely to be retrieved with visual recognition cues—which is the reason we all keep family albums of photographs to retrieve the Kodak moments of our past.

ACTION TAGS

The greatest trick Google ever played on us was teaching all our fingertips to learn their name. The images of flying in an IMAX theater can make you experience motion sickness. Video games, one of the most important advertising forms of the future, will deliver their value to advertisers to the extent that the embedded brands, integrated into the action of the games, become the tags for reliving the excitement of the game experience. Action tags reference the physical body, real or imagined. The Google experience is a form of kinetic imprinting. For ad film-makers, the focus is on how to use the camera to reach through the eye to activate the other senses of the audience, such as smell, taste, heat, and movement.

Product-in-use shots, bite-and-smile food shots, the images of cars accelerating around California coastal highways, accident scenes where your insurance man was there to hold your hand, are all obvious examples of advertising imagery that imprint an image into the procedural memory system. When the camera "consumes" a McDonald's hamburger on-screen, it's as if you—taking the point of view of the camera—ate the burger. Similarly, in other ads you drove the car, let your fingers do the walking, or reached out and touched someone. That's how it's recorded in your mind.

It is the interaction of memory and our projective imagination that creates the experiences of our inner life. Indeed, it seems likely that one of the chief functions of advertising is to create "false memories" of brand experiences that you never actually had in real life. When these imaginary experiences are mixed together in the mind with real experiences of the brand, the mind stores the false with the real in the same memory systems. Importantly, when these memories are later played back, the mind does not distinguish the false from the real.

Food advertising can constitute a form of "virtual consumption," which is why advertisers have long been taught to sell the sizzle, not the steak. Virtual consumption events multiply the number of experiences you share with a brand beyond the real ones. That's one of the reasons large advertisers enjoy such a strong business advantage over non-advertisers in terms of their ability to use advertising to strengthen brand relationships. You can create more memories for a product which the consumer may never have actually consumed.

It is important not to interpret the role of action tags literally, however. Not every food commercial needs to show a bite-and-smile shot. The role of metaphor can be important here. The retail giant, Target, produces advertising not just about style—all that cool color and dance are metaphors for the store experience so that you remember how much fun it was shopping at Target. For cars, the visual warping special effects on screen make you feel the sensation of the tight curve of the road, so that later you will "remember" what a fast car that was. For fabric softeners, the warm fuzzy hug from the Snuggle bear makes you remember that this product is soft enough for your baby's skin.

In general, while both emotion and action tags are about feelings generated in the audience, the difference is that emotion tags are centered on human relationships (including the relationship to the self) while action tags are centered on objects and physical behaviors reflecting what cognitive psychologists call "embodied cognition.".

In the language of ad researchers, the classical hierarchy effects model was: think-feel-do. Contemporary researchers debate the order of the first two constructs—does feeling come before thinking, or thinking before feeling? What's been overlooked is the "do" leg of the triad, the consumer consumption behavior, which is usually interpreted as taking place after the ad experience. What's new here is the understanding that the doing can also take place inside the ad, with action images mentally rehearsing those consumer behaviors the advertising is trying to motivate.

Finally, while there are three memory systems of the mind involved in the processing of experiences of all kinds, for brand building advertising a fourth kind of tag is needed to integrate the other three—the identity tag. Without a brand identity tag, advertising still might drive sales by growing the category, but it won't drive market share.

BRAND IDENTITY TAGS

Names are only one way of tagging a commercial so that your brand doesn't end up in the lost luggage of the mind. Visual icons, like the McDonald's golden arches, can tag a commercial. Sounds, like the Intel bong, do the same. Recognizable shapes, like the curves of the classic Coca-Cola bottle can tag a moment of falsely remembered refreshment. Even colors can tag memories—if the actors are drinking out of a blue can, and not a red one, do you know which brand of cola it is? And, of course, verbal "tag lines" can act as brand identity tags, such as Nike's "Just do it!"

A Simple Tool

How can we put these different pieces together to get a whole picture of how advertising creates meaning and memory in the mind of the consumer? First, let us show you how the Picture Sorts® provides us with a simple tool for identifying the "branding moments" in advertising film of all kinds, from television commercials to online video.

We know from extensive pre-testing that the Flow of Attention® and the Flow of Emotion® picture sort graphs provide different and complementary insights into how an audience interacts with film both in terms of the cognitive processes of selective attention, and with respect to their emotional response to advertising images.

If we plot both Flow of Attention and Flow of Emotion visual information in a grid, like that shown below, we can cross-reference the two dimensions of how the audience thinks and how the audience feels about each image in the ad. What we get is a scatter plot, confirming the independence of the two measures. Pictures plotted in the upper right hand corner of this grid are special—they represent the moments in the commercial that are both high in audience attention and emotional engagement.

Our published research on long term ad effects strongly suggest that these are the branding moments of the ad. Only these key images from the ad enter the long term memory of the consumer to form the long term image of the brand. In other words, these images are the memory "tags."

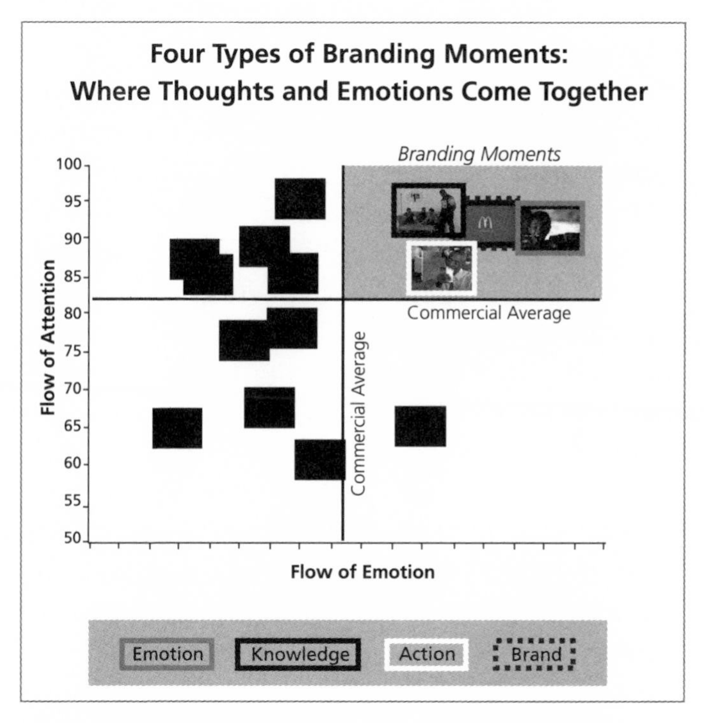

The four types of memories: Emotion, Knowledge, Action and Brand.

Content analysis of the branding moments can now be used to code for each of the four types of branding moments, or memory tags, we have described. This classification of images can be done using the judgment of skilled researchers, or more precisely, using consumer input based on a third-dimensional picture sort, the Flow of Meaning. The output of this analysis can be created in the form of a four-tiered histogram shown below, which highlights the cumulative branding moments across a number of commercials in a fast food campaign.

This graphical display gives brand mangers a new tool for managing advertising campaigns. Each of the four tiers can be thought of as a memory "bank" into which brand images must be deposited by advertising. A given commercial might, for example, deposit one or two or even three images in the Knowledge Bank. Another might make deposits in the Emotion Bank. A third commercial might deposit images in the first two banks but make the heaviest contribution to the Action Bank. To be well-branded, each of the commercials must also make deposits in the Brand Identity Bank.

Importantly, this leads us to a new form of "triple-entry" book-keeping for the three different memory systems of the consumer. It seems likely that, over time at least, an ad campaign should try to keep the image deposits roughly

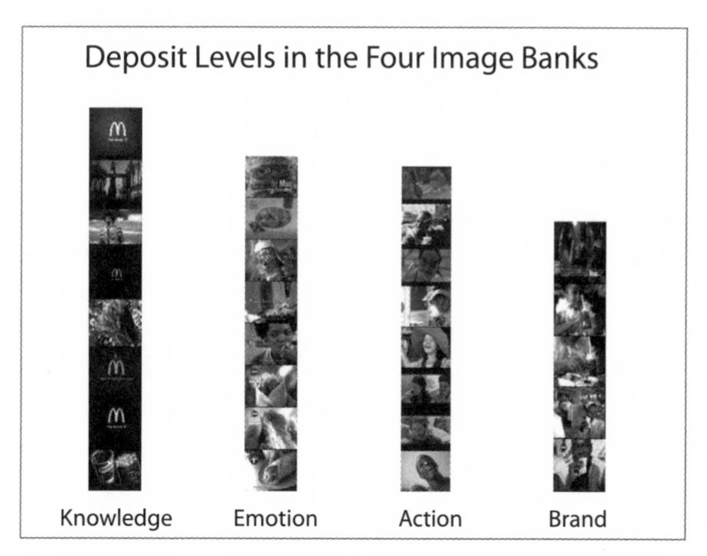

A bookkeeping system for tracking brand memories.

in balance. To build a complete "representation" of a brand in the mind of the consumer all three memory systems must be engaged. If deposits are only made in the Knowledge Bank, you are building a concept, not a brand. Similarly, if deposits are only made in the Emotion bank, without regard to rehearsing consumption behaviors in the Action Bank, or without occasionally grounding the brand in product news for the Knowledge Bank, the brand image will be similarly incomplete and out-of-balance over time.

In the end, this discussion about the different memory systems in the mind of the consumers leads us to a more refined and holistic view of advertising. In an age where the various media alternatives for reaching the consumer seem to be growing exponentially, and where the focus of advertising research is shifting to the measurement of integrated advertising campaigns, its useful to remember that all forms of advertising must do their work against the mind of the brand customer, measured one at a time. Perhaps it is time to turn Marshall McLuhan on his head to achieve an understanding of the new advertising realities: the mind, not the media, is the message.

XI

Four Dramatic Structures of Emotional Television Advertising

XI

Four Dramatic Structures of Emotional Television Advertising

On an intellectual level, television commercials work by telling us what we are supposed to think about a product or service; on another level they work by showing us how we are supposed to feel about a brand. Good storytelling, which unites ideas with emotions, lies at the heart of advertising effectiveness. For television, that means constructing a visually compelling story with moving pictures.

In an interview with the *Harvard Business Review*, Robert McKee, one of the most respected screenwriting lecturers in Hollywood, discussed some of the structural principles involved in telling a good story and pointed out the benefits of applying this knowledge to the practice of management. Most executives make the mistake of attempting to persuade using lectures replete with statistics, facts, litanies of bullet points and quotes from authorities. McKee argues convincingly that executives could be more persuasive using dramas—compelling stories packed with emotional power. For the ad business, understanding the role of the brand in the context of the different structures of storytelling lies at the heart of how to analyze a television commercial.

Along similar lines to McKee, the ad researcher Bill Wells classified all television commercials into two fundamental types: lectures and dramas. This simple categorization brought some clarity to the debate about the role of reason and emotion in advertising. The lecture type tends to be simply a linear presentation of features and benefits designed to convey a rational argument for buying the brand—a unique selling proposition. When we talk about dramas (both light and comic, as well as those more serious in emotional tonality) we must recognize that structural issues are more complex. Good stories can be told in more than one way.

In fact, from our pre-testing experience we have identified four distinct structures associated with effective emotional advertising. The role of the brand in each of these four types of stories is quite different.

The Flow of Emotion and Advertising Response

To explain these four structures we must first describe how we go about measuring the emotion in television commercials. For McKee, "a story expresses how and why life changes." To measure the emotion generated by a commercial story, therefore, requires a dynamic variable, one that captures how the audience's feelings change as they move through the film. We call the measure we use the Flow of Emotion.

The metaphor employed here is to model emotion as a "fluid" which is pumped through an ad—that is, the more emotionally engaging a commercial is visually, the more volume of emotion is pumped in. To slightly expand the metaphor, emotion is thought of as coming in two flavors, positive and negative, so that the dynamic tension between the two can be analyzed to understand the dramatic structure of a particular commercial. We visualize that structure by superimposing two curves: one represents the percent of respondents who choose the top two boxes (positive end of the scale) and the other represents the percent choosing the

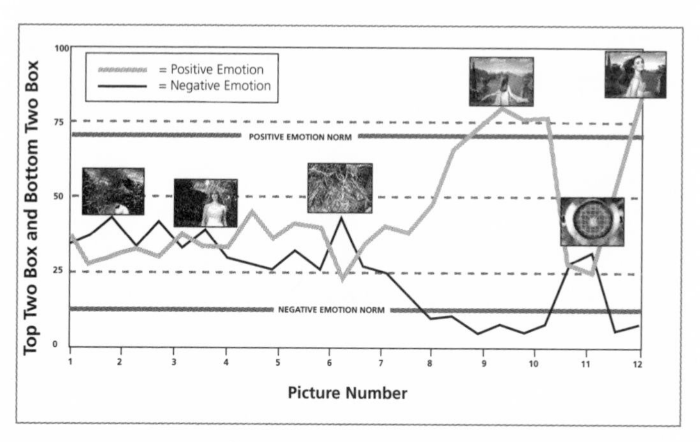

Ameritest Flow of Emotion graph.

bottom two boxes (negative end of the scale).

The average level of these positive and negative flows is the area under each of the two curves. The relationship between these averages and commercial performance measures on two pre-testing systems is shown in the table below.

	Positive Flow of Emotion	Negative Flow of Emotion
Liking	0.46[1]	-0.51[2]
Ameritest Measures		
Attention	-0.08	0.13
Branding	0.19[1]	-0.24[2]
Communication (strategic message playback)	0.31[2]	-0.21[2]
Motivation (weighted purchase intent)	0.58[2]	-0.57[2]
Millward Brown Measures		
Attention	-0.17[1]	0.33[2]
Branding	0.29[2]	-0.27[2]
Communication Effect	0.51[2]	-0.59[2]
Overall Effectiveness Index	0.44[2]	-0.33[2]

Notes: [1]Significance >95% confidence, [2]Significance >99% confidence.
N = 68 Unilever commercial's

Flow of Emotion and Commercial Performance as measured by Ameritest and Millward Brown.

The Flow of Emotion does not strongly predict attention-getting power but it is strongly predictive of motivation or persuasion. This is highly desirable since attention and motivation are conceptually distinct constructs. It is easy to think of commercials that break through the clutter but don't motivate you to buy, as well as those that have a compelling strategic message but don't get your attention. However, there is a significant relationship between the emotion flows and both measures of branding, and an even stronger statistical relationship between the emotion flows and measures of communication effectiveness and motivation (purchase intent).

We interpret this to be like the concept of "working energy" in physics, where the distinction is made between the total energy of a system and the energy available to do work. The total emotional energy of an ad may contain a component of entertainment value or even borrowed interest for the purposes of attracting attention, but the flow of emotion as measured here relates primarily to the 'working emotion' in the system that is available to build the brand.

Four Dramatic Archetypes

The dramatic structure of a television commercial may be thought of as organized emotion. In our pre-testing work we have identified four types of emotional organization or dramatic structures which, in general, can be found in effective commercials (commercials that have scored well on pre-test performance measures)—the Emotional Pivot, the Positive Transition, the Build, and Sustained Emotion, as shown below.

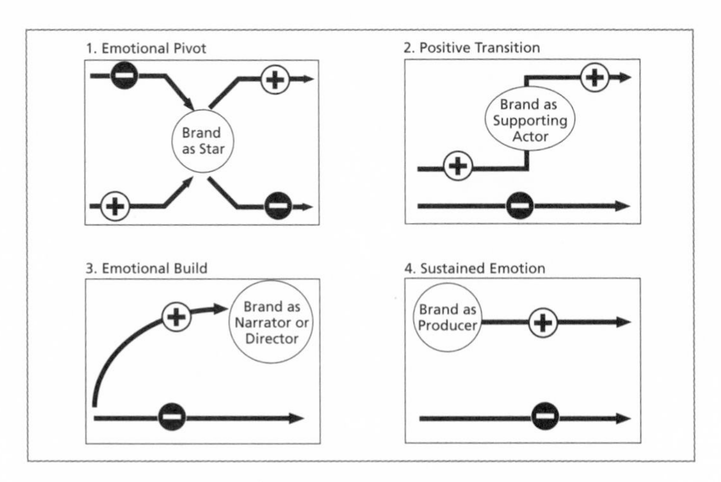

Four archetypes of dramatic structure.

The Emotional Pivot

This dramatic structure involves a "phase transition" in audience emotional states, from a beginning negative state to an ending positive state. It is characterized by strong negative emotion ratings in the beginning of the execution, which then vanish abruptly and are replaced by strong positive emotions by the end of the ad. The point in the ad where the negative emotions flip over to positive emotions is called the "emotional pivot." Problem/ solution commercials are one genre of advertising which have this type of emotional structure.

The Positive Transition

This structure also involves an abrupt or discontinuous change in emotional states, but this time from a low-level positive state to a higher level positive state—like an energy jump in quantum mechanics. Thus, the flow graph for this type of execution looks like a step function. Executions that make use of a reveal technique, where there is a moment of sudden realization that the ad is about something completely different that what one originally thought, provide examples of this type of dramatic structure.

The Build

The third type of dramatic structure involves an increasing flow of positive audience feelings climaxing in an emotional high point at the end of the ad. Humorous commercials with a strong visual payoff produce examples of this type.

Sustained Emotion

The fourth structure represents commercials that simply make you feel good from beginning to end. The flow graph shows a high positive, but flat pattern, indicative of a high volume of emotion being pumped through the ad. Montage commercials with strong music tracks yield examples of this type.

It should be noted that lecture type ads will look like this last type of emotional ad in terms of the flow graph, with the main difference being that the focus of audience attention in the ad is on rational information content rather than esthetic or emotional content.

Each of these structures may be thought of as an elementary building block which in longer pieces of film may be combined in different ways to create more complex stories, though most thirty-second commercials are short enough that they represent fairly pure examples of each of these types.

In analyzing an ad, you should be careful to distinguish between emotional effects intended by the creative—the purposeful use of negative emotions in an emotional pivot—versus unintended effects that represent opportunities for polishing or improving the ad.

Four Different Roles of the Brand

Notice that in two of the four dramatic structures the brand identifier is introduced in the middle of the commercial, as part of the action in the film, while in the other two structures the brand is a book-end, either at the beginning or the end of the ad. The timing of the introduction of brand identifiers—e.g., package, name, logo—is key to defining the role of the brand in the four different structures. A simple way of thinking about the differences is to think of the brand in terms of four different Hollywood types.

Brand as Star

The most obvious role for the brand is that of

the star of the little movie that is a television commercial. In this type of drama, the emotional pivot, the plot is quite simple. Negative dramatic tension is created in the beginning of the ad, then the brand arrives on its white horse and makes the negative feelings go away, so that the audience leaves with a happy ending. If the brand arrives at just the right time in the story, which is at the boundary between the negative emotional state and the positive emotional state, then the brand receives the credit and is perceived as the cause of this change or resolution of emotional tension. The brand clearly becomes the hero of the spot.

Brand as Supporting Actor

In this second type of story, the positive transition, the brand is not the star but plays the role of supporting actor. It is the Sancho Panza to the consumer's Don Quixote. The consumer, by projection, is given the starring role. The brand is part of the action, however, necessary to advance the scene and create twists in the plot. The role of the sporty car in some automotive advertising, for example, is to take ordinary life and elevate it to a higher plane of experience—which is, in the end, the promise the brand is making to the consumer as driver. Again, timing is a key point with this type of dramatic structure: the brand should arrive at the boundary between the low emotion state and the higher emotion state—so that the brand receives the credit and is perceived as the cause of the enhanced consumer experience.

Brand as Director

In this third type of story, the build, the brand is not an actor in the story but is acknowledged in only the credits at the end of the film. The brand is the director, unseen but an always-present intelligence, building a story to give meaning or definition to the experience promised to the consumer. Many of the IBM blue letterbox commercials are of the director type.

Brand as Producer

The fourth type—the thrilling exciting hilarious celebration of amazing sights and sounds you've never seen before—brought to you by—presented to you by—the brand!

It's the brand as the producer of sustained emotions, the rock concert promoter of good vibes, the P.T. Barnum of emotional end benefits. And it's up front about telling you so. No shyness here. (But remember, substitute rational selling propositions for emotions in this model and—hey presto!—you suddenly have brand as lecturer.)

All four approaches to emotional advertising work effectively in the sense of scoring well on measures of performance, yet these four types represent a considerable repertoire for deploying emotions in the service of building brands. This analysis is confirmation of the idea that advertising can work in more than one way, particularly on an emotional level. What this means from a practical perspective is that creatives should be empowered to depict and to attempt to evoke the full spectrum of human emotion, from despondence to elation. It is also a reminder to students of advertising—and good storytelling—that structure and content are also important, regardless of the type of advertising we are talking about.

XII

What is "Information?"

XII

What is "Information?"

In a meeting at a medium-sized baked goods company the advertising agency realizes that the newly minted CEO, promoted from the financial side of the business, is operating with a mental model of advertising that you might call the "news program" model. It is quite evident he believes, that if you have nothing new to say about a brand, you shouldn't say anything at all. The reason to spend money on advertising, he believes, is quite simply to introduce new products or to announce product improvements. Not surprisingly, the ad team invests a great deal of effort in explaining the role that emotion has in strengthening the relationship between a brand that is already established and the consumer.

At a large fast-food restaurant chain which does a great deal of new-product advertising, a product manager and an agency creative director are engaged in a familiar debate—how much screen time in a commercial should be devoted to showing the product? The creative director makes the case that the first job of advertising is to attract attention and build new-product awareness, which is the point of investing time in attention-getting, non-product visuals. But the client wants to "light the money!" The new product itself is the attention-getting "news" in the ad, he argues, so they should spend as much time as possible showing the product in order to motivate the consumer to try it.

Both of these stories illustrate the balancing act involved in creating effective advertising. Debate can be framed in a variety of dichotomies: rational argument versus emotional appeal, attention versus persuasion, strategy versus execution. The creative tension generated by these antipodal points of view can sometimes energize breakthrough thinking, but confusion frequently results from the failure to recognize that every piece of human communication is a double helix of information content. To see why, we need to ask ourselves at a deeper philosophical level, what exactly "information" is?

SEMANTIC VERSUS ESTHETIC INFORMATION

Students of information theory distinguish between two kinds of information that are present in the universe— semantic and esthetic information. Technically, semantic information is the part of a message that can be translated as you cross over from one channel of communication to another; esthetic information is the part that is lost in translation. The old adage that a picture is worth a thousand words is wrong. Every picture contains information that cannot be put into words, which is the esthetic information content of the visual. There are no words for the feeling I get when I look now at a picture of my six week-old grandson practicing his first smiles as I push him in a pram through Hyde Park in England on a sunny spring day. To capture and store those wordless feelings is the reason we take pictures.

Our day-to-day lives are made up of particular experiences. Individual one-of-a-kind experiences are the stuff of our interior universe. Where were you at 9 o'clock in the morning (EST) on September 11, 2001? Though I'm sure you recall the moment vividly, your answer to the question is totally different from mine—because it's a personal memory. The public facts of 9/11 have become a part of our history. But your private memories of it will die when you die.

Knowledge of the particular is fundamentally different from the type of knowledge that scientists deal with. Scientific researchers deal with repeatable, generalizable information that can be replicated from one experiment to the next. One-time only experiences are the realm of the artist. Both kinds of information—the general and the particular—can be true, but each represents a different reality. Scientists seek knowledge while artists seek emotional truth.

Semantic information, expressible in word

concepts and ideas, is outer-directed. It has as its frame of reference the objective world-out-there. Esthetic information, conveying emotion and sensory feelings, is inner-directed. Its frame of reference is the subjective "I," the Self. The first kind of information is collected from observable data; the second from insight. Both kinds of information are important for advertising brands.

The mind of the consumer can be thought of as continuously engaged in the process of defining the self and orienting it with respect to the outside world. A brand's image is constructed through emotional associations with the consumer's concept of the self. A brand's positioning is determined in the context of a universe of competing brands. One of advertising's jobs is to organically add image associations to a brand like the growth rings of a tree. The other job of advertising is to signal the brand's global positioning coordinates in order to anchor those images to a fixed place in the mind so that it's clear what the brand stands for. Volvo, for example, owns the word "safety" in the minds of car buyers. These two different jobs—building an image and positioning a brand—are performed by managing the yin and the yang of the two kinds of information communicated by a piece of advertising.

Another way to think about the information contained in an ad is to think about the concept of "news." The new and unfamiliar is the opposite of the old and familiar. Frequently, the mission of advertising is to get consumers to take a second look at a brand they think they already know, to put a fresh face on an old acquaintance. Persuasion, which Plato taught us in the *Phaedrus,* is the process of moving someone by small logical steps from the head nod of an accepted belief—the comfort zone of the familiar—to the edge of a new conclusion. A piece of communication that was made up entirely of new information would be completely incomprehensible. The familiar provides a necessary Rosetta Stone for translating new information into relevant concepts.

But just as in journalism, news in advertising is more than simply information you didn't know before. To be newsworthy, information must contain an element of surprise. News is "unexpected information."

Storytelling thrives on surprise. The turning points in a movie occur when characters don't behave as expected, when new information is introduced that changes the audience's understanding of what's going on. When that happens, according to the film-writing guru Robert McKee, a "gap" opens up between expectation and reality, releasing emotional energy that drives a plot forward. In the Bazaar scene in the film *Casablanca* when Ilsa informs Rick that she was already married to

Victor Laslo when they were having their love affair in Paris, Rick's emotions turn from hopeful positive to dark negative. This new information revealed a gap, like the blind spot in a rearview mirror, between his mental picture of the faithless lover he imagines Ilsa to be and the faithful wife she really is, forcing him to completely re-interpret the wreck of their relationship.

Surprising information is important because it can change your mental model of the world around you. This is information that we pay attention to, for which the unconscious mind instinctively filters, because to do otherwise can be very dangerous. An animal that is not sensitive to the "news" in its environment will not survive long.

News is to semantic information as originality is to esthetic information. This is why creatives strive for originality, for fresh creative executions. Their goal is to communicate the information the client wants, but in a way they didn't expect. In a sense, the quest of the product manager for news and the quest of the creative director for originality is the same quest, though the information domain each operates in is quite different.

Information Processing by Brand Lifestage

From a communication standpoint, advertising for new products clearly differs in a number of fundamental ways from advertising for established brands. Coming in the critical first stage of the product life cycle, a new product commercial has the job of generating awareness of the product starting from a zero base. It must, therefore, communicate a large amount of new information. It must communicate the brand name; it must communicate the category; it must communicate the attributes of the product and how those attributes are different from other products in the category and what the benefits of those differences are. By contrast, advertising for established brands has the benefit of prior advertising or marketing history. Usually its job is to remind consumers of the brand and to reinforce existing attitudes and loyalties toward it. Typically, established brand advertising has much less factual information to convey than advertising for new products.

It is reasonable to assume, therefore, that consumers in general would respond differently to new-product advertising than to established-brand advertising. This assumption has been confirmed empirically by a number of researchers in recent years. As an example, in a famous analysis of a thousand television commercials, academic researchers Stewart and Furse found that recall scores and persuasion scores were highly correlated for new product ads, whereas for established brand commercials the two measures were uncorrelated.

Interestingly, such differences not only confirm that the information content of the two kinds of advertising is different, but also suggest that how the mind of the consumer actually processes the information content of new-product ads is different from how it processes the information in established-brand ads. For example, because the rational or semantic content of new product commercials is less familiar, we might expect that the brain has to work harder to process the information.

To explore differences in cognitive processing, we analyzed a sample of 41 packaged goods television commercials, 23 of which were ads for well-established brands and 18 introductory spots for new products. The Flow of Attention® was used to deconstruct audience attention to the different types of information contained in the advertising.

The information content of each ad was determined by frame-by-frame coding of the individual pictures used in the picture sorting task. A simple two-way classification scheme was used where the dominant information content of each picture was classified as either P or E type. P-type pictures were pictures containing explicit product-related content such as the name, the package, visualizations of product attributes or benefits, and product demos or pictures of the product in use. E-type pictures were basically all other visuals in the execution. The images in E-type pictures can be thought of as representing much of the esthetic content of the video portion of the commercial.

Examples of the information patterns produced by this coding are illustrated below.

Commercial 1: E P E E E E E E E E P P P P E E E E P
Commercial 2: P P P E P P P E P E P P P
Commercial 3: E E E E E E E E E P E E P

Information type, frame-by-frame.

Each series of P's and E's represents the sequence of pictures taken from one commercial in the order shown, and coded according to our binary categories. As can be seen, the proportion of P- to E-type pictures present in a commercial, and the order in which each type of picture occurs in the flow of commercial images, varies considerably from ad to ad.

When we analyzed our sample of commercials shown in the table above, we found that new product commercials contained substantially more P-type information than established brand commercials. Less than half, or 47%, of the visuals in established brand commercials were of the product, or P-type, while 69% of the visuals in new product ads were, a level nearly one-and-a-half times higher. This is consistent with the commonly held perception that new product ads tend to be loaded with rational "information."

The types of visual information actually processed by the viewer, as measured by the percentage of pictures recognized in the sorting task, was also different for the two kinds of ads. More product imagery was recalled from new-product ads, 41% versus 29%, while more non-product executional imagery was processed in established-brand ads, 37% versus 19%.

In the Flow of Attention, the average number of images recalled was much less predictive of commercial performance on dimensions such as attention, branding and recall, than the number of peak points of attention—the mountain-tops of the sine-wave type attention curves. More of these attention peaks were associated with stronger attention-getting power for the ad as a whole, and more peaks containing product imagery were associated with better branding and recall scores.

Our analysis of peak experiences suggests that new-product ads are indeed processed differently than established-brand ads. We see the same number of P-type visuals in the viewer's peak experiences of both categories of advertising, 17% for new products and 16% for established brands, despite the beginning imbalance of P-type information in favor of new-products ads. This suggests that even for established brands, explicit product imagery plays a role in focusing the consumer's attention and anchoring the emotional, esthetic imagery in her mind.

However, for established-brand ads, the executional E-type information occurs in peak experiences at a rate three times higher than for new-product ads—a rate much higher than we would expect given the beginning imbalance of information types between the two categories of ads.

Published research has shown that it is only the rational, product (P-type) imagery in Flow of Attention peaks that drives day-after-recall scores. To the extent that the product imagery is also relevant and motivating to consumers, this would explain the correlation between persuasion and recall scores found by Stewart and Furse for new-product ads. But for established brands, the emotional imagery is more likely to play a role in driving motivation. Published research has shown that emotional engagement can be a strong driver of purchase intent for established brands. Since emotional (E-type) imagery does not drive day-after-recall scores, this explains why recall and persuasion are uncorrelated for established-brand advertising.

From a theoretical standpoint, P-type information is the type of information we would expect to produce the cognitive or learning response predicted by the classic "learn-feel-do" hierarchy-of-effects model of how advertising works. This is exactly what happens with viewer processing of highly rational new product ads.

On the other hand, E-type imagery (esthetic or emotion-generating) is the type most frequently processed at peak levels by viewers of established brand ads. That is three times the rate of the semantic, P-type information. In terms of a hierarchy of effects, this is the "do-feel-do" model that was developed in the 1980s as an alternative to the original learning model of advertising. Importantly, these findings are consistent with the assumption made by many advertising practitioners that established-brand advertising often works using an emotional rather than a rational mechanism.

However, one of the variables left out of this simple analysis is the question of which of these new or established-brand ads were effective? In a follow-up study we analyzed a second group of new-product ads, half of which were determined to be quite strong and the other half quite weak.

SUCCESSFUL NEW PRODUCT COMMERCIALS

In this analysis, we looked at test data for 20 new-product ads for 10 different restaurants in the QSR category. These measures included attention-getting power and motivation for each ad. Counting the number of pictures used in the picture sorting decks, we conducted a frame-by-frame analysis of how much time was spent showing the new product, including ingredient shots, food prepping shots, bite and smile, etc.

We found that above average new-product ads spent one-third more time showing the product (using the frame counting method) than below average commercials. 56% of the visuals in the 30-second commercials showed the product in the successful ads, while only 42% of the visuals showed the product in unsuccessful ads.

Moreover, the successful ads showed the product more without trading off attention for motivation. In fact, the successful ads were above average in both, while the unsuccessful ads where below average in both.

These are, of course, only average differences and do not provide a formula for developing new-product ads. One of the most successful of the ten strong ads showed the product only 23% of the time while one of the least successful ads actually showed the product 58% of the time. But the strong correlation between the amount of time the new product is shown on screen and commercial performance reminds us that new-product ads form a distinct genre of advertising, more rational in its information content, which must be taken into account when developing new creative work.

More generally, when discussing the content of advertising we are reminded to think more broadly and deeply about the information. Each of our five senses contains information that cannot be translated into the other four senses—smell has a language all its own that is incomparably different from the language of touch, or sound, or sight. The language of advertising film conveys emotional truth to our eyes that our ears cannot completely understand. Pictures are not the same as words. To create effective advertising we need both.

XIII

How to Construct Persuasive Selling Propositions

XIII

How to Construct Persuasive Selling Propositions

Persuasive sales arguments begin with a "head nod". Plato taught that in his *Dialogues* when he showed how, with a series of short steps in logic, it is possible to lead a person from that initial point of agreement to a concluding position they would have been uncertain about at first had it been put directly to them.

This may seem to be only a matter of semantics. But semantics are what advertisers are concerned with when they determine unique selling propositions to fix a brand's positioning in a competitive marketplace. Mastering semantic clarity along with emotion, its equal partner in the art of advertising, is one of two strategic keys for building successful brands.

Brand leadership is fundamentally concerned with managing meaning. How do the performance claims and support points communicated about your brand "fit" into the consumer's belief system? What are the resulting higher-level values your brand stands for in the mind of the consumer? Have you defined those values in ways that are meaningful to the contemporary consumer? These are all questions of semantics— because semantics is the study of meaning.

Consumers are "logical" in their way, but consumer logic is not the same as Aristotle's logic. Therefore, to persuade consumers, advertisers must develop sales arguments on the consumer's terms. Researchers, then, must help the ad team understand which "trains of thought" consumers use to arrive at a particular position with respect to the product category.

This chapter describes a tool for helping with that task, the semantic network. Think of a semantic network as a "road map" to the consumer's mind. Just as a road map shows places and the pathways connecting them in a given geographical area, so a semantic network shows ideas which consumers associate with a given product category and the linkages between those ideas. The basic ideas underlying semantic networks have been well known in the academic world for more than 30 years. However, only in the last decade has the business world been putting these ideas into practice and applying them to marketing and knowledge management issues.

Importantly, this technique does not require the use of new questions or additional interviewing time in the data collection process, but rather is a means of adding value to the research with a new method of analysis for data that has probably already been collected in some other study.

In the mid-1960s, Ross Quillian first implemented what would later become known as a semantic network in his dissertation on the design and use of computer programs to store word meanings. The computer program itself embodied a theory of human language comprehension and paved the way for further work in Artificial Intelligence. Shortly thereafter, Quillian and his associates revolutionized the field of cognitive psychology by championing the study of semantic memory, i.e., memory for general information, knowledge about the world, and cultural knowledge.

Applying a similar approach to marketing applications, Harvard Professor Gerald Zaltman shows examples of how qualitative interviews provide material for the creation of "consensus maps." In a similar vein, but on a quantitative level, semantic networks provide marketers with a map of the mental models which different consumer segments hold about their product category.

Semantics: the Rational Side of Market Communications

The significant aspect of semantic nets for advertising is that they are concerned with the relationships or linkages between objects, concepts or events. In terms of language or semantics, the structural relationships between words can be interpreted as their semantic meaning.

In more general terms, it can be used as a representation of knowledge. As such, it can be used as a basis for understanding learning, that is, how new facts get added or fitted into our brains, and retrieval or recall, that is, how our brains determine what knowledge is relevant in solving problems or making choices.

The basic assumption is that the ideas which consumers hold about a given product category do not exist in a vacuum but rather are embedded in a context of related ideas. The key to using a semantic network is to understand the connections that consumers make between one thought and another.

Constructing a semantic net is a way of "parsing" a message to get at the deeper structure. This structure represents the meaning or significance of the brand message in the context of the belief structure of the category.

How to Build a Semantic Network

The raw material for a semantic network is drawn from brand attribute ratings. The ratings are collected in typical consumer questionnaires that attempt to describe consumer brand perceptions with five or six point rating scales. These kinds of ratings can be found in a wide variety of quantitative consumer studies, such as diagnostic pre-tests, tracking studies, or general attitude and usage surveys.

The data that is analyzed is a matrix of correlations, rather than the metrics that are usually reported, such as average scores or top box/top two box percentages. In this analysis attention should be focused on the relationships between variables, rather than on the levels of agreement to particular rating statements viewed one at a time. As in traditional factor analysis, correlations are interpreted as distance metrics, providing measures of the strength of association or linkage between the various pair-wise combinations of mental objects (such as product features and benefits, personality traits, etc.) in the set of constructs being rated.

Unlike factor analysis, which is usually used as a form of data reduction to collapse the differences between highly correlated items into a few underlying dimensions, with semantic network analysis the focus is on doing the opposite: the objective is to "explode" the differences between correlated items in order to explore the context of closely related—but not synonymous—ideas. The method of constructing a semantic net follows a mechanical, iterative procedure to identify the hierarchy of relationship between consumer perceptual categories.

To begin the process of constructing a semantic network, start with a criterion variable or "bottom-line" type of item, such as purchase intent. Then, using a stringent statistical cut-off point, you should identify the few ideas that are most closely correlated with the starting, criterion variable. These two or three or four variables are the primary drivers and represent the first level of relationships in the map.

The next step is to identify secondary variables that are connected to the primary drivers. In other words, in round two start with each of the driver variables and identify a small subset of the remaining variables that are most highly correlated with these.

Then the process is repeated again. Correlations are used to identify those ideas that are most closely linked to the secondary variables, and then the ideas that are related to these tertiary variables, and so on, until the set of variables in the dataset is exhausted.

Typically, in moving from the few important correlations between the criterion variable and the primary drivers, to the correlations between the drivers and other descriptive concepts, the overall degree of inter-relatedness between ideas increases. This normally results in a corresponding increase in the number of high correlations. As a rule of thumb, therefore, the cut-off point is raised slightly (using judgment) so as not to blind the analyst with too many relationships. This adjustment is usually allowed once, and after that you should stick to a reasonably fixed cut-off point for identifying "significant" correlations.

Finally, after this very mechanical procedure, a degree of artfulness comes into play. This is the right-brain task of graphing and organizing the various connections on a piece of paper in as compact and efficient a way as possible. Examples of these graphs follow throughout this chapter.

An obvious limitation of this kind of road map of the consumers mind is that it is two-dimensional. Physically, at least, the human brain is 3-D. A truer representation, it would seem, would look more like the space filled wiring of neural ganglia. Indeed, you could build a model of a semantic net out of short bits of wire, and by lifting up the ends, bend them around to bring the ends together and close the connections that are awkwardly displayed on paper. What you might get is a three dimensional, multifaceted polyhedron.

Application of Semantic Networks

What follows are several examples used to illustrate semantic networks. These examples are drawn from a variety of consumer research projects conducted for various clients over the past few years. Each of the networks in these examples was constructed from quantitative datasets based on a range of sample sizes, from a minimum of a hundred consumer interviews, to over a thousand interviews.

Example One: Identifying Drivers of Purchase Intent

The first simple example of a semantic net involves a snack product based on the familiar party mix that you make with peanuts, pretzels, cereal biscuits and seasonings, usually prepared around Christmas time in vast quantities for your friends. This party mix comes ready-to-eat in a box, and therefore is a convenient snack anytime. Because conven-

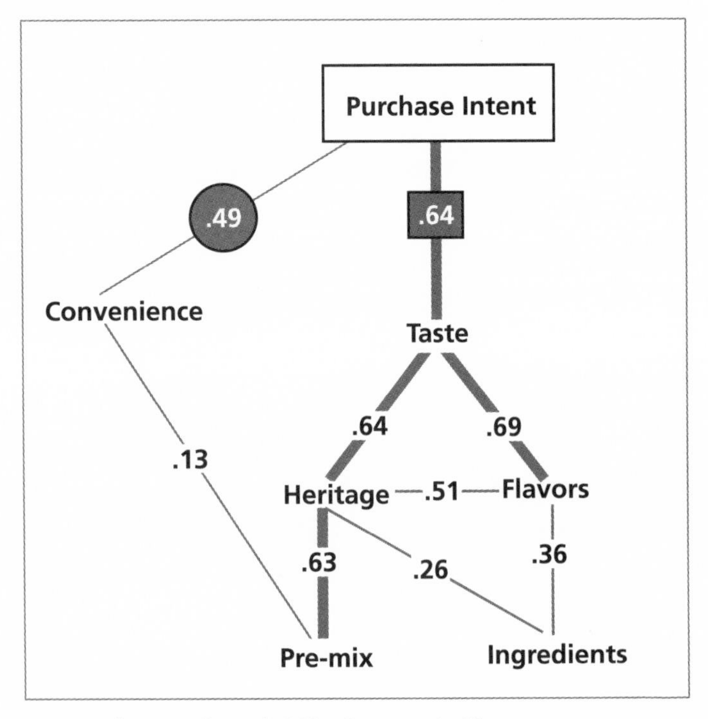

Example 1: A Snack Mix Semantic Net.

ience is the original reason-for-being for selling the product pre-mixed in the box, the original communication strategy developed to advertise the product was based on convenience.

The simple semantic map shown in this example was constructed from a set of brand ratings from a pre-test control cell. Notice that there are several "mental paths" that might be followed to reach the consumer. Taste is the perceptual variable most strongly linked to purchase intent for the party mix, with the highest degree of correlation of 0.64. Convenience is an important but secondary benefit, indicated by a lower correlation with purchase intent (of 0.49.) Moreover, it is clear that taste could be supported in several ways, e.g., premix—heritage—taste; while the convenience idea is supported only by the product attribute that this product comes in a box.

Example Two: Identifying Barriers to Purchase Intent

In this case, a semantic network was used to explore a range of possible ways to sell butter. Butter is an interesting product to try to market in that it is the only example we could think of where the unbranded product usually costs more than the competing, branded alternatives—that is, margarine.

The overall preference item "Butter is the product for me" was chosen as the criterion variable or starting point for the semantic net.

What we found was that "freshness", "taste", and the ingredient dimension that "good cooks use it" were, in that order, the most strongly linked items to preference for butter.

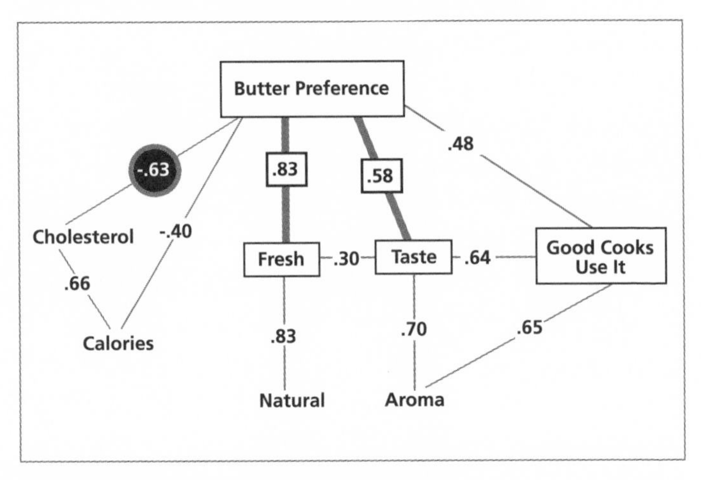

Example 2: Semantic Net for butter.

There are a number of important insights that could be gleaned from this graph. First, concerns about cholesterol and calories are negatively correlated to butter preference. In this case negative correlations can be interpreted to represent significant barriers to usage that marketing must overcome.

Note the strong linkage in consumers' minds between cholesterol and calories (+.66). While it is true that versus margarine, butter does contain more cholesterol and thus may not be as good for you, it is a fact that butter and margarine contain exactly the same number of calories. And yet consumers assume that butter contains more calories than margarine. Why? Apparently, because of an association they make in their minds between calories and the cholesterol content of butter.

If you were to ask the typical consumer exactly what cholesterol is, the answer you might get would be something like a yellow, globby, fatty substance—that's full of calories! So, one way to advertise butter would be to educate consumers about this misconception of the caloric content of butter. And while the perception of high cholesterol could not be addressed with advertising head-on, since it is a true negative to health, it might be possible to isolate that concern, by breaking the links to other negative misconceptions consumers have, so that it might wither on the vine so to speak, or at least be minimized as an issue that has to be dealt with by advertising.

But a second, more important observation that can be made from this graph is that freshness, based on the natural origins of butter, is more strongly linked to butter preference than taste is. This appears to be somewhat surprising, since we would expect good taste to be the primary benefit for any food product. So what's going on?

Perhaps, it's simply a matter of what the old advertising master Leo Burnett would have called "inherent product drama": of good versus bad. Most consumers would agree that butter tastes better than margarine. But margarine is used more often than butter because of the "bad aura" that butter has developed as a result of consumer concerns about cholesterol and the misconception about its calorie content. To overcome this bad aura and increase butter usage, advertising would need to communicate on an emotional level something good about butter. Under the circumstances, taste does not automatically qualify, since many consumers can translate buying butter for its taste as a form of "indulgence", which is just another kind of sin. A better strategy for lowering the cholesterol barrier might be to point out that butter is a fresh, natural dairy product, while margarine is artificial and factory-made.

Example Three: Developing Alternate Strategic Selling Paths

To help develop possible strategies for selling milk, a semantic network was constructed for the National Dairy Association to provide answers to four basic questions:

1. What are the motivating ideas that consumers hold, to a greater or lesser degree, about the product?
2. What are the initial points of agreement about perceptions of the product—that is, what product claims will elicit "head-nods" of agree-

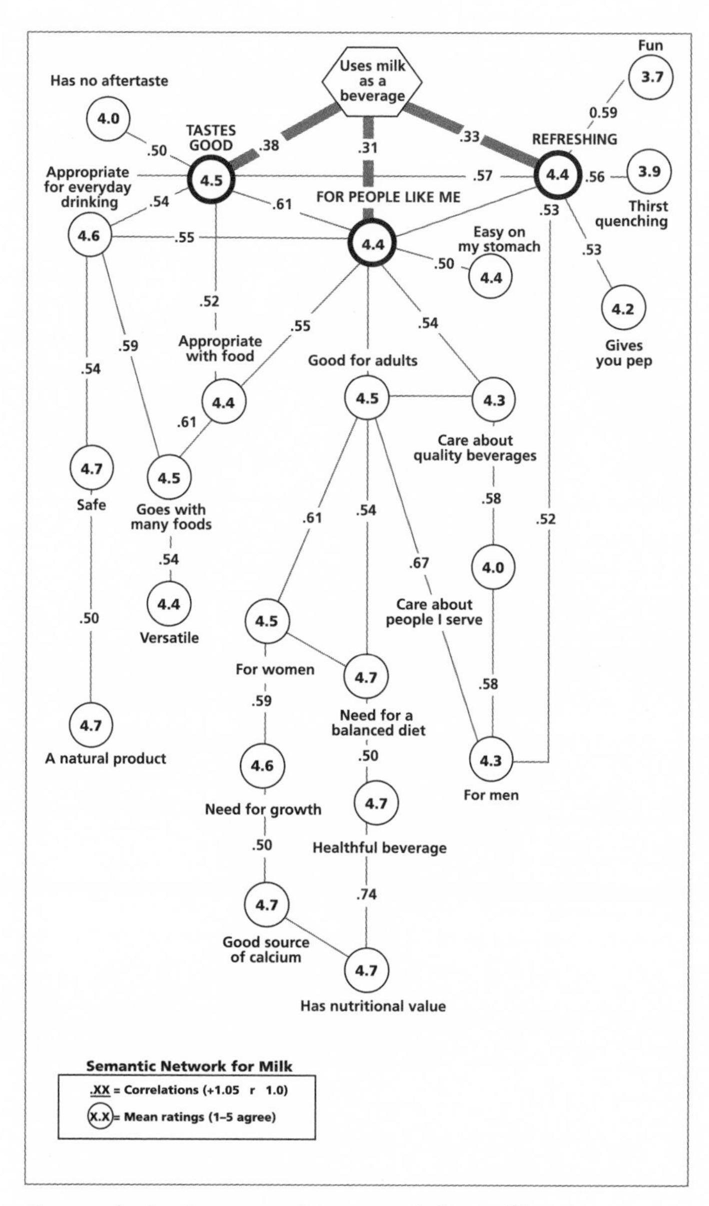

Example 3: A semantic network for milk.

ment from the consumer?

3. What are the points of leverage that can be used to move consumers to product ideas about which they are less likely to agree?

4. What is the shortest path to follow in taking the consumer from an initial point of agreement to a motivating idea about the product—without requiring "great leaps in consumer logic?"

Taken together, this information from semantic networks produced a guide for developing persuasive ad campaigns to win more business from consumers.

MOTIVATING IDEAS

Two types of measures are shown on this semantic map. (Shown above)

The numbers within the circles are mean scores on a 5-point agreement scale that the given idea describes milk. The numbers next to the linkage lines are correlation coefficients. These are indicators of the closeness or degree of association between ideas.

Three primary drivers were identified in this study. These are the three ideas most closely linked with respondent ratings of milk as a beverage for personal consumption.

The first is taste. Agreement that milk tastes good among light/medium users was a moderately high 4.5 on a 5-point scale.

The second is refreshment. On this dimension milk also receives a moderately high rating of 4.4 on a 5-point agreement scale.

The third dimension we call "emotional relevance." This is our rough translation of the item "for people like me." There is undoubtedly a psychological component to milk usage due to its association with motherhood, childhood, the comforts of home, etc. Unfortunately, none of the items that we had to work with represent this area very well. This item seems to come closest in meaning to that area. As support for that interpretation, we note that this item is associated in the network with other items descriptive of "caring" and a sense of well being (i.e., health items).

Finally, we note that all three areas—taste, refreshment and emotional relevance—are roughly equal in their linkage to milk usage as a beverage.

Persuasive Pathways

In analyzing the semantic network for milk, we identified four paths that seemed to offer interesting strategic alternatives for persuading light/medium milk users to drink milk more often.

1. Safe to Drink Every Day
2. Milk Goes Great With Food
3. Part of a Balanced Diet
4. Energizing Refreshment for Men

Below we sketch out these paths in terms of

a step-by-step consumer argument. Before we do so, however, we should point out two things. First, the semantic "argument" is not written out in advertising language; indeed, it is not even written in the language of a good concept. Instead, what the net provides is the logical skeleton around which more polished concepts could be written. Second, the semantic network does not tell us which of the four paths is best. To determine that, one needs to test these four strategic concept areas among consumers. What the semantic network provides is a disciplined approach to constructing distinctive—and from a consumer standpoint, "logical" selling propositions for driving milk consumption.

Pathway 1: Safe to Drink Every Day

Supporting Argument:

1. Because it's a natural product.
2. Milk is safe.
3. So it's appropriate to drink every day.
4. (And it tastes good too.)
5. So milk is for people like you.

Therefore: Drink milk more often.

This argument starts with a very strong "head nod" from the consumer: milk is a natural product (Agreement level = 4.7). From there, the path runs easily "downhill" to "Emotional Relevance"—i.e., "Milk is for people like you." This pathway can be thought of as having a certain amount of leverage

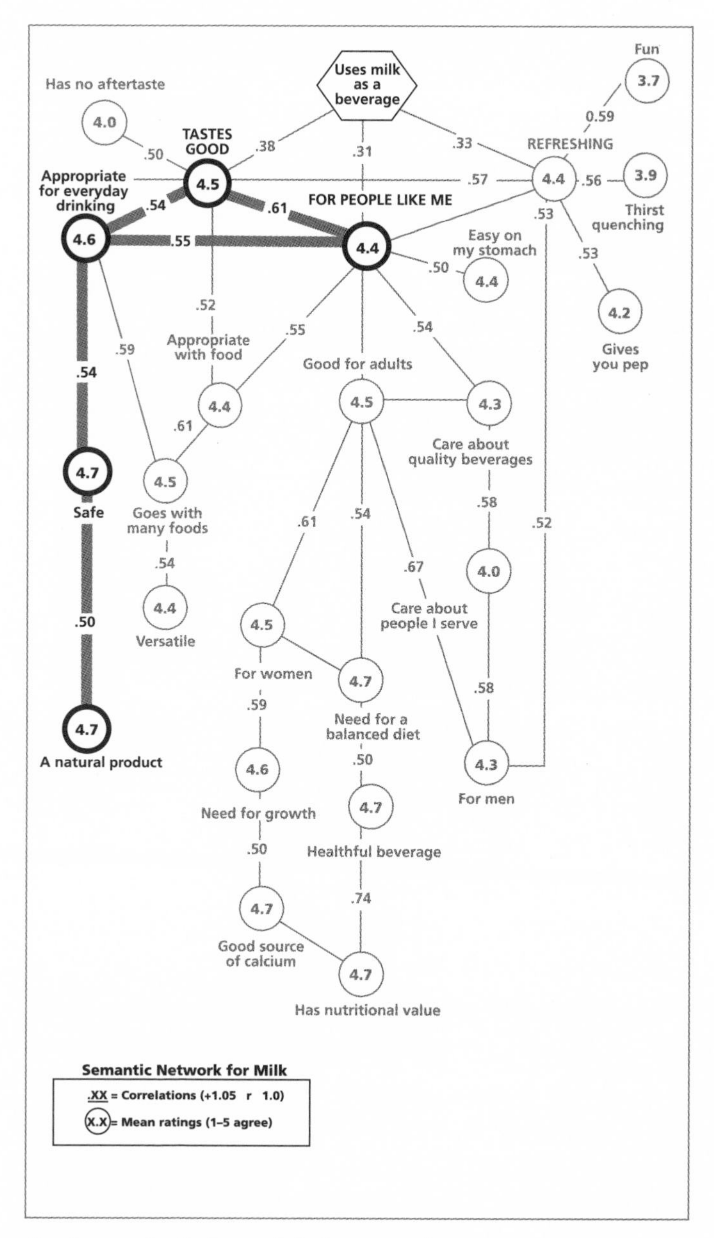

Pathway 1: Safe to drink every day.

because consumers will more easily grant us the first point than the last point: Natural Product (4.7) For People Like Me (4.4)

This area is interesting because it may capitalize on a concern that some consumers might have that man-made products, such as soft drinks, may have harmful cumulative effects. This is a hypothesis, which might be explored further with additional consumer research.

Pathway 2: Milk Goes Great With Food

Supporting Argument:

1. Milk is versatile.
2. It goes with many foods.
3. Milk is appropriate to drink with food.
4. It tastes so good.

Therefore: Drink milk more often.

This Pathway can be thought of as running along "level ground" in that consumer agreement with the opening point is equal to consumer agreement with the final point: Versatile (4.4) Tastes Good (4.5)

Nonetheless, the path may be well worth traveling because of the opportunity available, via advertising, to dramatize the opening point by showing milk being consumed with a wide variety of foods. A particular strength with this strategic approach is that—if the advertising is successful—many food products around the house can become strong psychological cues reminding consumers day after day to drink milk more often.

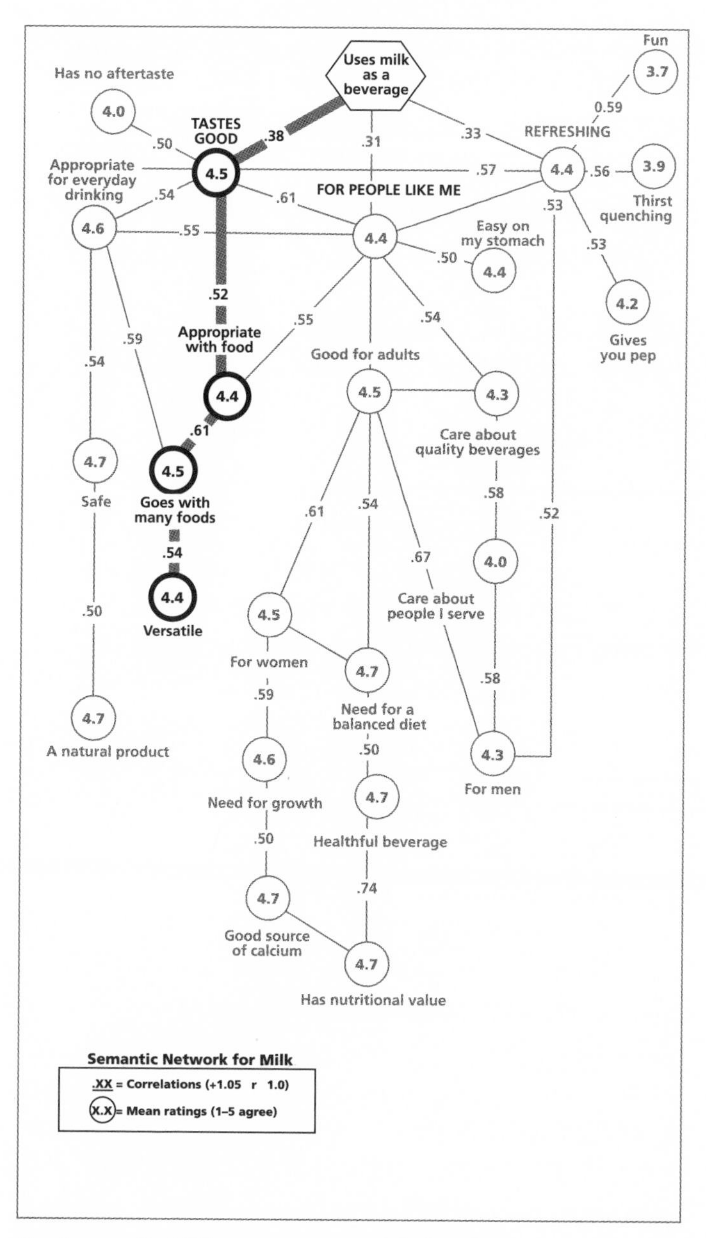

Pathway 2: Milk goes great with food.

Pathway 3: Part of a Balanced Diet

Supporting Argument:

1. Milk has nutritional value.
2. It's a healthful beverage.
3. It's needed for a balanced diet.
4. For instance, milk is a good source of calcium.
5. Women need calcium.
6. So milk isn't just for kids, it's good for adults.
7. For people like you.

Therefore: Drink milk more often.

Like the first path, there's an inherent leverage in this downhill path: most consumers will grant you that milk has nutritional value:

Nutritional Value (4.7) For People Like me (4.4)

Pathway 4: Energizing Refreshment

Supporting Argument:

1. Milk gives you pep.
2. It refreshes.
3. And for men,
4. It's good for adults like you,

Therefore: Drink milk more often.

Unlike the other three paths, this one appears to run slightly "uphill". Consumers are less likely to grant you the milk "kick"—i.e., "milk gives you pep"—than the ultimately motivating item of refreshment: Gives You Pep (4.2) Refreshing (4.4)

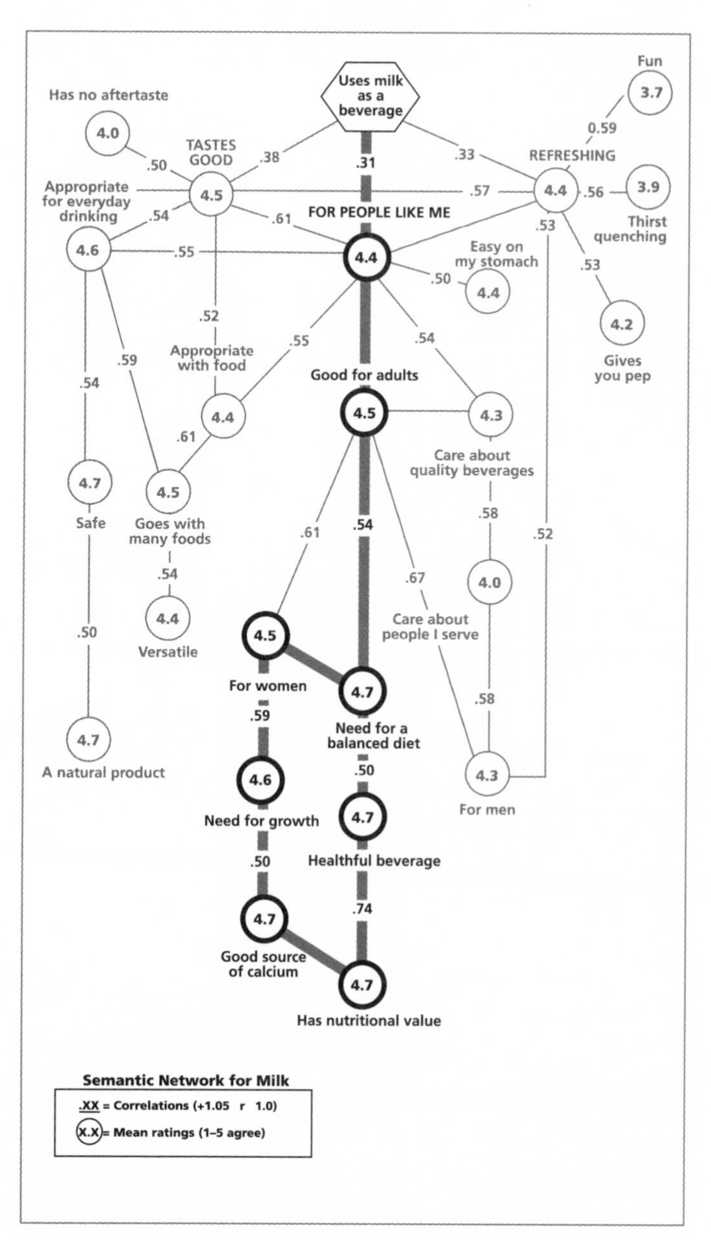

Pathway 3: Milk is part of a balanced diet.

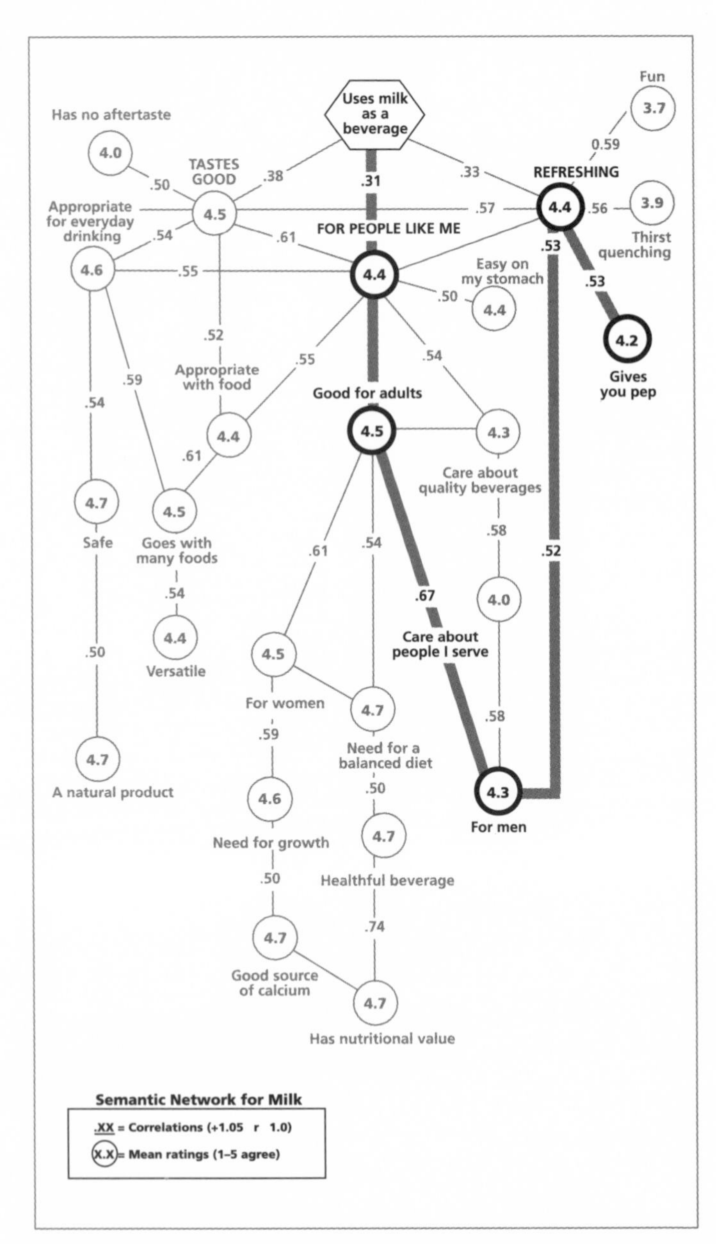

Pathway 4. Milk is an energizing refreshment.

While this is certainly a valid strategic area, it requires that advertising work harder, to possibly change, and not simply reinforce, the ideas consumers associate with milk. It is highly dependent therefore, on a believable and energizing advertising execution to strengthen the linkage between energy and refreshment in order to motivate consumers to drink more milk.

By working outward from these ideas, we developed four stepping-stone strategic paths for consumer persuasion, each of which begins with a relatively non-controversial "head nod" point of agreement. The four paths are:

1. Safe to drink every day. Begins with "milk is a natural product" and plays on negative perceptions of artificial beverages.

2. Milk goes great with food. Begins with "milk is versatile" and can use a variety of everyday foods as psychological cues to remind consumers to drink milk.

3. Part of a balanced diet. Begins with "milk has nutritional value" and can use the calcium benefit story as an added benefit for women.

4. Energizing refreshment for Men. Begins with "milk gives you pep" and can use additional masculine associations of fun and refreshment.

These are the four strategies, which seemed to offer the smoothest logical path for consumers to follow to a positive feeling about drinking more milk. With each semantic spine in place, advertising executions could then be developed to wrap emotional flesh around the semantic skeleton.

Example Four: Identifying the Effects of Persuasive Advertising

In this case history of a bar soap, a semantic analysis was conducted that had a fundamentally different objective from the preceding examples. The goal here was to find out how two very different advertising ideas impact the semantic belief structure of consumers. What linkages would be made stronger by the new advertising? What new linkages would be created?

This application used a baseline semantic network constructed from the brand attribute data collected in a pre-test control cell.

In two pre-test cells, consumers viewed a test ad and brand attribute ratings were also collected as a standard part of the test. Correlations between brand attributes in the two advertising cells were then compared to those from the control cell. For each of the two ads, linkages that were strengthened (i.e., had significantly higher correlations) are highlighted with heavy black lines.

The two ads produced different semantic effects. Ad B appears to strengthen or reinforce more of the semantic linkages than ad A. It also appeared to be creating new connections; for instance, the idea of "good smell" is now linked to the idea that this is "soap for the entire family" and, importantly, it is now directly linked

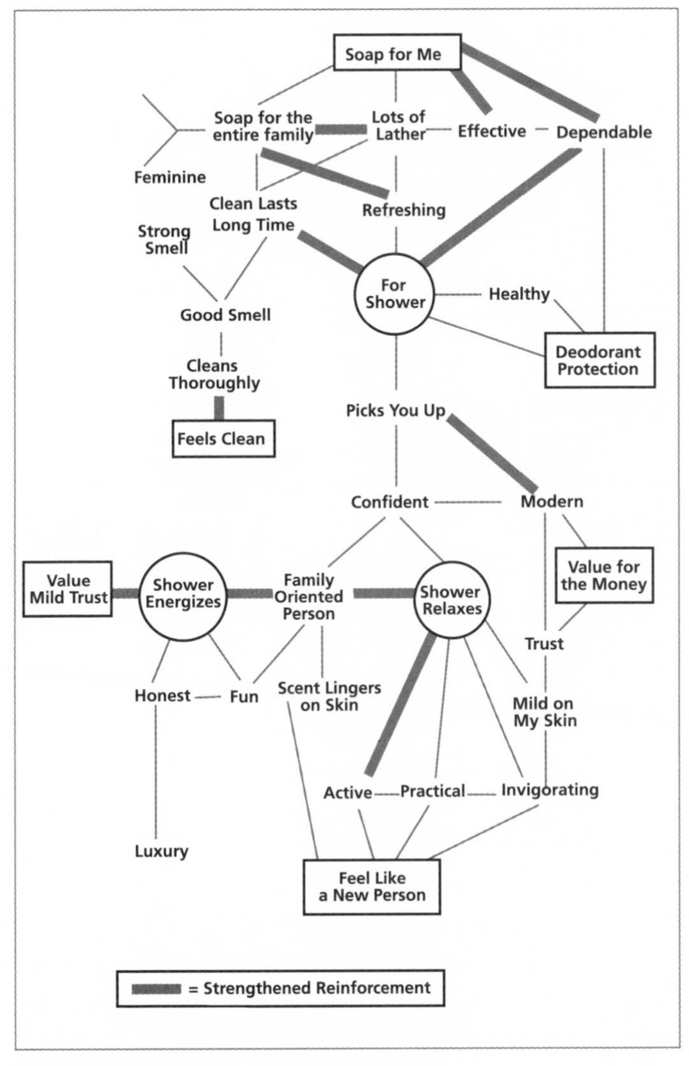

Soap Commercial A: Semantic Net.

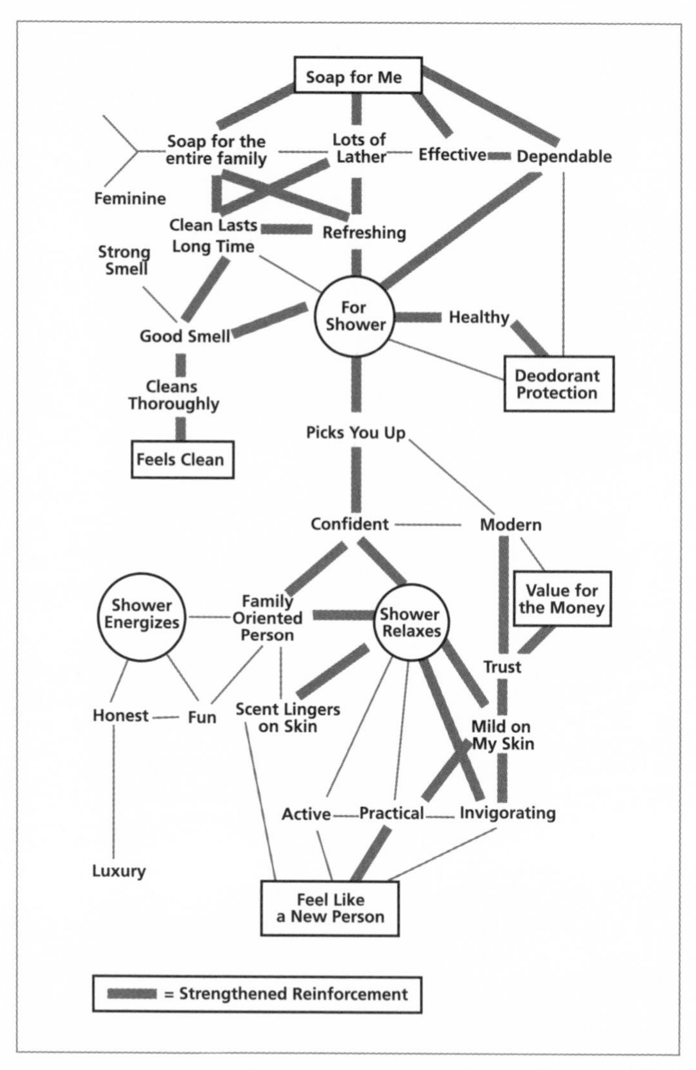

Soap Commercial B: Semantic Net.

(with a correlation above our cut-off point) to the preference variable, this "soap is for me."

Also, as another observation, there are a

greater number of connections being strengthened. In a semantic sense, one might say that Ad B is a "bigger idea" than Ad A because it's better connected.

To sum up, semantic network analysis provides a disciplined, quantitative approach to exploring the connections between semantic concepts in the mind of the consumer. As our examples have shown, this can be useful for identifying brand-differentiating options for advertising strategy development. Moreover, because this analytic approach does not require new data but rather is a new way of looking at data that may have already been collected, it is an economical way to find persuasive selling ideas.

XIV

When to Introduce the Brand

XIV

When to Introduce the Brand

One of the most important creative decisions to be made in the design of a television commercial is determining the right time to introduce the brand into the flow of the ad. Many traditional copytesting researchers recommend the "early and often" rule. Their research suggests that commercials that identify the brand name in the first five seconds of the ad score best.

Creative teams have long resisted this rule, frequently wanting to withhold the identity of the brand to the very end of the ad. Their argument for delaying the introduction of the brand is that consumers don't want to watch hard core sales presentations, but rather need to be seduced by the entertaining qualities of commercials. They argue that consumers must be drawn into a brand story before revealing the sponsors name. A variant of this "misdirection" approach is based on the following brand switching argument. If you are a regular user of brand A, then as soon as you see in the opening seconds of a commercial that it is for competitor brand B, you will tune out the rest of the ad because you have already made your brand choice in the category and don't want to be bothered with second-guessing yourself. Therefore, to overcome consumer defenses and get users of brand A to take a second look at brand B, this advertiser should withhold the brand identity as long as necessary to get the consumer interested in their brand's story.

An advertiser must overcome the viewing audiences' defenses, not unlike the way a professional coach must devise strategies to win a football game. If a coach runs on first down every time, the defense will move up and crush the play before it begins. The winning coach has to have a sophisticated Play Book. He has to create misdirection and use the defense's strategies against them. Run a play action pass, a reverse, a middle screen. Catch the defense over-committing and over-pursuing. Likewise, advertising pros must go to their creative Play Books to win the battle for the hearts and minds of the consumer.

Our experience in testing advertising provides us with many examples of television commercials that generate high Brand Linkage scores when the brand is introduced in the middle, when it is not identified until the end, or when it is introduced in the beginning of the ad. This suggests that the traditional strategy to always introduce the brand in the opening few seconds of a commercial is based on too simplistic a view of the game.

Coaches spend hours studying film to learn their adversaries' tendencies (run on first down), philosophical beliefs (running or throwing priority, attacking or flexing defense), and preferred plays (which teams rely on the West Coast Offense to spread the defense). Likewise, ad pros spend hours studying ad film to learn consumer cognitive viewing strategies, their reactions to different kinds of emotional moves, and when the consumer's eye is, or is not, on the brand.

From our experience, we can say that a weak branding score is usually a fixable problem. Unlike low scores for Attention or Motivation, which may be due to a weak creative concept or a poor communication strategy, a weakness in branding can almost always be strengthened in the editing room—if you understand the underlying structural principles that determine well-branded advertising executions.

Three Keys to Brand Linkage: Focus, Fit and Timing

There are two principles of branding that we refer to as focus and fit. From a focus perspective, we know from our mathematical modeling of brand linkage scores that somewhere in the flow of the commercial there must be at least one moment—what we call a "single-minded branding moment"—where the identity of the brand being advertised is at the center of the audience's visual field of interest. ("Single-minded" means there is no within-frame competition for attention to the brand identifier. Unfortunately, this is a common problem.) In short, there must be at least one moment where the audience's attention is focused solely on the identity of the brand that's sending them a message.

The second principle is that an advertising idea should be custom-tailored to fit the particular brand being advertised. In other words, your distinctive brand should be able to wear the ad like a like a millionaire athlete wears a custom-made suit, not like something purchased off-the-rack that another brand could wear equally well. Generic creative concepts do not produce well-branded advertising executions.

In both cases quantitative diagnostic research can be used to measure how well an advertising execution focuses attention on and fits the brand. Focus is measured with an Ameritest Flow of Attention® graph—which, like the video instant replay of a football game—is used by professionals to analyze and improve their performance on screen. It's an online picture-sorting methodology that is used to freeze time. It gives us a stop-action view of how audience attention flows and focuses from moment-to-moment on the different images in a commercial. Fit is measured with a simple rating statement where the consumer is asked to rate the ad on a continuum from "it could be an ad for almost anything" to "it could only be an ad for this particular brand."

A third principle of branding addresses the timing of when a brand should be introduced into an ad. The timing of a brand's arrival on the screen is not arbitrary; it's a well-determined function of the creative choices that you make about the kind of brand story you want to tell. And it's driven by the emotional structure of the ad.

Timing and Dramatic Structure

From our analysis of consumers' emotional responses to television commercials, we have identified four archetypal structures that can be used to transfer an audience's emotional response from a television commercial to a brand. (See Chapter XI on the four dramatic structures.) These represent four different plays that the creative coach can use to move the brand forward in consumer emotions in order to score a sale. Each of the four can be powerfully effective—but each of the four structures calls for a different, right time to introduce the brand in the running flow of the commercial.

The first play is the "kickoff," where the brand is brought on the field at the very beginning of the commercial and positive emotions are engaged to generate as much momentum as possible for the full run of a thirty-second ad. The second play is the "pivot," where negative emotions are deliberately built up in the opening moves of the play. Then, at the critical moment when the brand arrives those emotions are reversed, leaving the audience with strong positive feelings toward the brand by the end of the ad. The third play is the "transition," which starts with audience emotions in a mild, positive state (e.g., fun) until the brand appears to jump audience emotions to a higher, more intense positive state (e.g., excitement). The fourth play is the "end pass,"where audience emotions fly toward the brand, which is waiting in the end zone of the commercial, to receive the accolades of the fans cheering in the stadium.

These primary structures have been identified empirically through the use of a second type of picture sort instant replay, the Flow of Emotion®. Pictures from an ad are sorted not on recall, but rather on a respondent's positive and negative feelings towards each image in an ad.

In longer commercials, these plays can be used in combination to construct more complex advertising experiences. And while each type can work well, the choice of which one to use depends on the overall marketing strategy for winning the game. A creative pro, for example, takes into account the life stage and the

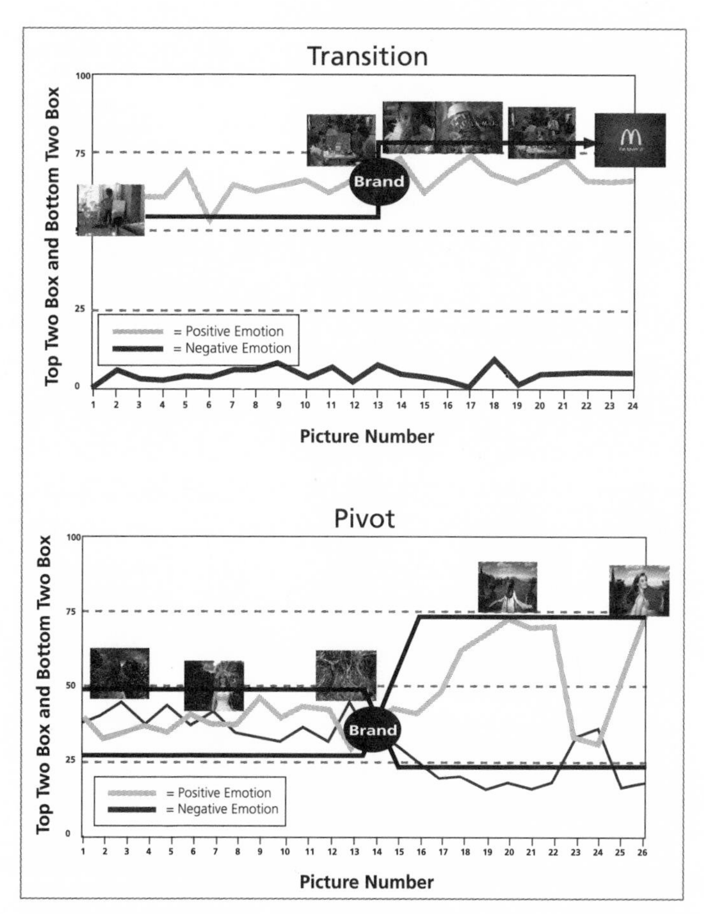

Flow of Emotion for a transition-type ad and a pivot-type ad.

inherent energy of the brand being advertised in timing the brand introduction. To see why, let's examine each play in detail.

The Kickoff

This presentation-style advertising is a particularly effective play for launching a new product. The goal of introductory advertising is to position an unknown brand clearly in the consumer's mental map of competing alternatives in the category. Positioning a brand is like identifying your team with a particular city—the Bears are from Chicago, the Cowboys are from Dallas, and the Packers from Green Bay. A positioning anchors a brand experience in the semantic or verbal part of the brain. By definition, a commercial for a new product must send information about the product concept to a new hometown address or positioning in the brain. That's why, for example, the commercial should first cue the category (e.g., the city) before introducing the brand name (e.g., the street address) of the new product.

A new product is a rookie that has to prove itself with functional performance before an emotional relationship with the crowd can be formed. For that reason, a new product commercial tends to be loaded with factual information—features, benefits, product advantages versus the competition, what the package looks like. Rational information like this is most easily processed by the semantic side of the brain in a linear sequence where it can be filed away in memory for future recall. This is the reason why kicking off the brand name in the first few seconds of this type of commercial is a good idea.

The Pivot

You open the ad by intentionally creating negative tension—you make your audience squirm, engage, get involved.

Two young people are sitting in a dark room. They type furiously on their laptop computers in some hidden place. The guy breaks into the corporate payroll system. "Whoa I got in!" "Look at what that VP makes compared to that VP," the woman responds. "I bet he doesn't know that!" "Sure he does," the guy says as he pops the return key. "I just e-mailed everyone in the company." Then a super appears on the screen: "You Are So Ready for IBM."

Problem/solution commercials have been a very popular genre of advertising. Using drama to make a problem seem important is one way of making the solution seem important. Indeed, for some established brands, pre-emptively "owning" the consumer problem may be the marketing strategy rather than selling one specific solution.

Pivots in our inner emotional states can be quite rapid, with one emotional state flipping over to its opposite in the blink of an eye, like an intercepted pass. The tipping point between one emotional state and another can be quite precise, like 32 degrees Fahrenheit for water turning into ice. Such a boundary point between emotional states is the center of maximum drama.

This is the precise moment when a brand should be introduced in a pivot-type ad. By placing the brand at the boundary between a negative emotional state and a positive emotional state, the brain unconsciously draws the conclusion that the brand is the cause of the transformation from negative to positive—and so the brand becomes the hero of the spot! In contrast, we have a number of empirical examples of commercials that were poorly branded because the brand was introduced five seconds too soon into the dramatic storyline.

The Transition

The creative director knows life looks like that—everybody flowing in one direction, all bunched up and pinned in. So he chooses a positive transition design. The guy in the ad is driving along in his new 4X4 SUV. It's a sweet ride, but life is a congested highway. Then he pops the curb, climbs a 60 degree incline, and flies down the other side of the mountain. His life was not bad, but the brand surprised him with an exhilarating change.

In this type of advertising there is no role for negative emotion, but nonetheless the structure represents a movement from one emotional place, a low positive, to another place, a higher positive or different, more intense emotion. Commercials that attempt to reposition established brands in emotion-space or those that communicate a "new and improved" message might be examples of this category of advertising.

In many ways commercials of this type are like pivot ads in that the brand plays an explicit role in the story's action. Again, if the brand is timed to arrive at the precise boundary of the quantum-jump from one emotional state to another, the brain will interpret the brand as the cause of the transition to a more positive state. And as a result, as with pivot ads, the appearance of the brand would be expected in the middle, not at the beginning nor at the end, of the ad.

The End Pass

A guy walks into surgery all scrubbed up. A nurse dramatically puts the surgical gloves on him. He goes to work on the patient, saving his life. But wait, who is this guy? A nurse asks him what hospital he's from. "Oh, I'm not a surgeon," he says confidently, "But I did stay at a Holiday Inn Express last night."

The End Pass is a powerful play, but it's a somewhat risky play for a new product launch or a small brand with little to spend. There is a chance that consumers who do not stay involved to the end of the storyline will not learn the brand's identity. This would inhibit the build in awareness and thus trial or penetration of the brand.

TIMING AND BRAND LIFESTAGE

This type of advertising is usually used to add to a brand's image by telling brand stories of a humorous or dramatic nature. Its content is almost entirely emotional—though the emotions still have to fit the positioning established by the brand early in its lifestage. Usually power brands have earned the right to do this kind of advertising through large investments in media over time or by developing such a distinctive, recognizable style of advertising that the consumer has no trouble predicting who the brand will be when it appears, inevitably, at the end of the commercial. An example of a power brand would be IBM, which rarely shows its name before the end of its blue letterbox television commercials.

At the most basic level, positioning a brand and building a brand image are the opposing creative principles of advertising. Positioning anchors a brand in the mind by establishing rational context within a relevant frame of competing brand claims. It requires clarity and consistency of communication. Positioning is about semantics—or how, on a conceptual level, a brand fits clearly into the mental map that the consumer has formed of the category.

In contrast, *image* is the part of a brand that grows and flowers with each new ad execution to create emotional connections to the consumer's inner Self—so that a consumer will come to feel ownership of a brand over time. Brand image requires freshness and variety of expression. Brand image is about aesthetics—or how you touch a consumer emotionally.

In terms of the job that a television commercial has to do, the balance of effort involved in positioning a brand and building a brand shifts as a function of the brand's lifestage. (*See below.*)

Semantic information content tends to be higher at the beginning of a brand's life; emotional content tends to be higher as the brand matures. It is within this framework, the longer view of the marketing timescale, that the creative decision about which dramatic structure to use in a particular commercial must be made. On multiple levels, therefore, creating well-branded advertising is about getting the timing right.

Creative Choice Varies as a Function of Brand Lifestage. Some Common Plays:

	Lifestage		
Dramatic Structure	New Product	Established Brand	Power Brand
Kick-Off	X		
Pivot		X	
Transition		X	
End-Pass			X

Choice Varies as a Function of Communication Content

XV
Rehearsing Ideas With Rough Ad Testing

XV

Rehearsing Ideas With Rough Ad Testing

The typical industry rationale for pre-testing commercials at a rough level of finish (e.g., as animatics) can be summed up in five words: screen out bad ideas economically. In short, rough pre-testing has been used as a "go/no go" early warning system to minimize waste and limit the time and expense allocated to fully produce an execution. Put another way, if a rough commercial doesn't score well, then go no further—with the assumption, of course, that the research score of the animatic is predictive of its score as a fully-finished commercial. Testing roughs is economical considering that the average cost of an animatic is roughly a tenth of the cost of a fully finished commercial.

Many advertisers realize cost efficiencies in this business process by learning about the creative at rougher levels of finish at the outset (e.g., using animatics, photomatics, stealomatics, etc.). As client and agency converge in their satisfaction with a creative idea at this more preliminary inexpensive level, more successful efforts are taken to higher levels of costly full-production.

In general, previous research on the validity of rough testing has focused on the comparability of scores for rough and finished ads, demonstrating the predictive value of working with ads at lower levels of finish in order to filter creative ideas in the early stages of the advertising development process. However, from our perspective, this is only half the value of pretesting. The other important benefit of working with rough commercials is to use the diagnostic information from the test in order to optimize the performance of the final film, a subject about which much less research has been published.

As Peter Senge points out in his book on learning organizations, *The Fifth Discipline,* "The almost total absence of meaningful 'practice' or 'rehearsal' is probably the predominant factor that keeps most management teams from being effective learning units." In applying this management philosophy to the development of effective advertising, a good business practice is to rehearse the creative in rough form first.

Both academic and industry researchers have found that there are more similarities than differences in the general effectiveness of rough and finished versions of the same execution on such performance measures as attention, motivation, semantic communication, and emotional communication. The implicit theory underlying these studies is that roughs should be used to filter rather than optimize.

We were unable to locate any published research to date on the optimization function of roughs. Accordingly, what follows is an empirical analysis of the benefits of "rough rehearsal" from our database.

Specifically, we compared commercial performance scores across the following four mutually exclusive groups which, taken together, represented the complete testing history for a specified set of brands over a relatively short, recent time period:

Group 1: Ads that had been tested only in animatic form, with no subsequent testing of the final film for those ads that were selected for production [More than 50 ad pre-test results];

Group 2: Ads that had been initially tested in animatic form and were eventually re-tested as final film commercials. These data represent the performance of these ads as animatics, early on in their developmental lifecycle [n=14 ad pre-test results];

Group 3: The same ads in group two that had been initially tested in animatic form and were eventually re-tested as final film commercials. These data represent the performance of these ads as final film commercials, later on in their developmental lifecycle [n=14 ad pre-test results];

Group 4: Ads that had been tested only in film form, with no previous animatic rehearsal. [More than 50 ad pre-test results.]

The composition of the four groups reflected roughly equal proportions of new versus established brands and was not dominated by the test results for any one or two brands. Indeed, the sample represented a wide range of brands in the home care product category (laundry detergent, softener) and in the personal care product category (hair care, face care, hand and body lotion). Finally, it should be noted that this sample represents all the animatic-film test pairs for this set of brands over this time period and is not just an after-the-fact subset of ads for which improvements were found.

The statistical results of our study are shown in the table below. Since these results are of a proprietary nature, all raw percents were converted to indices. All statistical test results reported below were based on raw percents.

All Pre-Test Results on Evaluative Measures

	"Animatic-Only" vs. "Film-Only" Pre-Tests	"Animatic-Then-Film" Pre-Tests	"Film-Only" vs. "Film-After-Animatic" Pre-Tests
Attention	110	115	114
Brand Linkage	102	106	112
Branded Attention	112	122	128

COMPARABILITY OF ANIMATIC AND FINISHED FILM SCORES

First, we compared the group of ads that were tested only in animatic form but not re-tested in film form (if they were in fact produced), with the group of ads that were tested only in film form, without animatic rehearsal first.

These results are consistent with previously published research by other ad research suppliers showing that animatics produce scores nearly as strong as the scores of finished film. This provides support for the argument that animatic testing provides an efficient method for filtering advertising ideas, since the average performance of animatic and film ads are essentially equivalent. It should be noted, however, that we are only talking here about an average result. This is not the same thing as saying that all advertising concepts can be equally well expressed in animatic form—an issue of concern to agency creatives striving to find fresh film techniques to express their advertising ideas.

IMPROVEMENT FROM REHEARSAL TO FINAL PRODUCTION

Next, we examined the scores of the fourteen animatic-film pairs. The film version of the ads in this group scored +22% higher on Branded Attention than the animatics. Importantly, there was statistically significant improvement on all three evaluative measures of Attention, Brand Linkage, and Branded Attention.

The explanation for this is that the animatics that were eventually re-tested in film were initially quite average performers that, for a variety reasons, went forward into production. To allay management concerns about the original average scores, therefore, these ideas required additional testing after they were produced.

In general, insights provided by the diagnostics would have suggested that these advertising ideas might be "diamonds in the rough." As a result, changes were made in the ads that resulted in improved film scores. In short, there was a larger than expected increase in branded break-through performance for the same ad concepts as a function of rehearsal.

THE VALUE OF REHEARSAL

Finally, when we compare the performance of final film for commercials that were tested first in animatic form versus commercials that skipped the rehearsal step and went straight to final film, we see the value of the rehearsal process.

Film ads that were rehearsed first in rough production scored +28% higher on Branded Attention than commercials that skipped the rehearsal step and went straight to final film. Again, we note statistically significant improvements in their Attention, Brand Linkage, and Branded Attention measures.

THREE CASE STUDIES

What follows are three case studies—taken from the sample of 14 ad pre-test results comprising the two ad groups described above—showing the benefits of "rough rehearsal" based on careful consideration of diagnostic insights from the Ameritest Flow of Attention® measure.

Case 1, Suave Hair Care: Improving the Opening to Enhance the Attention Score.

Opportunities for Improvement: The key challenge for this ad was softness on the Attention Score. Flow of Attention results (as seen below) showed that there was no initial hook to engage viewers at the outset of the commercial. To compound this problem further, the animatic had music but no voice-over for the first twelve of its entire thirty seconds.

What Changes Were Made: Engaging close-ups of a child having fun on a merry-go-round were inserted at the outset of the commercial to enhance viewer interest and generate positive emotion. Additionally, the voice-over narrative started seven seconds earlier in the film version than in the animatic. Finally, the key discriminator—You don't have to spend a lot to get a lot—was added to the copy to more clearly communicate the Suave point of difference.

Benefits of Rough Rehearsal: As shown in the

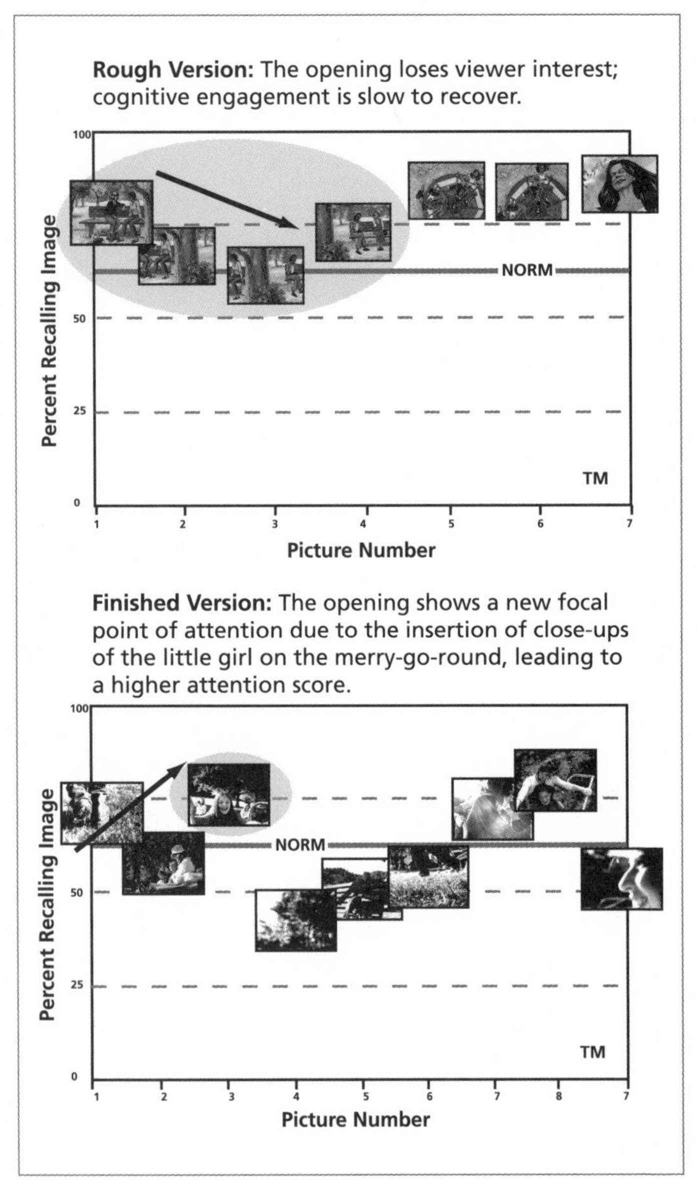

Suave Hair Care before and after Flow of Attention graphs showing improved opening sequence.

exhibit at left, Flow of Attention results showed less of a drop in cognitive engagement at the outset of the final film ad compared to the animatic. In short, an opening that was slow in the rough version received added momentum in the film version thanks to the fun-filled, close-up images of the child on the merry-go-round. The Attention Score increased 21%

Case 2, ThermaSilk Hair Care: Improving a Transition in the Middle to Enhance Brand Linkage.

Opportunities for Improvement: The key challenge for this ad was a soft level of Brand Linkage, possibly because viewers weren't processing the abrupt brand slate that occurs in the middle of the commercial. The dip of the Flow of Attention is shown in the upper panel of the image below. In addition, the "real hair" shots do not stand out in the latter part of the ad, possibly due to the abrupt transitions between the "thermal world" and the "normal world" shots, suggesting that viewers have a superficial understanding of the heat-activation benefits of the product.

What Changes Were Made: The transition introducing the brand slate in the middle of the ad was made less abrupt, moving smoothly from a shot of thermal-imagery hair to thermal-imagery product to normal product. To better communicate how the product works, the brand descriptors "Heat Activated" was added

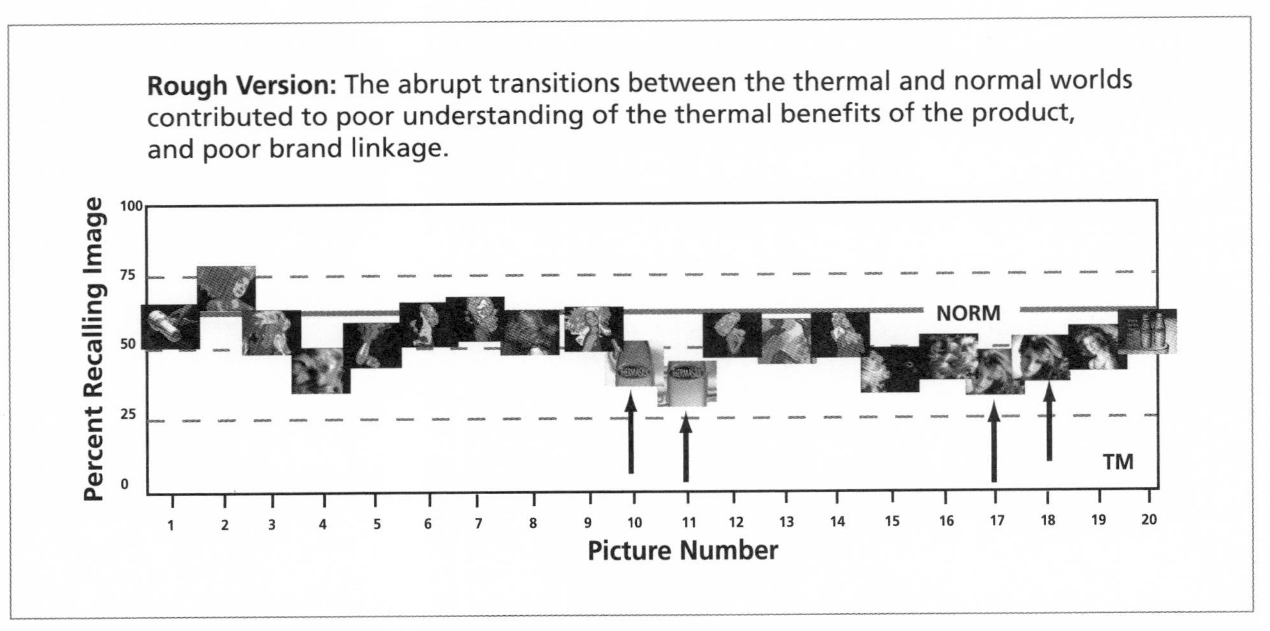

Thermasilk Hair Care Flow of Attention graph for rough version showing need for improvement (marked by arrows).

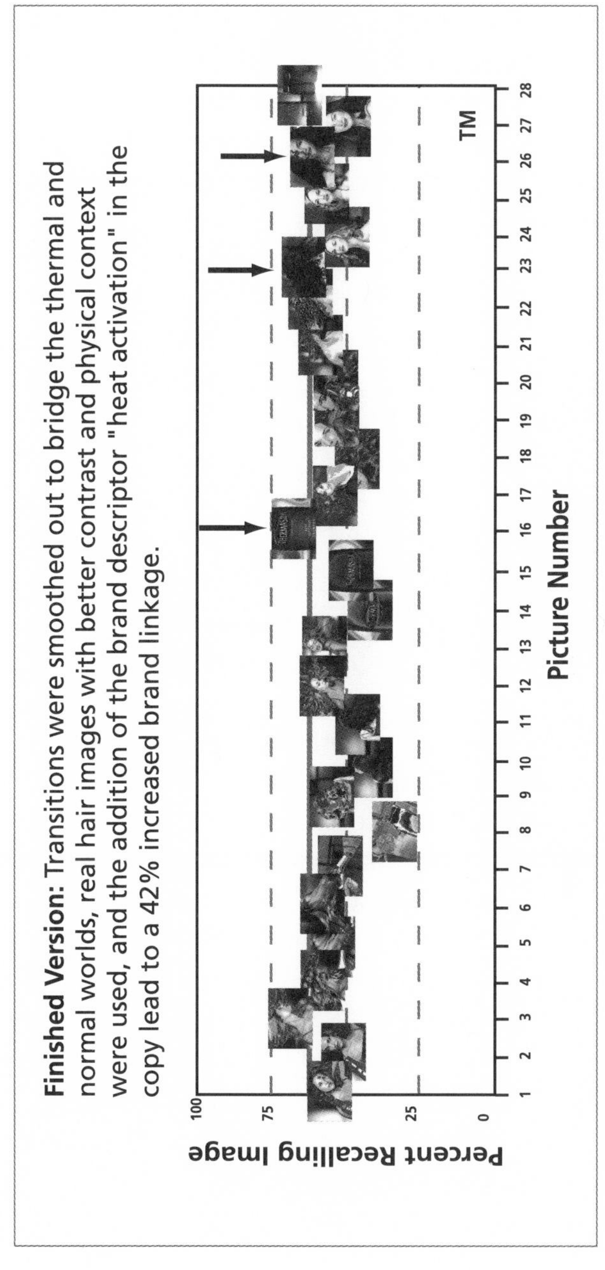

Thermasilk Hair Care Flow of Attention graph for finished film version showing areas of improvement (marked by arrows).

in the copy of the film version. Additionally, to clarify transitions between the "thermal" and "normal" worlds, more visual contrast and a more extended physical context was used (i.e., showing a complete head or profile rather than close-ups that were difficult to identify). Also, more screen time was devoted to the shots of "real" hair.

Benefits of Rough Rehearsal: Flow of Attention results (as seen below) showed that, compared to the rough version, viewers of the finished version were focusing on the brand slates in the middle of the commercial. The smoothed transition was easier to follow. Furthermore, viewers were not tuning out the real hair shots in the finished film version. Branded Attention increased 42%.

Case 3, Degree AP/Deo: Improving the Ending to Enhance Brand Linkage.

Opportunities for Improvement: The key challenge for this ad was its soft Brand Linkage. Flows of Attention results shown below, indicated that viewer engagement began to wane near the end of the commercial when the branding slate was presented, and coincidentally, right after the story had been positively resolved. This commercial, in effect, had run out of story before running out of ad. There was also a focus of attention on the heat-seeking gadget rather than the brand. As a result, this

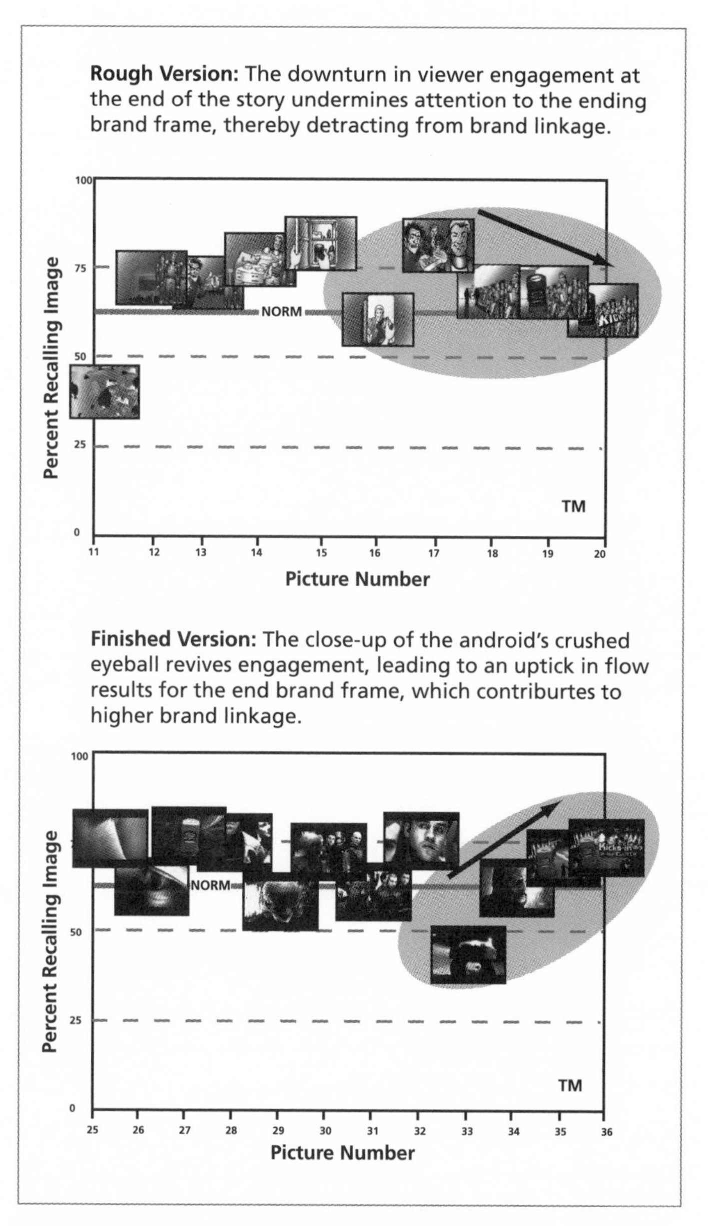

Degree Deodorant, before and after Flow of Attention graphs showing improved ending sequence.

ending brand slate was poorly recalled.

What Changes Were Made: The storyline was extended so that the story ended when the ad ended. In addition, inserting the shot of the android's crushed eyeball re-energizes the momentum of the story and once again draws the viewer into the experience of the ad. Flow of Attention results (as seen above) showed that viewers were fully engaged right up to and during the ending brand slate.

Benefits of Rough Rehearsal: Flow of Attention results showed no downturn in cognitive engagement at the end of the film version compared to the animatic. And once again, Brand Linkage increased 25%.

From a pre-testing perspective, the results detailed above underscore the improved effectiveness of advertising that can be realized based on rough rehearsal. Also, from a financial perspective, we can calculate an approximate dollar value of this rough rehearsal process. These days a major advertiser will spend approximately five million dollars in media costs to air a typical television commercial. What our findings suggest is that an advertiser can spend less than $50,000 on the rough production and research of an advertising idea in order to gain more than a $1 million improvement in the audience impact of the final commercial—a twenty-to-one return on investment!

Thanks to our rough rehearsal process, ads that would have been discarded based on an examination of "report card" measures alone were salvaged and improved. These results also support the general business practice of leveraging diagnostic insights at every step of the advertising development process.

XVI
Why Length Matters

XVI

Why Length Matters

For decades television advertisers have debated the pros and cons of different commercial lengths. This important debate has been fueled mostly by rapidly rising media costs. In the 1950s, the dawn of the age of television, the standard TV spot was 60 seconds in length. Then the tsunami of media inflation hit and the 60-second spot was forced to contract. The '70s saw the emergence and eventual dominance of 30-second TV ads. Quickly following its 30-second parent we saw the birth of the 15-second spot. Even shorter lengths of film continue to emerge as today's media mix supports anything a creative mind can imagine.

As advertising video has begun its migration from the television screen to the web, one of the economic variables impacting the media plan is that it costs no more to place a 30-second video on the web than it does a 15-second video, or for that matter a seven-minute video. On the Internet, creative considerations rather than media purchasing power become paramount in the decision of how long a video to produce.

30 SECONDS VERSUS 15 SECONDS

A generation ago when major advertisers first began to experiment with 15-second commercials, a great deal of ad research was conducted to help manage the transition to this shorter form of advertising. At the time the most widely used scorecard measure of advertising performance in the U.S. was day-after-recall scores. A number of research companies pretested ads and reported that you could get roughly three-fourths of the breakthrough power, or recall, with a 15-second ad that you could with a 30-second ad.

This was a rather remarkable finding. After all, why not half? Why three-quarters? With half the visual real estate, containing half the information, you'd expect to get half as much impact with half the advertising. If you can get three-fourths of the memorable impact with only half the film time, which costs roughly half as much in media air time, it seems that shorter commercials represented an extremely good buy.

Of course, agency creatives were quick to argue that not all brand stories can be properly told in as short a time as 15 seconds—complex selling propositions or emotional ads, like a piece of symphonic music, take a certain amount of time to build involvement. In terms of film experiences, the 15-minute version of Star Wars would probably not have had as much impact on audiences as the original feature length version. Nevertheless, based on published research on average commercial performance and simple economics, it's surprising that the default length of a television commercial today isn't 15 seconds.

The current worldwide leader in advertising research, Millward Brown, takes a somewhat different position than the older American research firms. It estimates ad breakthrough not with a day-after recall score but rather with a derived measure of attention-getting power. Its position is that, based on ad quality or creative considerations alone, there is no difference in attention-getting power, on average, between a 30-second or 15-second commercial. In pre-testing, for example, the same set of norms is used to evaluate the breakthrough power of a 10-second ad as is used to evaluate a 60-second commercial.

That is not to say that Millward Brown believes that a short commercial will have the same impact in the marketplace on brand awareness as a longer commercial. Its argument is economic rather than psychological. In estimating the efficiency of a 30-second commercial versus a 15, it uses a rule-of-thumb adjustment that goes like this: 100 GRPs purchased for a 15-second ad is equivalent to only 50 GRPs purchased for a 30-second spot, because 15 seconds cost half as much as 30 seconds. In the absence of insights about how consumers engage with shorter versus longer ads, it is hard to say what insights or guidance Millward Brown's pre-testing experience would provide regarding the value of different video lengths on the web.

Research data from Ameritest suggests that there are indeed psychological factors that come into play in designing advertising film of different lengths—factors which, as we will shortly see, are determined by the limitations of the cognitive processing powers of the human brain.

In other published studies, where there has been an opportunity to compare the attention scores for identical sets of 30-second commercials tested in both pre-testing systems, we have found the Ameritest and Millward Brown breakthrough attention measures to be highly correlated—even though the two approaches to measuring attention are quite different. Ameritest exposes a test commercial in a clutter reel of control ads and asks the question, "Which of the commercials that you just saw did you find interesting?" The percentage of respondents mentioning the test ad gives the measure of attention. Millward Brown does not use a clutter reel format but rather simply exposes the ad by itself and collects several rating statements on enjoyment, uniqueness, involvement etc. that are then weighted together to calculate an attention score.

In the case of commercial length, it appears the use of a clutter reel does make a difference in measuring attention—just as it did in the real life settings of on-air recall testing. Ameritest finds it necessary, like some other testing companies, to provide different norms for 60's versus 30's versus 15's, etc. (We also use a similar clutter format for print testing and find it necessary to provide different norms for print ads of different length, such as one page versus two-page ads.)

To explore the psychological reasons why longer commercials produce higher levels of attention, a recent analysis looked at a subset of commercials representing an important class of the duration problem: 15-second ads which were cut down from original 30-second executions. Presumably, unlike commercials which were conceived from the beginning to be 15 seconds in length, these were advertising ideas for which creatives intuitively felt a full 30 seconds were needed to tell the story, but which, due to the pressure of media budgets, were also re-edited to 15-second lengths as well.

From our pre-testing database of packaged goods ads nineteen pairs of 30's and 15's were identified. This set is a small but highly controlled sample of ads representing the same brands, the same communication strategies, the same creative concepts, and are even filmed by the same directors. The table below shows the differences in scores between the two commercial lengths. Confirming the older findings of the recall-testing companies, we find that the shorter ads have eighty percent of the breakthrough or attention-getting power of the longer versions. But there is no difference in terms of brand linkage or motivation.

:15s are roughly 80% as effective as :30s in generating attention

	Attention	Brand Linkage	Weighted Motivation
Base Size	*(19)*	*(19)*	*(19)*
:30 commercial	47.7	80.4	33.4
:15 commercial	39.5	84.7	32.6
:15 effectiveness	**83%**	105%	98%
Significance level	0.03	0.34	0.75

Note: the database consists of 19 "pure pairs" for which the :15 is cut-down from the parent :30.

FREQUENCY OF BRANDING MOMENTS

To understand what is going on with these attention scores we need to think about what attention is. When we think of attention we are focusing on only a small fraction of perceptions, thoughts and feelings that we become conscious of—i.e., what we attend to—out of all the information, both from outside and inside of our bodies, that is continuously being received and processed by our brain, both above and below the level of consciousness.

One of the ways to think of how an audience watches advertising film is to think of viewers as consuming information. It's a back and forth process. The consumer bites off a chunk of information, chews it, digests it to give it meaning, and then goes back for another bite of information.

What is important for capturing the attention of the conscious mind is not the raw content of the ad but rather the amount of meaning it contains. To continue our food metaphor, think of this as the nutritional content, and not just the calories, in the film. In a clutter of competing ads, the consumer devotes more attention to the most meaningful ads. Meaning is, of course, in the eye of the beholder. The true test of the significance of the information in an ad is how much attention, either on a conscious or unconscious level, the audience decides to allocate to it. Only the information in an ad that is important to the audience is transformed into thoughts and emotions that ultimately come together to form the meaningful memories that nourish brands.

Diagnostically, we visualize the moment-by-moment information processing of video by an audience with a Flow of Attention graph®. Generally, this information consumption curve is wavelike in shape. While it is not actually an electrical brainwave, it can be thought of as a representation of one of the hidden biorhythms of the engaged mind. It has been shown repeatedly that there is a strong mathematical relationship between the number of peaks in an attention curve and the overall attention-getting power of the ad as a whole. Depending on the type of visual content of the peaks, the frequency of attention peaks is also predictive of day-after recall. In fact, the tempo of the peak moments in an attention curve is predictive of our internal perception of subjective time. The more peaks, the more information processing, and the viewer experiences the sensation that time flies by more quickly when watching more enjoyable works of film.

This moment-by-moment structural analysis of film can help explain the psychological differences in the performance of films of varying lengths. The 30-second commercials we examined have, on average, four peak moments of audience attention. The 15-second versions have, on average, three peak moments of audience attention. The ratio of three out of four is consistent with the earlier findings of recall testing companies and the eighty percent efficiency in commercial attention-getting power that we found in our own system.

To understand why commercials half as long would contain three quarters as many peak moments of attention, we might look at examples of "directors' cuts" in the movies. When time is not a limiting factor, as in the DVD release of a movie, directors will tend to add back a great deal of content that was left on the cutting room floor when a film had to be edited down to fit the parameters of the theatrical release version. Under the discipline of creative constraints, these extra minutes of film are judged by the director to be of lesser importance in telling a story. Similarly, when a piece of commercial film needs to be tightened up, images that are less powerful in conveying the strategic idea, that may be somewhat redundant or that might, in fact, cause some viewer confusion and contribute to "internal clutter," are ruthlessly eliminated. Good creatives intuitively understand what the most important moments in the film are—what the audience focuses on in the attention peaks—and will tend to fight to retain these moments in the shorter film. Since attention to an ad as a whole is driven by the number of peak moments in the film, one consequence of this tighter creative focus is that the shorter ads will tend to have more peaks per unit of time and therefore to generate proportionately higher attention scores.

It is also interesting to note why recall scores, which are generally uncorrelated with attention scores, tend to produce the same efficiency ratios for shorter pieces of ad film. Unlike attention scores, recall scores are only driven by the presence of semantic information in the attention peaks and not by emotional content. By semantic content, we mean product-related content such as visualizations of functional product features and benefits, product-in-use shots, product demos, packaging or visuals containing the brand name. Since recall testing is a measure of semantic learning, recall scores are driven by ad content that literally teaches us something—factual information or concepts that can be stored in the semantic or rational part of the brain. Recall testing is not a measure of the emotional "information" content of an ad—and it is just this type of information that tends to be squeezed out when ads are shortened. Not sur-

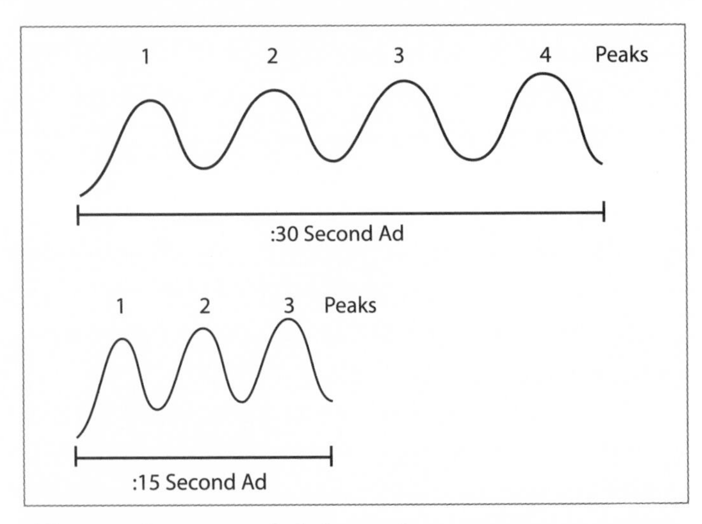

15-second commercials have three quarters as many peak branding moments as 30-second commercials.

prisingly, in producing shorter versions of ads we would expect clients to insist on retaining the rational product content at the expense of the emotional, aesthetic content of the film. The relatively strong performance of 15-second ads on recall tests confirms this.

BUILDING BRAND PRESENCE

Despite the pressure of ad budgets to produce shorter commercials, the average advertiser today would still much rather create a 30-second commercial than a 15. Why do advertisers think longer ads are better?

The stock creative answer is that you need more time to tell a complete brand story. Intuitively this answer feels right, but it doesn't really explain why more time is needed. For that question we need a deeper understanding of how memories are created in the brain and how different kinds of memories work together to create a brand presence in the mind. The following theoretical discussion presents one hypothesis to explain the importance of video length in advertising, with the caveat that additional research needs to be done to validate some of the ideas presented here.

We've all had the experience of being with someone physically who is not mentally or emotionally present. "Where are you?" we ask a friend who is lost in thought. Or, you're walking down the street and the person with you is talking on her cell phone, connecting with someone hundreds of miles away and not with you. Or, you might be presenting to someone who is busy checking emails on their Blackberry. Their attention is divided between you and someone else. In this age of multi-tasking it's useful to realize that awareness can be fractionalized—but we all know that communication is most effective when one person is wholly present to the other.

When a brand is wholly present to the consumer we mean that all the different parts of the brain that might contribute, on a conscious or unconscious level, to the purchase decision that has been touched by advertising. The traditional approach to thinking of brand-name awareness or top-of-mind awareness as an essential precursor to sales is too thin a construct, too one-dimensional an approach to thinking about how advertising does its work. Like recall testing, such awareness metrics only probe the semantic contents of the mind.

Currently, memory researchers describe at least three different memory systems in the brain that are relevant to advertisers: (1) the semantic memory system, where you store facts, concepts and language; (2) the episodic memory system, where you store emotions and autobiographical memories; and (3) the procedural or somatic memory system, where you store learned behaviors, such as how to tie your shoelaces, drive a car, or play a video game, and the physical sensations of the body, such as the feeling of a hug.

In marketing terms these three types of memory might be thought of more simply as Knowledge memories, Emotion memories and Action memories. For example, if you were to try to understand the meaning of different images from a bread commercial you might find that a package shot with a super of how many vitamins it contains communicates the factual idea of "healthy" (Knowledge memory); while an image of mom taking a hot loaf out of the oven to serve her family conveys the emotional idea of serving "love" (Emotion memory); and a close-up of fingers tearing a crusty piece from the loaf that allows us to virtually feel how "fresh" it is (Action memory).

For advertising, a fourth type of memory is also needed: an image that identifies the brand and serves as a "tag" for the other memorable images in the commercial, so that they can all be filed away in the proper place for future retrieval as your brand's portfolio of memories.

This set of four keys is needed to unlock all the doors of brand perceptions: one brand identifier image plus an image for each of the three memory systems of the brain. Advertising ideas and images that enter all the multiple memory systems of the brain make a brand real to us. Thus, when we imagine a brand in our mind's eye in this multi-dimensional way it becomes wholly "present" to us.

As we have seen, 30-second commercials turn out to be just the right length to deliver, on average, four peak brand-building moments. Fifteen-second commercials deliver a less complete brand story, touching on only three of the four. Since every commercial, regardless of length, must contain a brand identifier, this means that even a good 15-second commercial will tend to leave out one of the three memory types, falling short on either Knowledge, Emotion or Action imagery.

A simple way to think about this is to imagine that the job of your advertising is to make image deposits in the different memory banks of the mind. To build brand presence, each new ad campaign needs to deposit a memorable image in the Knowledge bank, another image in the Emotion bank, and a third in the Action bank. And each commercial needs to be properly tagged with a brand identifier.

To keep a brand wholly present in the mind, these image accounts need to be kept roughly in balance over time. This task can be accomplished in a variety of ways—by constructing a good 30-second commercial with the four different types of brand memories, or by rotating through a set of 15-second ads that complement each other. The decision as to which approach to use should be made not only on economic but on creative considerations.

On the Internet, where these economic considerations do not apply, much remains to be learned about the most effective length of web video. creatives must learn to strike the appropriate balance between the short attention span of the audience and the need to create four dimensional brand memories. Like the dreams of the Velveteen Rabbit, the goal is to make the brand real, or wholly present, in the mind of the consumer.

XVII

Film Tips for Branding Television Commercials

XVII

Film Tips for Branding Television Commercials

We have all had the experience of hearing someone say, "I saw a great commercial on television last night but I'm not sure who it was for." A professional's reaction to that statement is to conclude that the advertiser probably just wasted money because the essence of great advertising is that it builds brands. Advertising that does not communicate the identity of the brand in a memorable way cannot be great advertising, no matter how entertaining or emotionally arousing the film is. Brand Linkage is the business concept that the experience of a television commercial should be linked somehow to the experience of a brand in order to grow the business.

Why is Brand Linkage Important?

It is quite possible that unbranded advertising could drive sales in a category. That's why it's become popular in recent years to use television advertising to sell milk or raisins or a drug-free lifestyle. But if a commercial sells without branding, its' sales message and the benefits of that advertising will be expected to accrue to all the players in the category in proportion to the market share they currently have. To gain competitive advantage, a commercial must be branded. An effectively branded commercial will grow an advertiser's share of market in addition to any possible effects it has on the size of the market. Put simply, an effectively branded commercial will increase an advertiser's slice of the category pie, and if the pie grows too, so much the better!

THE VISUAL

The key to visual communication is understanding that all communication is interactive. Half of the experience of watching a television commercial is what ideas and images the advertiser puts into the ad. The other half is what the viewer brings to the party based on his or her own life experience, beliefs and attitudes. That's why upfront strategic research is so important to the communications process. Visual perception is not a passive recording of stimulus material. The eye is not a camera, rather it is an active processor of visual information. According to an old saw, "...there is no such thing as immaculate perception." Visually effective advertising that builds brands begins with a proper respect for the intelligent eye of the viewer.

The following guidelines are based on research findings from the study of the flow of viewer attention to the visuals in literally hundreds of television commercials. These are not intended to be hard and fast rules for commercial filmmaking, but merely summarize our experience with what works in television advertising. Keep in mind that if you choose to ignore any particular guideline in a commercial that you are creating, you should do so deliberately, breaking rules in order to achieve the intended creative effect that you have in mind.

Visualization: Visualize the brand identity, don't just say it in the copy.

While it is obvious, it's importance bears repeating: since television is primarily a visual medium, the key to effective Brand Linkage is visualization. If you have a problem with Brand Linkage in a commercial, trying to fix it by only making changes to the copy usually doesn't work. What follows are visual examples of "branding moments" in advertising.

In each of the following examples, the brand name is prominently displayed in a direct package shot or logo shot, and is the central focus of the visual.

Visual branding moments.

Framing: Establish the category frame of reference as soon as possible.

Just as framing a picture is important for achieving a particular aesthetic effect, framing the communication of ideas in a commercial is important for achieving a branding effect. At the beginning of a commercial you can be sure the viewer's mind is anywhere but where you want it to be. The average respondent is not waiting to receive a message from you, or from any other brand. To prepare each member of the audience to receive a message from the brand, it is important to provide category cues early so that the viewer will be in the correct frame of mind for processing the communication correctly.

The example shown below is the opening shot for a hair care commercial. It provides explicit visual cues that set up the viewer to expect further information about the hair care product category.

The major exception to this rule is the Reveal. This technique of deliberately keeping the viewer in the dark about the real subject of the commercial until very late in the sequence, achieves a dramatic, surprise ending. The reveal is particularly useful for old, established brands where the execution is used to draw non-users in to take a "second look at the brand" since cuing the brand too early may cause non-users, who think they've already made up their minds about the brand, to tune out.

Continuity: Create a unified selling proposition.

Continuity consists of weaving the threads of the different ideas in the commercial together in order to create a unified whole. The most obvious continuity structure from the world of filmmaking is the convention of beginning a sequence with a wide shot, cutting to a medium shot and finally to a close-up. To translate this idea into the world of advertising, you need to remember that continuity consists of weaving together different selling ideas into a unified selling proposition.

In the example above, continuity in constructing a selling proposition would consist of beginning a sequence with a categorical situation, cutting to the brand, and finally delivering the sales message. Another example of a continuity device would be a problem-solution commercial. Montage, another continuity device, involves the use of multiple brief images that express and often emphasize a single meaning or brand emotion. MTV type montage advertising can be quite effective, but only if continuity is maintained by focusing single-mindedly on one branding idea. Violations of continuity, or the "logic of the sale," are often root causes of problems with Brand Linkage.

Focusing: Make sure the brand is in a single-minded focal point of viewer attention at least once in the ad. Just as in composing a photograph, some elements in the picture will be in the foreground creating the focal points of a viewer's attention, and other elements will be in the background creating context. The same is true of a television commercial. The only difference is that the focal points of attention exist in time, rather than in space. The primary use of the Flow of Attention graph is to identify what images are in the foreground of audience thoughts and attention (images that are relatively high on the curve), and what images remain in the background of the audience thoughts and attention (images that are relatively low on the curve).

The key to effective Brand Linkage is that, for at least one clear moment in the thirty-second flow of images, the brand is in the center of the field of viewer consciousness. This is the branding image to which all the other thoughts and feelings created in the film will be linked.

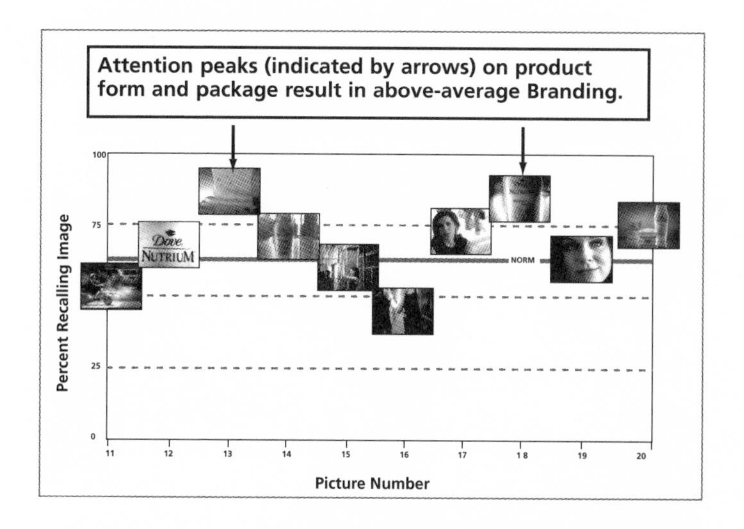

Transitions: Lead the viewer's attention to the brand.
Shots exist in relation to other shots. When considering the placement of the brand in the flow of images in the commercial, it is necessary to consider the rhythm of ideas that come before and after.

The concept of rhythm is connected with that of expectation. Rhythm implies that after one event occurs in the Flow of Attention, the viewer expects the following event. It is essential to note that the looking forward is not with certainty, but with expectation.

Discontinuities in the Flow of Attention generally occur when the sequence of ideas and images change direction unexpectedly, without a proper transition. For example, simply cutting to a shot of the brand at an unexpected moment in the flow can result in poor recall for that brand image and weakens Brand Linkage.

In an example of the Flow of Attention results for a Suave hair care commercial ("Loft" :30 shown below), the party scenes are not well integrated. Moreover, the "hair beauty" shots are tuned out by the viewer. All

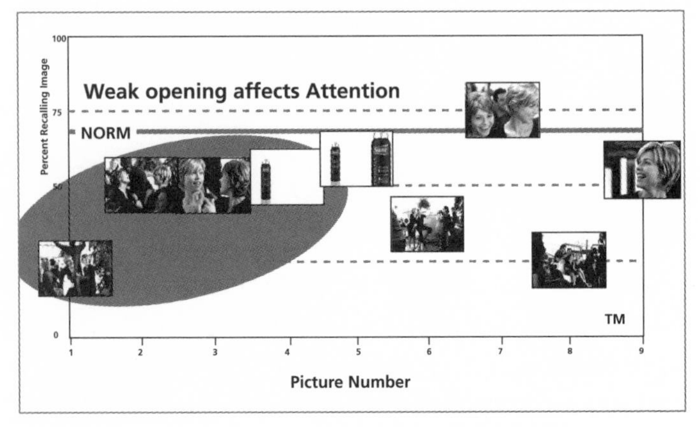

Flow of Attention for "Loft" :30, page 1 of 2.

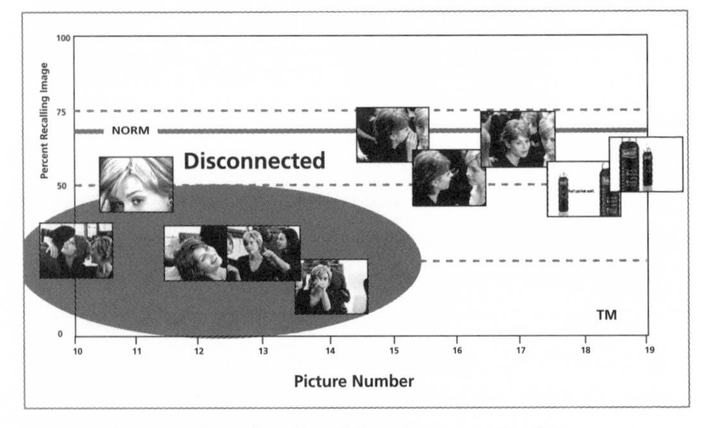

Flow of Attention for "Loft" :30, page 2 of 2.

of this disrupts attention and creates disconnects for the viewer.

Camera Distance: Use close-ups to move the viewer emotionally closer to the brand.
Camera distance is one of the key factors determining emotional response to the shot. Close-ups create an emotional intimacy or emphasis. More distant shots are cooler emotionally. Since one of the more important goals of advertising is to create an emotional bond between the customer and the brand, control of camera distance should be used to modulate the emotional distance between your customer and the brand. For example, as a visual rehearsal of the brand adoption process, you might use the camera to move viewer perceptions from the cooler, more rational and distant perceptions of the non-user of the brand to the close, emotional attachment of the brand's core user.

Zooming: Zoom in to make the viewer read the brand name, zoom out to shift attention to the visual.
Similar to the process of cutting from wide to medium to close-up, zooming in with a camera is a process of focusing the viewer's attention. Zooming in on a brand name (or a set of words in general) has the psychological effect of causing the viewer to read what's on screen. Conversely, zooming out shifts attention to the visual gestalt of what's on screen. Think of this

camera technique in terms of the process of being drawn into a book versus stepping back in a museum to look at a picture hanging on the wall. In the example shown below, as we go from the first shot to the second shot, the camera is zooming in on the product to focus attention on reading the brand name.

Zooming in *enhances reading and Branding scores improve.*

Camera Movement: Avoid panning across the letters of the brand name.

Panning across a long brand name is sometimes done to take advantage of the power of film to make the name feel more dynamic. However, this is a technique that may not create strong Brand Linkage. When people read, they perceive whole words as a gestalt and do not visually take in words one letter at a time.

Camera Angle: Avoid low angle shots of the brand.

Unusual camera angles can evoke strong viewer

emotions but they can also be confusing and imply unintended symbolic messages. Low angle shots of the brand convey power and authority, but also imply the attitude that the brand is talking down to the customer.

Within the frame: Avoid divided attention within the frame.

Because the amount of time that a given frame is on screen is under the control of the advertiser and not the viewer, you should not assume that the viewer will focus on more than one thought within the frame. In theory, copy and image should express a single thought.

An example of "in-frame" competition for attention. The bright product in the lower-right corner fights the bright tee-shirt to gain attention in this frame.

Duration: Pause on the brand to enhance attention.

The actual threshold of perception for registering a stimulus such as the brand, varies as a function of several factors from the contrast in the image to the response time of the particular viewer. The longer the brand is on screen, the more likely it is to become a focal point in the flow of attention as the image "burns in" to viewer attention. In other words, pausing on the brand is a good way to enhance attention. As a general rule, a brand that is on screen for less than half a second is unlikely to register with the majority of your audience.

Tempo: Register the brand on the beat of the editing tempo.

Getting the editing tempo right is one of the most artful and intuitive parts of filmmaking. In a sense, the film editor is engaged in a kind of virtual dance with the viewer. You can lead, but the viewer must follow. The importance of rhythmic structure in all forms of communication has been studied by a number of researchers. Rhythm and beat in language, for example, help us to organize the information in a face-to-face conversation to avoid cognitive overload by focusing on predictable, strategic moments in which to pay attention. In spoken language, the words you stress are the important ones, and you automatically speed up or slow down on the words in between so that the major points of stress form a regular chain of beats. Researchers have found that the beat is when speakers often convey key information and bring up new topics.

An early film theorist, Raymond Spotiswoode, suggested that a cut should be made at the peak of the "content curve," which is the point in the shot at which the audience has been able to absorb most of its information. If you wait too long for the cut, the shot begins to drag and get boring. If you cut too soon, most of the audience may miss the meaning and become confused. In the end, the meaning of the commercial is intended to be attached to the brand. Therefore, somewhere in the flow of the commercial there should be one clear moment where an impression of the brand falls on the beat of the editing tempo. The Flow of Attention graph shows the visual "beats" from your audience's perspective and reveals whether or not the brand is on one.

Repetition: Use repetition to strengthen branding

While in our view an important factor in determining branding is that a brand impression occur at least once in a clear focal point of viewer attention, it is true that simple repetition of the brand can improve memorability and therefore, the branding process. If you accept the notion that repetition is useful in a particular commercial, then the question becomes, "How many times should the brand identity be repeated?" As an opinion, let us suggest the rule of three. The logic for this is the same as the logic for using three vignettes per commercial. That is, once is a curiosity, twice is a coincidence, and three times begins to form a pattern. In the example below, these three frames appeared at different times during one ad. The advertiser used repetition to strengthen branding.

Repeating brand shots in an ad is one way to improve branding.

This also fits with the ideas of the respected advertising researcher Krugman who believed that, from a media buying standpoint, three exposures are needed to optimize the impact of a television commercial. He argued that the three exposures correspond to three questions that are subconsciously asked by the television viewer: 1st exposure: What *is* it? 2nd exposure: What *about* it? 3rd exposure: What *of* it?

Brand Identifiers: Identify the brand in a variety of ways.

To get good Brand Linkage in your advertising, it is necessary to focus the viewer's attention on a strong brand impression. This does not necessarily mean the brand has to be identified only by the brand name. One of the advantages that well-established brands have is that multiple ways of identifying the brand have been built up by advertising over time in the form of "advertising equities." For example, soon after it was introduced in IBM advertising, the "blue letterbox" became a telegraphic cue to the target audience that they were watching an IBM commercial. The following is a list of some different ways the identity of a brand might be cued in a television commercial:

- **Name:** This is, of course, the most straightforward way of identifying the brand. But for new products, or in some categories such as pharmaceutical, names that are difficult to read, or ambiguous in their pronunciation, can be difficult to work with creatively.
- **Slogan:** Which brand tells you to *Just Do It*? A well-known slogan is one way of contributing to the identification of the brand being advertised, as well as encapsulating an entire brand positioning.
- **Symbols:** Which brand is identified by the symbol of the golden arches? A symbol or visual icon can become telegraphic cues to the identity of the brand being advertised. Some symbols can also become mnemonics, or memory aids, for encoding, in a highly compressed way, a fundamental promise of the brand. For example, the Dove "milk drop shot" reminds consumers of Dove's heritage as a brand for healthy, soft skin.

- **Trade Characters:** Ownable brand characters such as the Snuggle Bear, Tony the Tiger, Mickey Mouse or the AFLAC duck.
- **Trade Dress:** Graphic elements that identify and therefore belong to the brand, such as the distinctive shapes of the Coca-Cola bottle or the Absolut vodka bottle, or in the soft drink category, the color red for Coke versus the color blue for Pepsi.

THE COPY

Our philosophy tends to emphasize the visual component of television advertising, based on the belief that television is primarily about the pictures, not the words. In part, our approach is intended to counteract what we believe is a historical bias of researchers who favor "copy-testing" television commercials. However, don't let that fool you into thinking that we believe copy is unimportant. Indeed, we believe that television is a multimedia or multi-sensory experience and all of the elements of the commercial need to work together to create a well-branded message.

In particular, we believe that one of the best ways to create brand building advertising is to use the medium effectively for storytelling. One of the most powerful aids to memory has always been the art of storytelling. Primitive people cemented their tribal relationships by passing on their core values and beliefs through the oral tradition of storytelling around the campfire. Today brands tell their stories with the bright, flickering images of television to create the lore and loyalty of a valuable brand franchise. To accomplish this, words are needed to focus the meaning of the images the viewer is watching.

Audio/Visual Sync: Make the Pictures and Words Work Together

To reinforce a communication point it is important that the information the viewer is receiving through the visual channel be coordinated with the information being received through the audio channel. For example, showing the brand while a voice over says the brand name out loud keeps the viewer's mind focused. To do otherwise, that is, to show one idea visually while conveying a different idea in the voice-over divides attention between the eye and the ear and forces the brain to choose one channel of perception over the other.

As an exception to this rule, sometimes an interesting effect can be achieved by creating contrast between what you are seeing in the pictures and what you are hearing on the audio channel. As a classic example of this, Woody Allen created a very funny comedy, "What's Up Tiger Lilly", by taking a serious, grade B Japanese action movie and dubbing comic dialogue over the original soundtrack. The unexpected juxtaposition of sound and image was quite effective. This technique has also been frequently used in television commercials where unexpected sound effects are played against predictable imagery to transform our experience of the ordinary.

Narrative/Brand Integration: The role of the brand should be clear, and essential.

The role of the brand should be clear and essential to the action of the story. That does not mean that the brand must be the center of attention all of the time—but it should never be an afterthought in the viewers mind. One way to tell if you have satisfied this requirement is to see if the viewer can play back the commercial in his or her own words without referring to the brand! If they can, the brand is not tightly woven into the narrative structure of the commercial and brand linkage is not likely to be strong.

Creating Brand Drama: Place the brand at the turning point in the drama.

One of the key elements of a good story is that it should create dramatic tension—for example, the struggle between good and evil. Sometimes in advertising negative emotions are deliberately evoked at the beginning of a commercial in order to make the ultimate promise of the brand seem more dramatic and larger than life. The important thing for this genre of advertising is that there be some resolution to the negative emotions and that the brand receives the credit for the resolution of the emotional conflict. In a commercial of this type there is usually a key moment—an emotional pivot point—when emotions turn from negative to positive or down to up, a kind of phase transition between the viewer's resonant emotional states. This moment is a key branding moment. It is the point in the drama when the brand gets to play the hero. From a brand linkage standpoint, this climactic moment is the time during the flow of the action when the identity of the brand should be clearly in the center of the viewer's attention.

The Music

Focusing Attention: Use music to focus attention on a branding moment.

Anyone who has ever watched a silent movie understands the importance of music in generating interest and emotion and carrying the viewer's attention forward in a piece of film. There is, in fact, experimental evidence that suggests a music track can actually increase the rate at which a viewer processes the visual information in a commercial. From a branding standpoint, one of the important uses of music is to create an accent—that is, to emphasize a key point in time, such as a branding moment, when the audience is cued by the music to pay particular attention to what is happening on screen.

Signature: Create a musical signature

One technique that can be used to strengthen brand identification is to create a recognizable phrase in the music track. United Airlines is an example of a brand with a strong music signature for their brand. Intel has succeeded in creating a highly recognizable musical "bong" both for their own advertising and to co-brand the co-op advertising they do with computer makers.

XVIII

Finding Ideas That Travel: What to Look for in Advertising Global Brands

XVIII

Finding Ideas That Travel: What to Look for in Advertising Global Brands

In broad terms, there are four potentially competing business objectives that must be kept in balance as a multinational corporation manages its international advertising.

- Brand Building by Speaking With One Voice
- Economies of Scale in Creative Production
- Maximizing Local Effectiveness
- Speed of Implementation

The main reason to do advertising at all is to build a brand. A global brand is one that stands for the same thing pretty much everywhere. While this does not necessarily require that identical advertising executions be used everywhere, it does require that the advertising communicates the same *meaning*, in terms of strategic messages and brand values, everywhere. In short, the brand needs to speak with *one voice.*

Advertising has to operate within given financial constraints. In general money saved in the cost of producing advertising executions can be put toward media buys to ensure that target audiences actually get an opportunity to see the advertising. The second objective, therefore, is to achieve *economies of scale* in the cost of creative production by re-using the same executions with minimal changes from one country to another. On the surface, this objective appears to line up with the first—in reality, as I have seen in our global pre-testing business, the same execution can work differently in different countries.

The most efficient advertising is advertising that makes each member of the target audience feel like the commercial is a personalized message sent directly to them. This is advertising the target audience is most likely to pay attention to, most likely to find relevant and emotionally engaging, and most likely to act on. Advertising that is developed in-country may have a home-court advantage in terms of how it scores on measures of performance—though we have seen that this is not always the case. The challenge of managing international advertising is to make the correct trade-offs between *in-country* customization versus *cross-country* efficiency.

Finally, the world of business is increasingly moving at Internet speed. Projecting ideas around the world rapidly is one of the keys to winning the global "street fight" for new business.

CREATIVE OPTIONS

From a creative standpoint, there are three fundamentally different approaches to the development of advertising execution that we have seen used with varying degrees of success. These are importing executions, local production and importing ideas.

Importing Executions

Commercials are produced in one country and imported by other countries for use in their local markets. The logic of this strategy is twofold. First, economies of scale are created by only having to produce one execution that can be used in multiple markets around the world. Second, and perhaps more important, the company can speak with one voice and project a consistent brand image around the world, hopefully leading to the creation of a global brand image.

The risks associated with this "one size fits all" approach arise from the fact that not all advertising can be expected to work equally well from one country to another. Failure can take various forms; advertising imported from one country to another can backfire by running afoul of cultural sensitivities in a foreign country. Trying to develop politically correct executions that work everywhere can lead to bland advertising that does not maximize local effectiveness, and third, an American-centric approach reminds one of the famous New Yorker's View of the World cartoon. Such ethnocentric uniformity ultimately can lead to a loss of perspective on the constantly changing world of opportunities facing the brand. At the very least, with an import strategy, a certain symmetry should apply. An execution that has been found to work very well in a foreign market should be a candidate for re-execution in the US market.

Local Production

The commercials produced are entirely unique to the country in which they are aired. The logic of this local "empowerment" strategy is that the in-country manager is closest to the market and therefore is most likely to be aware of cultural nuances and market conditions. In theory this leads to advertising with maximum local effectiveness.

In reality, the risk of this strategy is that the brand identity becomes fractured throughout the various markets; a result that is fundamentally at odds with the goal of a global brand. Local production also fails to create an economy of scale for creative production.

Importing Ideas

It is the *idea* behind an execution that gives it its meaning. If the goal of building a global brand is to make the brand stand for the same thing around the world then customers and potential customers everywhere should associate the same ideas with the brand. An execution and an idea are not the same thing; the movies *Seven Samurai* and *The Magnificent Seven* are the same story idea executed with a local cast for a Japanese and an American audience, respectively. In other words, there is a third strategy for managing global advertising.

Finding ideas that work globally—i.e., "ideas that travel"—is often the best strategy for achieving a balance in all four business objectives. First, using the same idea globally is a way of speaking with one voice. Second, finding good ideas is a significant part of the cost of creative development and can contribute to economies of scale in executing effective advertising ideas. Third, re-executing in a local market is a way of making sure that the idea has maximum appeal to the local market. Fourth, focusing management attention on rapidly deploying a single idea globally allows the modern brand to operate at Internet speed—a new requirement for doing business globally.

BARRIERS TO UNIVERSAL ADVERTISING

There are two fundamental reasons why an ad that performs well in one country may not perform as strongly in another. The first is based on executional considerations. Many of the details that go into making an effective execution may be fairly localized in their effects. A joke that is funny in one country may be offensive in another. A celebrity in one country may be completely unknown in another. If those kinds of factors appear to be central to the execution, so that taking them out fundamentally changes the commercial, then chances are you do not have a big, or global, advertising idea. A checklist of many of the executional variables that will affect how well your idea travels is shown at the end of this section.

The second reason that ads may not travel well is strategic. Obviously, a brands' positioning is defined with reference to its competitive set. The *competitive set*, and the brand's position within that set, may vary as a function of geography—e.g., you might be a market leader in one country, a minor player in another. Therefore, commercials designed to communicate strategic messages that reinforce a particular positioning can be expected to vary in performance internationally as a function of differences in the market context.

Keys to International Advertising: What We Have Learned

The Heuristic Model of Advertising is Global.

Analysis of an extensive international pre-testing database reported to the ESOMAR conference in Rome in 2001 validated with international data all the key relationships in the TV Advertising model presented at the front of this book.

What we found is that regardless of whether or not you are airing it in the US, Europe, South America or Asia/Pacific, an effective commercial can be defined as one that gets the Attention of its target audience, makes an impression of the Brand, and Motivates interest in doing business with the company. Moreover, regardless of which country you are talking about, the kinds of executions that get the attention of the audience are those that reward the viewer for the thirty seconds of time you are asking them to give you—by entertaining them, doing something they like, something that's different from anything else they've seen before. And regardless of which country, the way to motivate an audience is to communicate a relevant, believable, and brand-differentiating selling proposition in an emotionally dramatic way.

In other words, by validating the model with international data, it is clear that there is no need to re-invent in each country the research methods that have been developed for bringing discipline to the advertising process. Thus, while it may not be possible to always create universal commercial executions for global brand building, ad researchers can apply the same theoretical constructs for monitoring global advertising effectiveness.

What Has Worked

Brand image is determined with reference to the *self*—the "I" of the customer. A product has truly become a brand when it becomes "my product." The warmth and intimacy of the brand relationship is created in a variety of ways, from real experiences with the company to *virtual experiences* created by advertising. In fact, the "stories" that the best advertisers of global brands tell in their advertising does just that. This is in striking contrast to the kind of advertising that many business-to-business advertisers have been putting on air—a lot of computer graphics, montage, little narrative structure, emotionally bland.

In a content analysis of several hundred business to business commercials tested around the world we found that the following types of executions are superior in terms of their ability to attract the attention of the target audience:

- Focus on one idea
- From the customer point of view
- Utilizing humor
- Or Drama
- With lots of structure—i.e., stories
- Using characters

- In well-defined roles
- Dealing with problems of today (not the future)

Advertising that focuses on ideas or universal stories dealing with real human values, pays off in the long run compared to flashy video "technique" oriented ads that characterize so much business to business advertising. The challenge, however, is to generate this kind of advertising in a form that speaks to audiences around the world. In other words, it requires genuine insight into the human experience.

International Barriers to Executional Effectiveness

These are some executional variables that can affect how well a particular execution translates from one country to another.

1. Complex Language Ads that are heavy on copy or highly abstract verbal ideas are not likely to travel well. Ads with stand up presenters are likely to fall into this category.

2. Dialogue Does the dialogue carry the story or do the visuals? A good way to consider this question is in silent film terms. The more the story can be conveyed visually, the more likely the execution will translate. Dialogue heavy stories require extensive subtitles which can impede the viewer's ability to process information quickly.

3. Ethnic Characters There are clearly biases in many countries against members of other races or ethnic groups. Sensitivity to these issues is clearly called for in developing global executions.

4. Local Celebrities For executions that use a celebrity it's important to gauge the limits of their fame. For example, television stars are less likely than movie stars to be international celebrities.

5. Business Roles Different cultures conduct business in different ways and so the casting of business roles may not always translate well. For example, showing a female manager in charge may not play as well in countries where women have not risen in management ranks as much as they have in the US.

6. Culturally Inappropriate Cues Props or other objects in the execution may take on unexpected meanings in other cultures.

7. Local Settings Unless it is intentional, it probably does not help to have "made in the USA" stamped all over the execution.

8. Humor Visual or slapstick humor is likely to travel better than humor based on wordplay.

9. Music Music tastes vary widely and musical trends travel around the world at different rates. Therefore, music-driven executions may test differently from one country to another.

XIX

Five Research Strategies for Improving Advertising Productivity

XIX

Five Research Strategies for Improving Advertising Productivity

Like the children of Lake Wobegon, all advertising ideas are above average—if you believe the spin. But the statistical reality of the bell-shaped curve is that only thirty out of every one hundred ads you test will score above average. Forty out of a hundred must, at least the first time you test them, score only average.

No business wants to spend money on average advertising. Competitive advantage is gained in the marketplace only when you put your money behind advertising that is superior to your competitor's. But all too often, the tyranny of the calendar and the need to meet an air date arrives, and your advertising manager must confront the reality of spending millions of dollars on what is no more than an average performer.

Advertising is the business process by which ordinary products are made famous and turned into stars, and stars don't come cheap. How do you manage this expensive creative and frustratingly unpredictable process to beat the averages? As shown in the model below, you can bring research discipline to the creative process by using five different learning strategies to repeatedly achieve productivity gains in advertising performance.

TEST THE ADVERTISING CREATIVE WITH A VALID PERFORMANCE STANDARD.

Who would launch a new product into a national marketplace without first testing it among consumers? It only makes sense to apply the same logic to advertising, which is simply another product of human ingenuity and craft. One way of making sure that you are not putting money behind average advertising is to set a firm performance standard that says an ad cannot go on air unless it first achieves an above average score in pre-testing research.

One of the secrets for identifying superior creative performers is making sure that you use

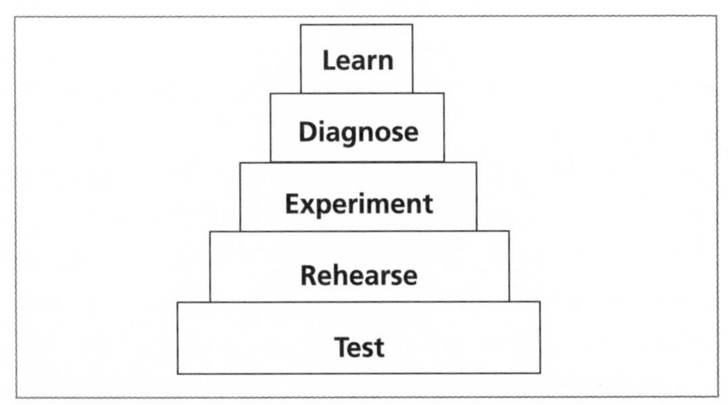

Five learning strategies for improving advertising productivity

valid measures in the research—are the measurements you collect actually related to effectiveness in the marketplace? To answer that question, advertising researchers have put considerable effort and expense into getting the research right.

REHEARSE THE CREATIVE IN ROUGH FORM FIRST. What stand up comedian would take their act directly to a national television audience like the Tonight Show without trying out their jokes in a small nightclub first? Yet many advertisers go directly into final production of their expensive commercials without any kind of rehearsal in front of a real audience. The point made by Senge in *The Fifth Discipline*, "The almost total absence of meaningful 'practice' or 'rehearsal' is probably the predominant factor that keeps most management teams from being effective learning units."

For that reason, large advertisers will test many advertising ideas at a rough stage of production first. Most television commercial concepts can be executed inexpensively in a cartoon form known as an "animatic", or with borrowed footage from other pieces of film in a form known as a "ripomatic." These rough versions cost only about a tenth as much as the final film and are usually good enough for testing purposes.

Rough production not only makes it cheaper to screen ideas, but it can also be used to make good ideas even better. Not all creative concepts are like the goddess Athena, who sprang fully-formed from the mind of Zeus. Sometimes a newborn idea has to come of age before being launched into the world.

In a review of fifty recent ad pre-tests, our experience suggests that commercials that had been rehearsed in rough production were + 28% stronger in terms of attention-getting power than those that skipped the rehearsal step and went straight to final film. What this means in financial terms is that we can spend less than $50,000 on the rough production and research of an advertising idea in order to make an approximately $1 million improvement in the audience impact of the final commercial. That's the value of rehearsal.

EXPERIMENT WITH CREATIVE ALTERNATIVES

All babies are beautiful in the eyes of their parents. The same is true for creative concepts. To find the best solution to your advertising needs, you must avoid the trap of falling in love with your first idea.

One of the benefits of rough production, therefore, is that it makes it cost-effective to test multiple options for an advertising campaign. Like new product development, creativity frequently boils down to a process of trial and error. Thomas Edison tried out over 3,000 different prototypes before hitting on the right way to make the electric light bulb.

According to the laws of statistics, if the first idea you test has a 30% chance of scoring above average, then testing two ideas gives you a 51% probability that one of them will score above average, testing three ideas gives you a 66% per cent chance, and testing four ideas gives you a 76% probability that at least one of your creative concepts will score above average on the first pass through the testing system. (This is based on the binomial distribution that arises from a series of Bernoulli trials.) For a new product launch, for example, where timetables are extremely tight and where you don't want to be forced into the position of launching with an average commercial for lack of better alternatives, it makes sense to plan in advance on testing multiple advertising concepts to gain favorable odds for success.

Optimize the Creative With Diagnostic Insights

Remember, the first time through the testing system you can expect 4 out of every 10 ideas to score at an average level simply because of the laws of probability. Sometimes though, the first execution of an idea produces a "diamond in the rough."

The in-going assumption about pre-testing research is that many of the ideas that make it as far as the quantitative testing stage have the potential to be winners, but for some flaw in the execution that's holding them back. The primary goal of diagnostic research, therefore, is to help identify missed opportunities.

There's a huge gain in productivity to be realized if you can rework an idea that scores only average and make it an above-average performer rather than throwing out the idea and starting over. Time as well as money is lost when you only use research as a filter for advertising ideas. The value of diagnostic pre-testing research, therefore, is optimization.

To begin with, diagnostic research is used to help the ad team answer the following question when confronted with a disappointing test score: Is this a little idea that has been well-executed, or is it a potentially big idea that has some executional flaw holding it back? Or in business terms, is this an idea worth investing additional time and money trying to fix?

For instance, some commercials in pretests score only at average levels on the performance measure of Attention, but score highly on diagnostic factors such as likability, originality or entertainment value—factors that normally are strongly predictive of above average attention-getting power. In those cases, look for some structural flaw in the flow of the film that might be fixed with a little re-editing. Think of it as the film equivalent of fixing a grammatical error in a sentence you is writing.

Next, the job of diagnostic research is to define the problem as precisely as possible—so that creatives know what to fix! For that reason, don't just engage in copy-testing. Use both verbal and non-verbal diagnostic techniques to provide insights into how a commercial is performing. For example, the Ameritest Picture Sorts® technique allows us to understand how a commercial is working as a piece of film. These film direction diagnostics, the "Spielberg variables", are particularly important because, at the end of the day, the actionability of diagnostic advertising research can only be found in the editing room.

In a review of the hundred plus ads recently tested in a major Unilever business unit, fifty commercial executions were found, on the first pass through testing, to score only average on key performance measures—the normal rate we would expect from the Bell Curve. Diagnostics, however, suggested that half, or twenty-five, of these "average" commercials had untapped potential. These commercials were re-edited based on the research findings.

As a quality control check, one in four had been retested. And all but one of the executions improved significantly, from average to above average, on key measures—an 87% success rate for improving commercial performance among these underachievers.

In terms of both time and money, therefore, the overall contribution to advertising productivity can be substantial if you take an optimization approach to using research. Looking at the hundred plus ads produced by this business unit during the review period, nearly half, or 43%, of the of the ads that were approved for airing were first re-edited, or optimized, based on research findings. The following chart illustrates how diagnostic research provided a way to save a large number of creative ideas that simply needed more polishing, while maintaining above average standards for performance.

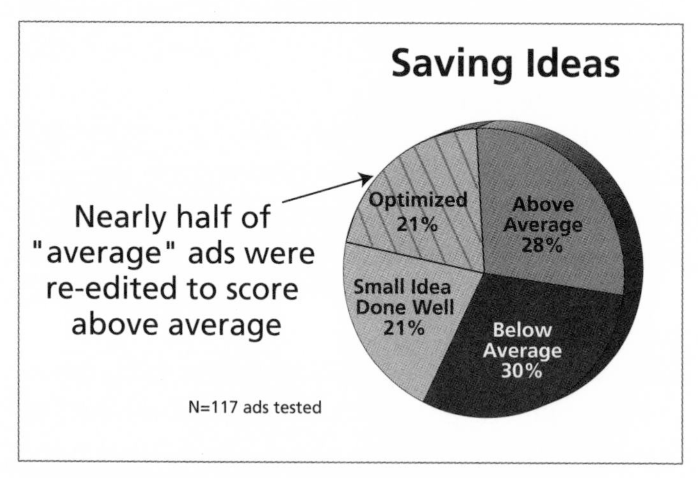

Optimize the creative with diagnostic insights

LEARN FROM THE COMPETITION

From a benchmarking standpoint, it's not enough for your advertising to outscore the commercials averaged together in some historical norm base. The reality is that you have to beat the other guys' advertising—right now! Your advertised share-of-mind is not just a function of your share-of-voice, or ad spending, it's also a function of the relative strength of your advertising creative when compared to the competition.

Some years ago, one of our major clients had a run of weak test scores for one of their deodorant brands. This led to much discussion about deodorant being a "low-involvement" category. It was theorized that deodorant test scores shouldn't be as high as in, say, the more glamorous shampoo category. To some, this line of explanation had the look and feel of a self-limiting mindset.

Then, a new marketing director who was a strong believer in research took over. He reasoned that the competition is selling the same kinds of products to the consumer in this so-called low-involvement category, so let's do some competitive intelligence and test some of their advertising to see their scores. Of course, the competition's advertising was found to significantly outscore his. With this new evidence, it wasn't long before his creative was scoring at a higher level.

Competitive testing gives you a way of experimenting with different methods of reaching the consumer at someone else's expense. And if you have more powerful diagnostic tools for understanding why the consumer is responding the way he does to these different approaches, you may end up actually knowing more about your competitor's advertising than he does, and you learn how to beat him.

The new marketing director was responsible for a number of brands besides deodorant. From the beginning of his tenure, he began a program for systematically testing competitive advertising in all of his categories. What he learned from this competitive research found its way into the performance of his own advertising. When the average performance of ads produced in the two years prior to the onset of competitive ad testing was compared to the average performance of ads produced in the two years after competitive testing was done, in those same product categories, the average had increased by +19%.

Test, rehearse, experiment, diagnose, learn—that's the research mantra for improving advertising productivity. The chart below illustrates the performance of two hundred commercials tested over a six-year period with this approach. A research system that simply filters advertising can raise or lower the hurdle for acceptable advertising performance, but it can not produce such a growth curve. This improvement in advertising performance over time provides evidence for the effectiveness of working systematically with the strategies of test, rehearse, experiment, diagnose and learn.

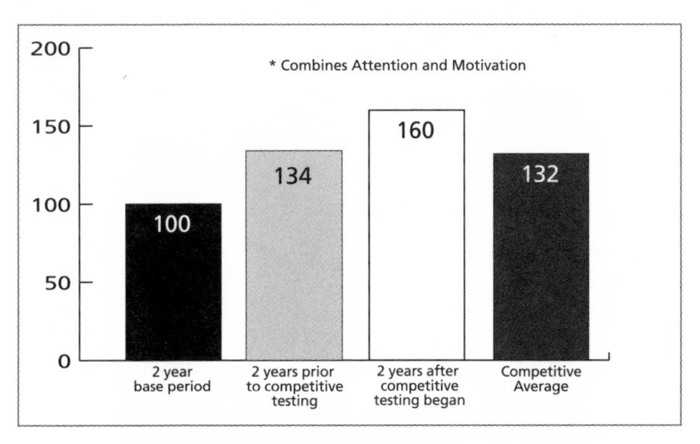

Ameritest Performance Index for 200 ads for one client showing a learning effect.

XX

How to Have a Successful Research Meeting With The Ad Team

XX

How to Have a Successful Research Meeting With the Ad Team

When I heard the learn'd astronomer,
When the proofs, the figures, were ranged in columns before me,
When I was shown the charts and diagrams, to add, divide, and measure them,
When I sitting heard the astronomer where he lectured with much
Applause in the lecture-room,
How soon unaccountable I became tired and sick,
Till rising and gliding out I wander'd off by myself,
In the mystical moist night-air, and from time to time,
Look'd up in perfect silence at the stars.

—Walt Whitman

Walt certainly knew what it was like to be a Creative, even if he never sat in a conference room listening to the research report. But not being a businessman, he might not have understood that creating stars out of ordinary products and services requires that the successful marketing manager must find ways to get the poet and the scientist to communicate effectively with each other.

This has never been more important than now, when senior management is demanding on behalf of the board of directors "figures, ranged in columns" proving the return on investment before your advertising budget gets approved.

Many bright researchers have been working hard on behalf of advertising managers and their agencies on the messy problem of how to improve the accuracy of advertising measurement, particularly in that emotionally charged arena of advertising research known as "pre-testing" or "copytesting." Knowing *in advance* that you have a piece of advertising creative that will return a multiple of the ad spend to the bottom line is much more useful than learning after the fact from tracking studies that, unfortunately, last year's advertising (from the previous agency) didn't work.

Researchers have tried out different measures for predicting advertising performance: recall, persuasion, attention-getting power, likability, communication and so on. All of these have been found to be somewhat valid up to a point and therefore important, but none of them have been found to be perfect. So one of the conclusions that many of us researchers have painstakingly arrived at is what creatives have been saying all along—that different ads can work in different ways and that there is no one simple formula for creating effective advertising.

Without getting into a debate about the pros and cons of different research measures, one of the overlooked implications of this conclusion is that for research to be a useful contributor to the process of developing effective advertising, creatives must make the effort to communicate to the researcher how *their particular piece of creative is supposed to work*. Only then can the appropriate research methods be deployed, and the appropriate interpretations of the data given, to properly understand whether or not your advertising is, in fact, working as intended. In other words, Research and Creative folks must collaborate with one another!

What Are the Barriers to Successful Collaboration?

In a word, *emotions*.

Let's look at the range of emotions that are likely to accompany various findings on ads that you will be researching. In general, if you test enough ads over time, the results, regardless of which research system is used, will follow a bell-shaped curve, as shown in the chart below. Ads that score in the top thirty per cent of ads tested will be described as "above average," which will undoubtedly be cause for great celebration. Time to pop the champagne corks! The advertising manager, the agency, everybody, including the researchers, all look brilliant!

Ads that score in the bottom thirty percent

of ads tested, unfortunately, will be described as "below average." This is, of course, cause for disappointment. Bad luck! Good try! But generally, if the research results are clear-cut in their meaning, most professionals will simply accept the verdict of the audience and move on to another idea. Emotionally, this is a *Zone of Resignation*.

The difficulty arises in the middle ground, the situation where the ad that was tested is described as only "average" or "at norm" statistically. Now, no one wants to be considered *average*, with its unspoken connotation of "mediocre." No ad manager wants to spend millions of marketing dollars behind an average advertising execution. At best, average advertising can be expected to cancel out competitive advertising, but it cannot be expected to grow the business substantially. There is no end-of-year bonus in that performance.

And yet, the research report isn't quite saying that the ad is "good" or "bad"—research reports are cautiously ambivalent about this. Perhaps it is only telling you that the work isn't quite done, that the creative execution needs a bit more polishing before its full potential is released. In this limbo state of average, there is a great deal of room for interpretation and for the various advocates of the ad in question to spin the data—or to question the limitations of the research methodology. But, given the

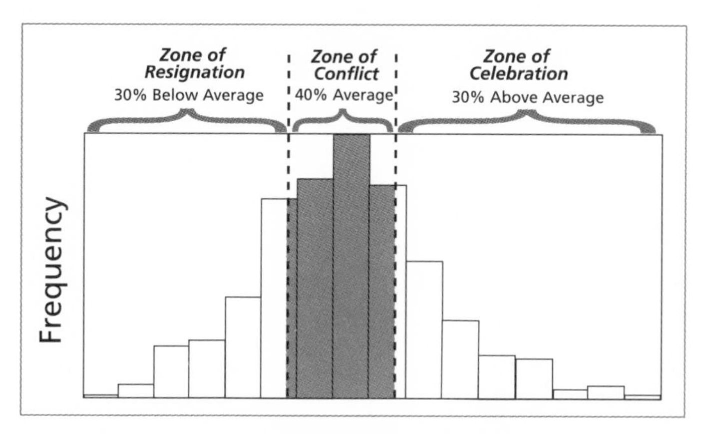

Ad test scores generate a range of emotions.

tyrannical pressures of the marketing calendar, there is also a great need for the advertising team to understand what to do next.

Emotionally, when research has to report average scores for an advertising test you are now in the *Zone of Conflict*. Unfortunately, according to the laws of statistics, you will find yourself in this emotionally-charged situation about forty percent of the time.

How you deal with the complex emotional dynamics of this situation will determine whether or not you have a successful research meeting with the ad team. And no matter how excellent the research was from a technical or methodological standpoint, the advertising research project is not finished until you've had a successful meeting with the ad team. It is only when research is actually listened to that it can make a useful contribution to the creative development process.

One common mistake in managing the emotions present in the room is to pretend that they do not exist. A research meeting is not a court of law where the advertising is on trial and the judge admonishes the jury to set aside their emotions and look reasonably at the facts of the case. We have long believed that the dichotomy between reason and emotion is a false one in advertising. Thought and emotion work together in creating effective advertising. Therefore, the separation of these two human faculties is equally wrong when research is used to evaluate advertising effectiveness.

Great work comes from people who are passionate about their advertising ideas—so how could we possibly expect the ad team members to be dispassionate about the research findings on their work? In our experience, one of the most reliable indicators that the ad team is learning from the research is the visible conflict of ideas—as long as that conflict is productive and not taken to a personal level.

Another barrier to the successful research meeting is the college lecture-room format of most research presentations. Whitman has already warned us of the likely response to that style of delivery from agency creatives. A sure sign of impending failure of the meeting is when the researcher assumes the role of expert professor and the ad team obligingly begins to ask questions about the research methodology, to take attention off the true, and in this case uncomfortable, subject of the meeting, which is the performance of the advertising.

Group Interaction: Dialogue is the Heart of Group Learning

A sign of impending success is when everyone in the room is fully engaged in a lively give and take of ideas as the group struggles to understand the significance of the research reporting on the audience response to the advertising. Each person in the room should participate fully in the discussion with the goal of understanding and insight, not in winning points or attempting to make a particular preconceived point of view prevail.

This kind of group interaction is what Peter Senge describes in his management book on learning organizations, *The Fifth Discipline,* when he talks about dialogue as being at the heart of group learning:

> *"The purpose of dialogue is to go beyond any one individual's understanding. In dialogue, groups explore complex issues from many points of view. In dialogue, individuals gain insights that simply could not be achieved individually."*

Senge borrowed this idea from the late British physicist David Bohm, who wrote an insightful little book on the subject called *On Dialogue*. According to Bohm, the concept of "dialogue" is concerned with:

> *"...a stream of meaning flowing among and through us and between us. This will make possible a flow of meaning in the whole group, out of which may emerge some new understanding. It's something new, which may not have been in the starting point at all. It's something creative."*

THE ROLES IN THE MEETING: UNDERSTANDING THE EMOTIONAL DYNAMICS IN THE ROOM

Dialogue, then, should be focused on logos or meaning, not analysis. It should reflect the fact that people come from different backgrounds and experiences, with different opinions, assumptions and mental models about how things work. Collectively, then, we are able to explore the complex issues of advertising from many points of view.

Indeed, many points of view are represented in the typical advertising research meeting. For the purpose of understanding the emotional dynamics present in the room, it is useful to review the different positions within the organizations that are likely to be represented in the meeting, as diagrammed below.

From the client side, three types of principal players might be present in the room, in addition to various assistants and observers. The first would be the senior marketing person in

Roles in the ad research meeting.

the room, such as the Marketing Director, who ultimately "owns" the brand and, therefore, would be the one who controls the advertising budget. The second would be the person charged with the day-to-day management of the brand and therefore, the one responsible for the development of strategy for the brand's advertising—the Brand Manager or Advertising Manager. The third important player in the room would be the primary client researcher on this piece of business, or these days, the "Consumer Insights Manager"—a title designed to reinforce the organizational emphasis on finding insights or the meaning of the research, and not just the collection and dissemination of data. This person, who is the research supplier's client, is responsible for the research contribution to the creative development process and therefore, in a very real sense, is the one who "owns the meeting."

From the agency side, there might be as many as four types of players present. First would be the Creative Director, who is the principal architect of the brand's advertising over time and, by virtue of her talent, knowledge and experience, occupies the position of the "advertising expert" in the room. Second would be the creatives, typically teams of writers and art directors, who actually came up with the advertising concepts being tested. Third would be the Account Manager on the business who is responsible for managing the business relationships with the client and for interfacing day to day with the creatives. Fourth, a key agency player these days is the Account Planner, whose job is to build bridges between consumer needs and desires and creative inspiration, which in the context of this meeting may mean filling the role of "translator" between the science of research and the art of advertising.

Finally, the research supplier might be in the room to present the research findings and facilitate the discussion—or this role might be assumed by the client researcher instead.

An emotional sensitivity to the different viewpoints in the room is critical to the creation of a successful dialogue. This is not the same as deference to hierarchy. As Bohm points out, "Hierarchy is antithetical to dialogue, and it is difficult to escape hierarchy in organizations." If the senior person is used to having her views prevail because of her position, then successful dialogue will not occur. If junior people are used to withholding their views because of insecurity, then dialogue will also fail. For successful dialogue to take place, all players must participate fully, though that does not mean that all must agree.

What, then, are some of the differences in the roles that the different players positioned in the room can be expected to perform? We conducted group discussions among client and agency personnel on the subject of how to have a successful research meeting. This is what they suggested.

The **Marketing Director** is the decision maker in the room and therefore her primary job is to actively listen rather than talk. If she makes her views known too early, she is likely to create a situation of "follow the leader," which is counterproductive to the purpose of dialogue. That being said, she does have a role at the beginning of the meeting to validate the objectives of the advertising. Since her business goals are at stake she should also clearly challenge the group for excellence and make it clear that she holds the work to the highest standards. Finally, at the end of the meeting she should take the responsibility to sum up learnings. This is important so that the group understands what she has internalized from the research findings that will affect her decision-making. She should set next steps so that the actions to be taken as a result of the research are clear to everyone and that the group can move forward.

The **Brand Manager/Advertising Manager** should provide the "set-up" for the meeting by reminding the group of the brand strategy and the objectives the creative is designed to achieve. As the "advertising buyer" on behalf of the company, the Brand Manager should be disciplined in examining the research to be sure that the advertising has met those objectives. But in performing the role of buyer-critic, it should be clear that all comments reflect a critique of the *work* with an eye toward identifying opportunities for improvement, and not criticisms of the people doing the work. A key role of the brand manger/ad manager is motivational; to be a cheerleader in order to get the best possible work out of the team.

The **Consumer Insights Manager/Client Researcher** validates the methodology through her endorsement and makes sure that the meeting is spent discussing what is important, namely the advertising, and does not degenerate into a confusing discussion of methodological minutiae. Her job is to help explain and clarify the research findings in order to illuminate the meaning of the research to the other team members. If there is a problem with the performance of the advertising execution, her job is not to tell the creatives how to solve the problem but rather is to *define the problem as precisely as possible* so that that the Creative Team can focus on coming up with appropriate solutions.

The **Creative Director** is the primary source of advertising expertise in the room and therefore should provide relevant mental models and examples for framing the discussion of the creative issues. This means providing a "big-picture" view of how a particular execution fits the client's objectives for the brand. The Creative Director should also set a positive tone for the meeting by signaling an interest in the consumer's response to the advertising, actively taking the lead by discussing the research findings.

The **Creatives** are in the most emotionally vulnerable and uncomfortable of positions, for it is their work that is being publicly critiqued. Simply being there to listen and learn signals their willingness to stand behind the quality of their work and their genuine interest in the success of their clients. As painful as it is, whenever a gap opens between the creative intent of the execution and the audience response to the execution, this represents an opportunity to learn a new insight about the consumer to whom they are trying to sell. As seekers of missed opportunities, creatives should actively participate in the discussion and not sit quietly in the room. By far, the best research meetings are those where the creatives do much of the talking.

The **Account Director** is the strategic partner of the Brand Manager and therefore the co-creator of the strategy. As the organizing hub of the agency resources her job is to keep the discourse grounded in the practicalities of keeping the advertising process on its timetable and within budget. But on an emotional level, her job is to provide moral support to the vulnerable creative spirit so as to encourage risk-taking and the inevitable missteps that are implicit in creating outstanding work. In research meetings, she will frequently come across as the "defender" of the work, championing ideas in order to provide the emotional momentum necessary to get an idea through to completion.

The **Account Planner** bridges the worlds of science and art by helping to interpret and translate the research findings in ways that the creatives find helpful. Since creative inspiration is frequently an intuitive or "inner-directed" process, the planner provides a counterpoint by bringing an "outer-directed" focus on the consumer, much like research, but typically with a more conceptual rather than technical orientation.

The Three Conditions Necessary for Discourse

Because advertising development is inherently a collaborative process, these roles will all tend to overlap. But it's important for understanding the emotional dynamics of the group interaction to understand the differences in viewpoints of the various stakeholders at the start of the meeting.

According to Bohm, three conditions are necessary for discourse:

1. All participants must "suspend" their ingoing assumptions and preconceptions;
2. All participants must regard one another as colleagues;
3. There must be a facilitator who holds the "context."

Conversely, the absence of these conditions will tend to undermine the successful outcome of the meeting. Regarding the first point, if participants take a "defensive" stance in the meeting, arguing from their fixed preconceptions, even in the face of research findings, their minds are closed to learning and the meeting will not accomplish anything useful. True learning occurs when you confront the gap between assumptions or expectations and reality. According to an old adage in business, it isn't what you don't know that leads to failure, it's *what you think you know that isn't true*.

The second point is a matter of trust. If one party doesn't trust the others to interpret the data correctly or draw the "right" conclusions, this will lead to attempts to control or spin the research findings. This represents a fundamental lack of respect for your colleagues that will, again, undermine the ability of the team to learn as a whole. Respect for differences in viewpoint and trust in the good intentions of all present are fundamental to creative collabora-

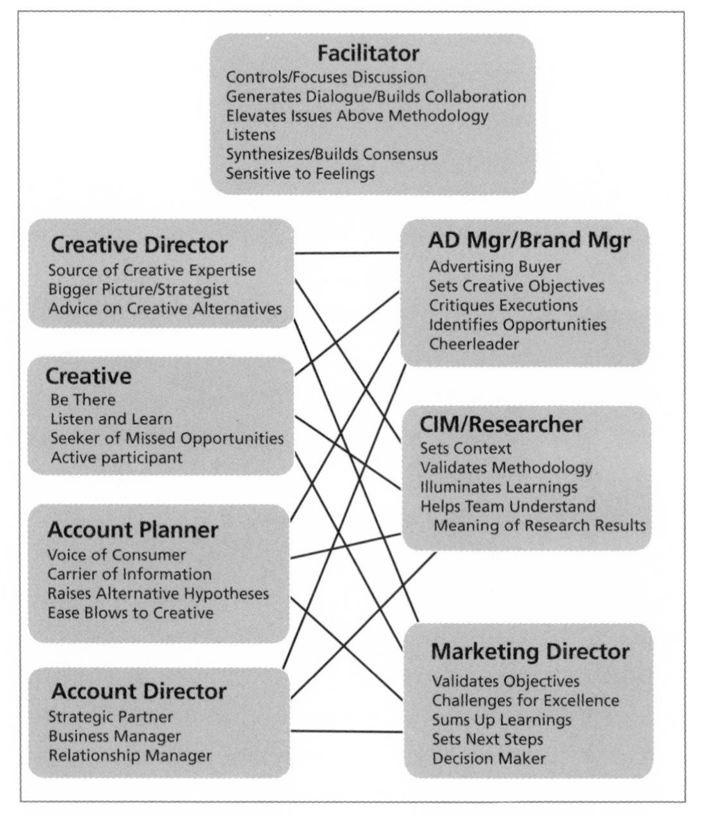

Relationships and roles in the advertising research meeting.

tion. Bohm points out the importance of taking the correct emotional stance in the meeting:

> *"We have been saying that people in any group will bring to it their assumptions, and as the group continues meeting those assumptions will come up. Then what is called for is to suspend those assumptions, so that you neither carry them out nor suppress them. You don't believe them, nor do you disbelieve them; you don't judge them as good or bad. Normally when you are angry you start to react outwardly and you may just say something nasty. Now suppose I try to suspend that reaction. Not only will I now not insult that person outwardly, but I will suspend the insult I make inside of me. Even if I don't insult somebody outwardly, I am insulting him inside. So I will suspend that, too."*

Third, it is important that a facilitator be present to empower the different members of the group to express their views freely and to keep the discussion focused on how the advertising is working. Indeed, the skills needed to generate true discourse in a research meeting with the ad team are really no different from the skills a focus group moderator brings to the business of generating insights from a group of consumers who have never met each other before. Admittedly, it's rare to find internal business meetings run as well as focus groups.

It is difficult for the Client Researcher or Consumer Insights Manager to play the role of moderator because of their need to be perceived as a member of the team, that is, as someone who is herself ego-invested in the success of the advertising. A mistake that Client Researchers sometimes make is to present themselves as somehow *objective* and therefore somehow indifferent to whether or not the research findings are positive or negative. Nothing could be further from the truth. There is a great difference between objectivity and the willingness to suspend your assumptions about the nature of reality. The Client Researcher cares as much as any other member of the ad team about developing winning advertising, and this must be communicated emotionally to the other members of the ad team in order to be accepted as a valued counselor. For that reason, the Client Researcher will often allow the supplier to play the role of facilitator, particularly when the results are controversial or negative.

As previously noted, the facilitator's role is not so different from that of a skilled focus group moderator, though, of course, she may also have to be able to answer questions of a technical nature about the quantitative research methodology that was used. In general, the facilitator must control or focus the discussion. In particular, she should elevate the issues above the methodology and keep them focused on the advertising. She should generate dialogue and build collaboration by actively listening, being sensitive to feelings and the emotional dynamics of the group, and by helping to synthesize the different threads of thought in order to build consensus around the meaning of the research.

The facilitator must be aware of the temptation to take the stage and focus the spotlight of attention on herself, to play the role of "expert." Shrewd advice to Facilitators is that, like the character played by Peter Sellers in the movie *Being There*, the more the other people in the group talk, the smarter you seem to get.

Causes of Failure and Success in a Research Meeting

To sum up, then, what are the sources of failure in a research meeting with the ad team? Here are some of the big ones:

- Lack of agreement on objectives
- Data is confusing/contradictory
- Research findings are seen as "black box" without face validity
- Discussion is focused on the methodology rather than the advertising
- Emotional dissonance
  - Creatives feeling attacked
  - Creatives feeling like they are being told what to do
  - Not knowing what to do as a next step
- Researcher comes across as a know-it-all

or as too academic
- Researcher tries to "play creative director"
- The researcher lectures the ad team, rather than generating discussion.

How do you know if you've actually had a successful meeting with the ad team? If the members of the ad team report the following positive experience:
- Everyone talked, particularly creatives
- All points of view were heard
- Focus is on learning, not report card results
- Positive emotions were created
- Clear understanding of how ad worked
- Clear understanding of opportunities for improvement
- Clear understanding of next steps.

In short, a successful research meeting means your ad team has received a communication back from their target audience and the gap, if it exists, between creative intent and audience response has been explored fully. In that case, the *Zone of Conflict* has become the *Zone of Opportunity.*

Glossary of Advertising Research Terms: How to Talk the Talk

Glossary of Advertising Research Terms: How to Talk the Talk

Action Standard
The minimum acceptable performance on key measures for an ad to qualify for airing. An Action Standard is not a single Hurdle Rate or a Norm to exceed, but may consist of several measures to meet or beat, singly or in combination.

Aesthetic Emotion
As defined by Aristotle, this is the kind of emotion produced by works of art where thought and emotion come together. Aesthetic emotion—also known as "working emotion"—is the key to building consumer relationships with a brand.

AIDA Model of Advertising Effectiveness:
This is one of several "hierarchy of effects" models that describes how advertising works. In a nutshell, this model says that consumers pass through several stages in a certain order on

their journey from prospects to customers. The first step is *Awareness* of the product or service. As the prospect gathers more information, this awareness becomes *Interest*. Then, over time, the interest morphs into *Desire* or a preference. And, finally, the desire (or Motivation) leads to *Action* (or actual purchase behavior). Critics of this approach point out that it isn't relevant to impulse purchasing (which follows an "awareness-action-desire" pattern).

Animatic

An inexpensive, cartoon-like rendering of a commercial concept that lacks the high production values of finished film. Testing animatics, instead of finished film, reduces the cost of testing multiple advertising concepts in order to identify winners. It provides creatives with the opportunity to rehearse their idea so it can be optimized in final production. This category also includes ripomatics, stealomatics, and photomatics.

Animatic Frame

Finished Film Frame

Archetype

This is an elementary idea or feeling that has "deep meaning," occurs in all societies and is readily understood. The great psychologist Carl Jung created this notion of archetype after observing the underlying themes and commonalities of myths across cultures. From a brand-building standpoint, archetypes are used to position a brand, serve as building blocks for brand persona/identity and inspire brand imagery for creative development. Examples from the marketing realm would be the Jolly Green Giant (based on the pagan "Green Man," who symbolized fertility and abundance) and the Marlboro Man (an icon of masculinity, freedom and independence).

Attention

This is one of the earliest perceptual/cognitive stages in processing stimuli that we are alerted to from any of our five senses. Attention occurs when we decide to tune in to certain stimuli for further processing in short-term memory, thereby tuning out other stimuli. In the 1890s, the great psychologist William James defined attention as "the focalization of consciousness;" a process to help one make sense out of the "blooming, buzzing confusion" experience of the world. In contrast, modern psychologists conceptualize attention in terms of processing capacity, resource allocation, and time-sharing.

Attentional Blink

A finding by neuroscientists that the brain will blink a metaphysical eye to shut out new information in order to process information in meaningful chunks, also called "spotlighting." The effects of the attentional blink are visualized by the peaks in a Flow of Attention graph.

Awareness

A measure of a respondent's conscious knowledge. Ad awareness is usually measured in tracking studies (either telephone or online) after advertising has run in the market. Usually, separate measures of unaided (spontaneous), aided (prompted), and top-of-mind awareness are collected in ad tracking studies. For example, Top-of-Mind Awareness refers to the percent of respondents who mention a given brand as the first one in response to an unaided brand awareness question. This relates to the concept of brand "salience."

Banner

All of the columns that run across the top of a page in a cross-tabulation. The industry standard is to include 16 to 18 points in a banner. For example, Gender consists of two banner points—Male and Female. There is typically more than one banner in a complete cross-tabulation job or "run." The banner points are usually the independent variables in a study.

Base

The number of respondents answering a particular question in a market research interview.

Bell Curve

Also known as the normal distribution or normal curve. Many variables tend to follow a bell curve, such as IQ, waist size, and pre-testing scores. This curve describes the values of a variable that have the following characteristics:

- Most of the values cluster about the average, with very few values extending far below the average and very few extending far above the average.
- The distribution of values is symmetrical relative to the average.
- Roughly 40% of all scores in a bell curve will be "average."

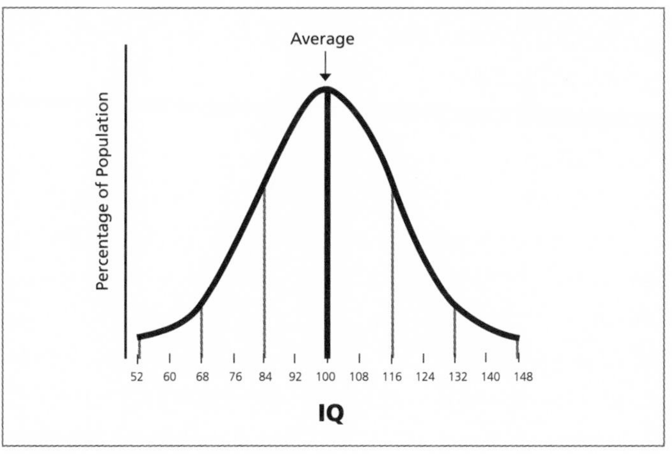

Example of a Bell Curve.

Benefit

The concept of looking at a brand feature from the point of view of the customer. Basically, benefits answer questions such as, "Why would that be important to me?" For example, the benefit of a special ingredient in a new shampoo might be the consumer benefit of beauty. It is an old adage in marketing that consumers buy benefits, not features.

Brain Waves

A physiological testing methodology measuring advertising effectiveness by examining the type of overall electrical activity of the brain (i.e., brain waves) through the use of an electroencephalograph (EEG).

Brand Attributes

The various aspects of product performance on which a target brand is likely to be evaluated by consumers versus a set of competitive alternatives. For a food product, brand attributes might include the concepts of taste and convenience. Usually ratings from ten to twenty features and benefits are collected in a pre-test. Differences across brand attribute ratings are used to assess the relative strengths and weaknesses of different commercials to position a brand within its competitive set.

Brand Image

The set of emotional and sensory inputs that a consumer associates with a particular brand in his or her episodic (i.e., emotional/autobiographical) memory system. Popularized by ad legend David Ogilvy, this notion of brand image is complementary to brand positioning, which represents a brand's place within the semantic (rational) memory system. One of the principal ways advertising works is by building a distinctive image of a brand over time, which forms an emotional basis for brand loyalty.

Branding or Brand Linkage

The degree to which the recipient of the advertising understands that the commercial message was from the manufacturer or source of the product or service. From a quantitative standpoint, it is a measure of the strength of the linkage between the advertised message and the brand. Advertising with a very low level of brand linkage sells the product or service *category* rather than the *brand*.

Brand Stretch

In order to grow a brand, advertising needs to take creative risks to stretch consumers' perceptions of the brand, but not too far. Advertising that goes "too far" creates a disconnect between the brand and the consumer. Advertising that follows a "Goldilock's principle" and is "just right" has one foot in the past and one foot in the future.

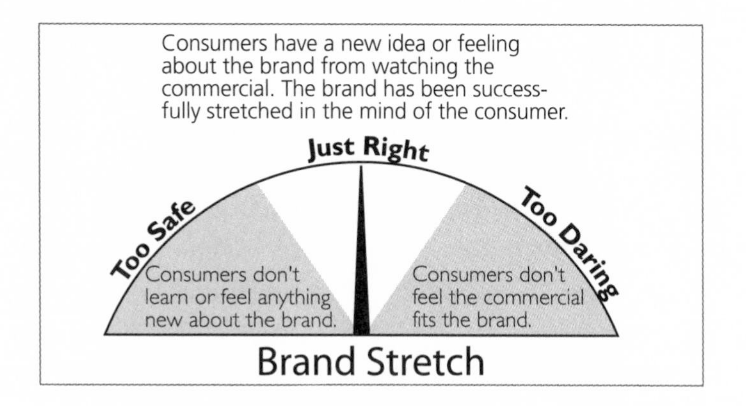

Branding Moment

Branding Moments are moments where thought and feeling come together in the ad. This is a theoretical concept put forward as a psychological mechanism for achieving long-term advertising effects. Branding Moments represent those peak moments in a television commercial, in both cognitive and emotional terms, when the advertising experience simultaneously enters both the episodic and semantic memory systems, thus linking both sides of the mind to the brand. These are the high points of aesthetic emotion where advertising imagery is given a clear meaning in terms of a brand's competitive positioning in the consumer's mind. Branding Moments can be identified by plotting the Flow of Attention against the Flow of Emotion.

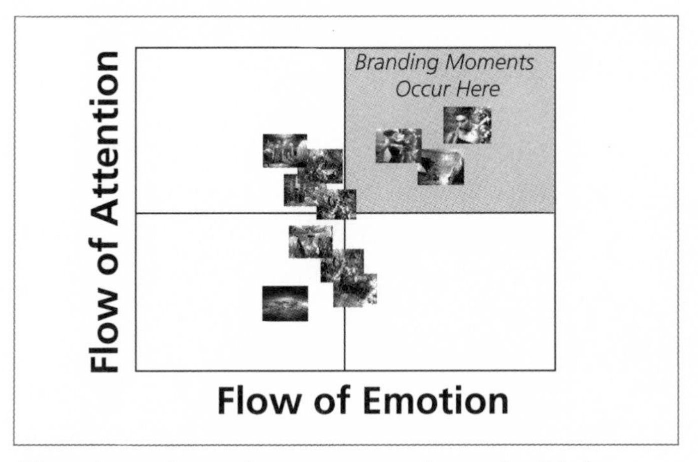

Thought and emotion come together to build the Brand Image for the long term.

CAPI

Computer Assisted Personal Interview. A PC is used to administer the survey to the respondent, and is controlled by the interviewer, who typically enters some or all of the respondent's input.

Cell

A research unit, sub-sample or group within a research study. For example, in a two-cell study, the first cell of respondents would be exposed to one ad while in the second cell, a different group of respondents would be exposed to a different ad.

Classification Variables

These are data that relate to product/ brand usage and lifestyle variables (as distinct from demographic variables). They are typically obtained at the end of a survey.

Click-Through Rate

The proportion of those exposed to a banner ad on the Internet who actually click through on the ad to go to the connecting web page. These days, click-through rates are usually less than one percent.

Closed-Ended Questions

A question in a survey that requires the respondent to choose one or more pre-listed answers.

Coding

The process by which open-ended verbal responses are converted into numeric categories so that they can be tabulated. Verbal statements made by respondents in an interview are collected. The ideas they express are classified into groups according to meaning. The nets and subnets created by these groupings can be used quantitatively to measure how effectively a commercial communicates its intended messages. Generally, this is a subjective, interpretive exercise. Dialogue between client and researcher is usually needed to reach agreement on the content of the various categories for consumer language.

Cognitive Unconscious

This is *not* Freud's repository of idiosyncratic sexual and emotional symbols, but rather the mental processes that are operating outside the realm of awareness. These processes are brought to bear upon our perception and experience of the world. Some marketers have argued that we are *unaware* of as much as 95% of our cognitive processing.

Commercial Ratings

A set of statements used to assess reactions to the execution itself, rather than perceptions of the brand created by the advertising (i.e., brand attributes). These would include statements capturing such dimensions of commercial performance as likability, entertainment value, relevance of the message, believability and confusion. In a standard interview, a common core of rating statements is asked across all ad tests. There are also optional statements that address specific creative issues or areas of concern about a particular ad.

Communications Brief

Also known as Creative Brief. (See *Communication Strategy*.) A document produced by the advertising team to summarize the intended message take-away and/or emotional effects of the commercial on the target consumer. Briefs will usually contain background information on the target consumer, a reference to the consumer insight(s) that leads to this particular advertising idea, product claims to be made, supporting reasons to believe these claims and other considerations.

Communications Strategy

Also known as Creative Strategy. The primary message take-away intended by the advertising team. The strategy is best expressed when focused on a single most important point to communicate, or the feeling that the consumer is supposed to take away after viewing the advertising. Getting the strategy right is half the job of developing effective advertising. It should be developed before the creation of advertising executions and is a key criterion for coding the respondent verbatims in the communication part of the pre-test.

Construct

Every field of inquiry, including market research, has theory and data. Theory refers to an explanatory framework that unifies key learnings from data, thereby providing understanding. A theory provides a connection between many separate elemental ideas or concepts. A technical name for an elemental idea or concept is a construct, or, more formally, a theoretical construct. For example, many pre-testing systems subscribe to a theory that identifies

Attention, Branding, and Motivation as key constructs that explain in-market purchase behavior. These constructs cannot be observed directly; they are defined by various measurement rules. Also known as Theoretical Construct.

Continuous Advertising Tracking

This methodology gathers information on ad awareness, brand awareness, and brand perceptions through interviews that are conducted on a continuing basis. The key benefit is that responses can be examined for any particular time period—for example, on a weekly, bimonthly, monthly, or quarterly basis—so that the impact of advertising flighting, sales promotions, or other marketing events can be lined up accurately with consumer responses. This approach is in marked contrast to the "wave" or "dipstick" method of advertising tracking, in which a limited number of interviews are conducted on a fixed monthly or quarterly basis. The downside of the wave or dipstick approach is that the timing of waves may inadvertently miss or fail to capture key marketing events.

Control Cell

A cell of respondents that receives no exposure to advertising, thus providing benchmark ratings of brand/service/product ratings which are compared against ad exposure cells to evaluate the impact of advertising.

Copy Sort

A parallel technique designed to complement the Picture Sorts technique to deconstruct the audience experience of a television commercial. The copy sort deals with words or copy rather than visual images. Three optional sorts may be used in sorting phrases and verbal ideas from the ad on the basis of 1) attention or recall, 2) relevance, or 3) feelings. Usually a five-point rating scale is used for sorts on relevance or feelings. In analysis, attention should be paid to both ends of the rating scale (e.g., top- and bottom-box ratings) in order to understand the dramatic impact of the language used in the commercial.

Correlation Coefficient

Also known as the Pearson Product-Moment Correlation Coefficient. Correlation is a measure of the relationship between two variables. It can indicate that as one variable increases in value, the other one decreases in value, showing an inverse or negative correlation. Alternatively, it can also indicate that as one variable increases in value, the other one also increases in value, showing a positive correlation. The numeric value of the correlation, i.e., the correlation coefficient, is a decimal that can range from plus one to minus one. The value of +1.00 represents a perfect positive correlation (the variables are synonymous), a value of -1.00 represents a perfect negative correlation (the variables are opposites), and a value of 0.00 represents a lack of correlation , (the variables are independent). For example, height and weight are positively correlated in that people who are tall tend to weigh more than those who are short.

Creatives
The people in an ad agency who actually make the ads, e.g., writers, art directors and producers.

Day-After Recall Testing
A method of testing advertising effectiveness pioneered by Burke and still widely used in the US by systems such as Ipsos-ASI and ARS. The memorability of the advertising is measured by asking respondents to remember the advertising a day after it has been shown on television by using category and brand retrieval cues.

Demographic Variables
Variables that relate to the lifestage, age, gender, income, marital status, employment, educational level, occupation, and household structure of consumers.

Diagnostics

A set of verbal and non-verbal measures that are designed to provide insights and understanding into how an ad is working. (In contrast, evaluative measures are used to make a go/no go decision.) Diagnostic measures are used to explore gaps between creative intent and audience response. They should be used to identify opportunities for improving executions that are performing poorly, and to explain the strengths of strong commercials so that future advertising development can build on that success. In general, diagnostic measures are used to gain insight into the pattern of results for evaluative measures. They tell you *why* rather than *what*.

Discontinuity in the Flow

A jarring or abrupt drop in audience attention to the visuals in the Flow of Attention graph. It suggests that the audience could be momentarily confused by the film and is not tracking with the intended flow of images. Discontinuities should be examined to distinguish between trivial breaks due to fluidity in camera movement, and more critical breaks due to poorly executed transitions between key scenes. Discontinuities are also to be distinguished from the continuously smooth rising and falling curves that form the natural rhythms of the Flow of Attention. (See ***Visual Connectedness***.)

Dramatic Structure

The narrative structure of a piece of advertising film intended to create a particular emotional effect on the audience. It is distinct from lectures or rational sales presentations made to the consumer. Ameritest has identified four archetypal dramatic structures in advertising that can be analyzed with the Flow of Emotion: 1) **Emotional Pivot**, 2) **Positive Transition**, 3) **Emotional Build**, and 4) **Sustained Emotion** (all listed in this glossary). Recognizing gaps between the intended creative structure of an ad and the audience's actual emotional response is a major diagnostic for advertising performance.

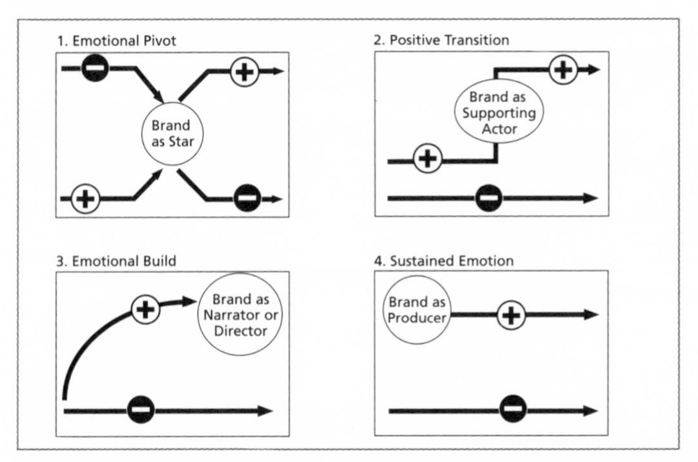

The four dramatic structures identified by the Flow of Emotion.

Emotional Build

One of four archetypal dramatic structures

identified by the Flow of Emotion. It is also known as Director-type advertising. This type of structure is characterized by a rising pattern in the positive Flow of Emotion as the viewer becomes more involved with the ad. It is sometimes associated with the reveal technique since the identity of the brand is generally withheld until the end of the commercial.

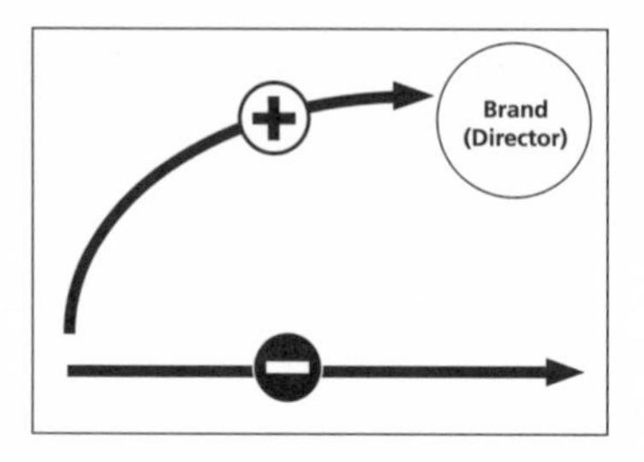

Emotional Pivot

One of four archetypal dramatic structures identified by the Flow of Emotion. It is also known as Star-type advertising. In this type of advertising, the commercial makes deliberate use of negative emotions early in the ad in order to establish emotional conflict or dramatic tension. The negative emotions are then

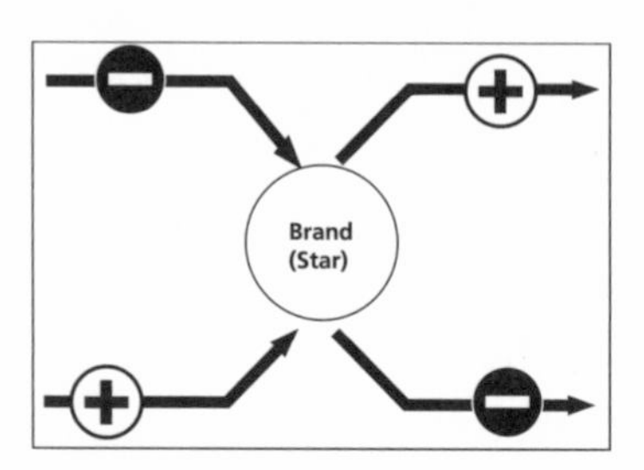

turned into strong positive emotions with the arrival of the brand, which is the hero, or star, of the spot.

Emotional Structure

The intended emotional or affective response to a commercial that is analyzed with the Flow of Emotion.

Entry Point for the Eye

This is the area or areas within a print ad that is first noticed by the reader and serves as a "hook" to draw her into the experience of the ad. Clear entry points are usually key to the Stopping Power or attention-getting power of print ads.

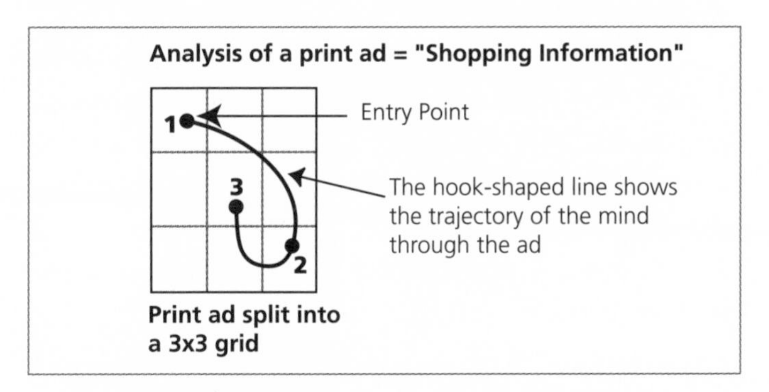

Episodic Memory

One of several human memory systems identified by Endel Tulving, a leading memory researcher and theorist in Cognitive Psycho-logy. This is the system where personal memories are stored and the concept of self is located, in contrast to the Semantic memory system. The Episodic system is key to understanding the concept of Brand Image and the workings of experiential advertising, and is generally accessed through qualitative projective techniques and, quantitatively, by the Picture Sorts technique.

Esthetic Information
One of two types of information present in every piece of communication, in contrast to semantic information. Esthetic information is personalized as it relates to internal states of mind, and is associated with emotional or sensory content. It is not translatable from one channel of communication to another. It is the part of the picture that cannot be put into words—the poetry but not the semantic content of language. You could think of this as information about what you experience through your five senses and/or how you feel about these experiences. Also known as Aesthetic Information.

Executional Peak
A peak in the Flow of Attention that does not contain product-related content, such as a package shot, product in use, product demo etc. Executional peaks usually contain the emotional or aesthetic high points of the

commercial narrative and are strongly linked to commercial enjoyment and attention-getting power.

Experiential Advertising
Advertising designed to associate a particular emotional or sensory experience with the brand as opposed to advertising designed to communicate rational selling propositions. Emotional advertising is a subset of this type of advertising as are commercials, such as appetizing food commercials, that are designed to evoke strong sensory responses from the audience. Experiential commercials create their strongest effects in the episodic memory system. Some researchers prefer to use the term experiential advertising rather than emotional advertising, because of the historical baggage associated with the latter.

Eye-tracking
A technology that uses a camera to record how a reader's eye moves through the visual layout of a print ad or package design. This technology is not portable and, consequently, is often used during in-person interviews at a central-location facility.

Factor Analysis
A family of multivariate statistical procedures that use correlation analysis to reduce

the number of variables in a set of rating scales. For example, factor analysis of a set of 30 rating statements might discover only 5 real, underlying dimensions (or *factors*) in the data. As an illustration, "the ad is clever and quite entertaining" and "the ad is lots of fun to watch and listen to" are correlated statements that are part of an "entertainment" factor.

Features
The functional attributes or dimensions of brand performance that consumers consider in making a choice among competitors in a given category. Communicating an important, believable brand differentiation feature can be a key rational component in developing highly motivating advertising.

Fieldwork
The data collection phase of a research study when respondent interviews are completed.

Fit
One of two factors (the other being "focus") that determine how well branded a commercial is. In a well-branded ad, the creative concept of the execution should be in character with or "fit" in with the underlying values of the brand.

Flow of Attention®
A proprietary technique developed by

Ameritest that measures the moment-by-moment attention of the audience to the flow of visuals through a commercial. By sorting images from the ad based on visual recognition some time after exposure to the commercial, this technique deconstructs the cognitive processes of selective perception involved in the commercial viewing experience. This technique is a powerful diagnostic for the performance of the commercial in terms of Attention and Branding.x

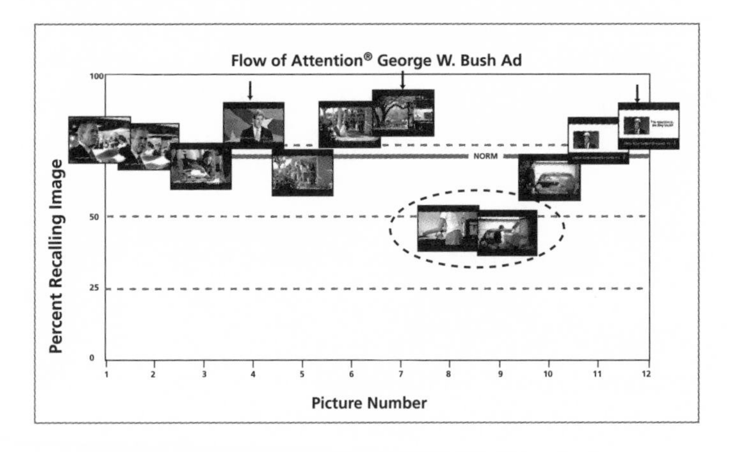

Flow of Emotion®

A proprietary technique developed by Ameritest that measures the moment-by-moment emotional response of an audience to the flow of visuals through a commercial. By sorting images from the ad on a feelings scale and examining the positive and negative responses to the images, this technique deconstructs the dramatic structure of the commercial in terms of

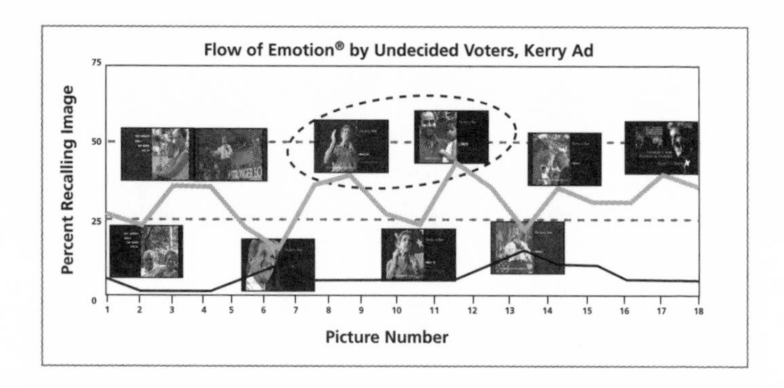

affect or emotional response to the ad, rather than rational response to the messaging. This technique is a powerful diagnostic for the performance of the commercial in terms of Motivation.

Flow of Meaning

A proprietary technique developed by Ameritest that measures the moment-by-moment flow of meaning in the audience response to the visuals in a commercial. In this technique, images are sorted into a number of different categories of intended meanings, which are pre-determined from the Creative Brief. This is a powerful diagnostic for pinpointing the source of different brand values communicated by the advertising. (See *Meaning of Images*.)

Frequency

A media measure that reports the *number of times* within a given time period that a proportion of your target audience is exposed to your advertising message. This is the companion concept to media *reach*. (See *Reach*.) The concepts of reach and frequency account for the breadth and the depth of the advertising media buy.

Gross Rating Points (GRPs)

Reach x Frequency = GRP's. This represents the total *media weight* spent behind advertising. It is a gross measure of the percent of households (or other universe such as adults, 18+, etc.) who have been exposed to an ad, and their average number of exposures, i.e., Reach (net percent exposed at least once) **x** Frequency (average number of times exposed).

Heuristic Model

A teaching model designed to provide a road map to help business managers understand how to think about different measures collected in

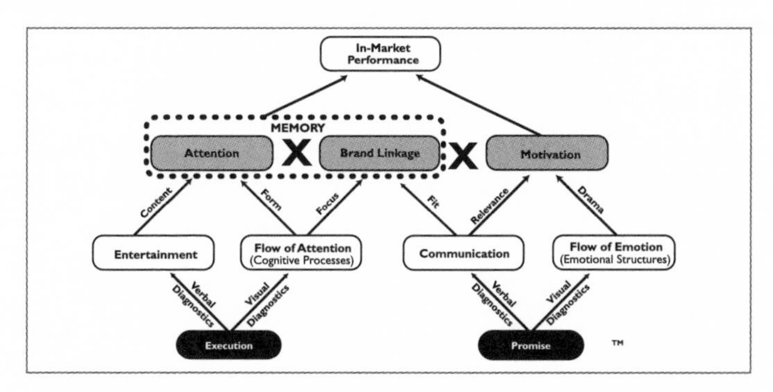

Ameritest heuristic ad model.

the Ameritest interview. It integrates advertising constructs and separates information vertically in terms of evaluative versus diagnostic variables, and horizontally in terms of executional versus strategic variables. It also shows how non-verbal picture sort variables complement traditional verbal measures.

Incentive

Payment to the respondent for taking the time to do an interview, usually either a small cash amount or the opportunity to win a larger prize in a lottery.

Incidence

This is the percent of the population who are in a given target group. For example, the incidence of male 21–24 year-old beer drinkers is 18%.

Index

A performance score generated by taking a raw measure from the interview and dividing it by the average performance on that measure from a particular database (e.g., an in-country database of ads tested) and then multiplying it by 100. An index of 100 means that an ad performs at an average level compared to ads from that particular database.

Involvement

The high and low involvement theory of advertising suggests that the consumer will invest more mental energy in some categories versus others in searching for relevant information, such as automobiles vs toothpaste. Low involvement categories are hypothesized to require more of an emotional than a rational sales approach.

Key Metrics

The performance measures used to evaluate advertising in the go/no go decision.

Laddering

A qualitative technique used for uncovering the underlying values operating in a given category. The technique usually involves asking the simple question, "Why is that important to you?" over and over again as consumer responses ladder from brand features to consumer benefits to consumer values. For example, the consumer benefit of beauty in the skin care category might ladder up to the consumer value of self esteem.

Lifestage

From a pre-testing standpoint, product lifestage is generally divided into the two categories of new products and established brands. New product ads generally work quite differently from established brand ads. For example, creative briefs usually call for new product ads to be "introductory" in tone. Some suppliers make additional distinctions among established brands, such as "relaunch" for ads designed to "reposition" an established brand, or "power brands" for brands that totally dominate a given category.

Mall Intercept

A data collection technique in which the interviewer screens potential respondents from within a mall and, if they meet the screening criteria, brings them to a central location facility within the mall for interviewing.

Marketing Mix Modeling or Analysis

The marketing mix refers to factors within the marketer's control that ultimately satisfy the needs of customers. Some pundits call these factors the four Ps—*price*, *product* (which includes packaging or services), *promotion* (which includes any kind of marketing communication, such as advertising, sales promotions, PR, etc.), and *place* (anything related to distribution—getting the services or products to prospects and customers). From a business standpoint, marketing mix analysis describes the effects of these factors on one another and on sales volume. What is the incremental value of each of these elements of the marketing mix? Which of these elements returns the highest amount of profit to the corporation? How would you reallocate your budget to these various elements to optimize your return on investment? This approach is used primarily for consumer packaged goods and requires advanced statistical analysis of sales data, spending data, and consumer response data.

Meaning of Images

Visual images are inherently ambiguous until the multiple possible interpretations of an image are collapsed into a single or dominant meaning by accompanying copy or by the context of placement in the story of the commercial. Determining whether or not a particular image in a commercial conveys appropriate meaning or brand value can be determined by a

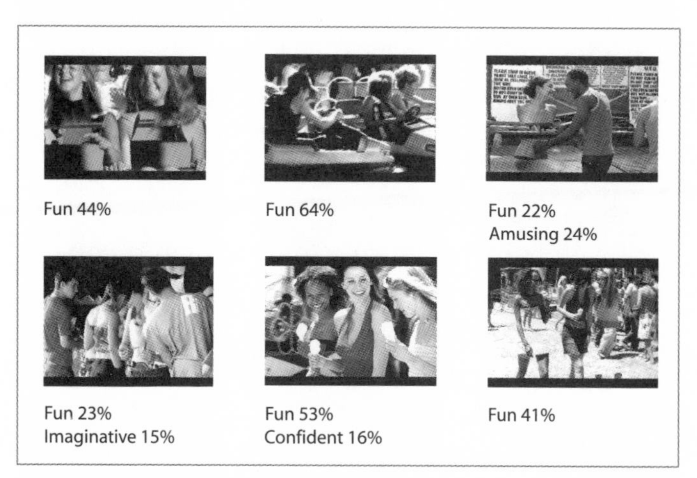

Data from a Flow of Meaning sort.

picture sort by having respondents sort images into different "buckets" of meaning. These results show the percent of respondents selecting a given concept as the one that best describes the image.

Metaphor

A general term encompassing many non-literal linguistic devices (e.g., analogy, simile) to communicate information. From a marketing standpoint, the metaphor is the royal road to the consumer's repository of unconscious thoughts about brands, products, and services. Projective techniques leverage metaphorical thinking to tap into these depths of knowledge.

Motivation or Persuasion:

Since the goal of advertising is to influence attitudes, intentions, and behaviors, motivation or persuasion is conceptualized as the final step in the decision-making process. Some modern theories suggest that there are two routes to effective persuasion. In a *central route*, consumers engage in careful and considerate rational processing that leads to a purchase decision. By contrast, in a *peripheral route*, consumers engage in what might appear to be impulsive decision-making based on positive or negative emotions in response to imagery, sounds, and language that are associated with the advertising messages. Not surprisingly, most theories of persuasion emphasize either rational or emotional factors.

NAIC

North American Industrial Classification code. The US Bureau of the Census has updated what had previously been called SIC (Standard Industrial Classification) codes. This is a numerical system in which six-digit codes are used to represent all possible industries or types of businesses based on the products and services they provide. For a complete list in downloadable text file format go to http://www.census.gov/epcd/naics02/naicod02.txt

Nets

When coding verbal content from open-ended questions, a net counts people, not ideas. The net counts the actual number of respondents who play back a particular idea at least once. It eliminates the double counting of people who express the same idea multiple times, possibly in slightly different ways.

Norms

The average of scores taken from the database of other commercials tested in the same way, which are presumed to follow a normal or bell-shaped curve. Norms are used to provide a benchmark for interpreting evaluative scores or diagnostic rating statements.

Offline Research

Pre-test research conducted in person, at a central location or a convenience sample of consumers intercepted at a research facility within a mall, rather than on the Internet.

Online Research

Pre-test research conducted over the Internet. In general, ratings collected online cannot be compared to ratings collected offline without some further adjustment factor. Experimental work to compare online with offline data collection shows that Picture Sorts are comparable for either method of data collection.

Open Ended Questions

Questions asked that are designed to collect respondent thoughts in their own words, rather than with pre-determined choices or rating statements. Communication of strategic messages is assessed by coding verbatim playback from open-ended questions. Also known as "open ends."

Panel

A group of respondents who are recruited to participate in consumer research at regular intervals over an extended time period. The two most commonly used types are national mail and national online panels.

PAPI

Paper and Pencil Interviewing. In this traditional approach, the respondent completes a paper questionnaire.

Peak Visuals

These are the most salient points in the visual experience of a commercial. Peak visuals are the highest recalled visuals in the local neighborhood of pictures plotted in the Flow of Attention graph. Peak visuals can also be identified with the "beat" of the film experience, which many film editors intuitively think of as the fundamental unit of structure in film storytelling. Peak visuals are also related to the concept of the "attentional blink" in neuroscience.

Persona

The human face or personality that advertising projects onto a brand. The brand persona is collected through the use of a checklist of personality traits. Some examples are *contemporary, traditional, friendly* and *smart.*

Picture Sorts®

A proprietary tool developed by Ameritest that is used to deconstruct the audience's visual experience of a television commercial. Different Picture Sorts are used to diagnose different strengths and weaknesses of the commercial. Three types of sorts are the Flow of

Attention, the Flow of Emotion and the Flow of Meaning. Special sorts are also conducted depending on potential creative issues. As a diagnostic tool, the Ameritest Picture Sorts have been validated against all the major pre-test report card measures.

Place

The emotional place where a brand lives (as distinct from semantic positioning). A brand place such as Marlboro country, or the Green Giant's valley, or the Keebler Elves' tree becomes a stage for telling a brand's stories and a mental container for storing a brand's values and memories.

Positioning

The place a brand occupies in the mind of the consumer in the context of the brand's competitive set. First popularized by Reis & Trout in their book, *Positioning*, this marketing concept deals with the semantic memory system. Because positioning is a semantic or verbal construct, a brand's positioning can easily be measured with traditional verbal rating statements in a pre-test.

Positive Transition

One of four archetypal dramatic structures identified with the Flow of Emotion. It is also known as Supporting Actor-type advertising. In this particular dramatic structure, the audience experiences a quantum leap in emotions, from a low positive emotional state to a high emotional positive state, as a function of the action of the brand.

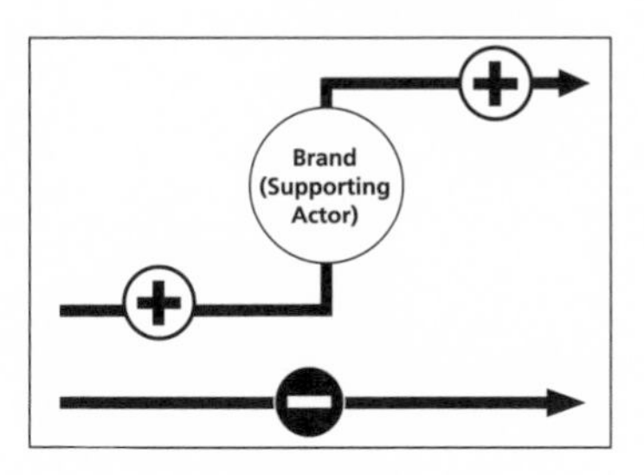

Pre-testing

Testing television commercials prior to airing them or moving them to a higher level of finish. The first goal is to qualify the ad as strong enough to meet company action standards for final production or airing. (See ***Action Standard.***) The second goal is to identify opportunities to improve the performance of the advertising through editing.

Pre-recruiting

A method of recruiting respondents and making an appointment for the respondent to be interviewed, versus recruiting respondents from the mall or street to be interviewed immediately. Pre-recruiting is often used for specific samples outside the general population that can be difficult to find, such as business professionals, physicians, etc.

Precision

Usually refers to the number of "significant digits" that are reported in decimal numbers for quantitative variables. There is a lesser need for precision in advertising research in which subjective perceptions are measured, with most practitioners sticking to one significant decimal point.

Probe

A follow-up question designed to clarify the meaning of respondent answers to a question that has just been asked.

Product Drama

The use of the power of film to promise the emotional or sensory experience a consumer might have in consuming a product. It is the role the product visuals play in creating the virtual consumption experience which is a "false memory" of a positive brand experience generated by advertising.

Product Peak

A Flow of Attention peak where the visual contains product-related content, such as a package shot, product in use, product demo, etc. Ads that test well in Day-After Recall testing systems tend to have a high proportion of product peaks compared to executional peaks, which indicates a focus on rational rather than emotional communication.

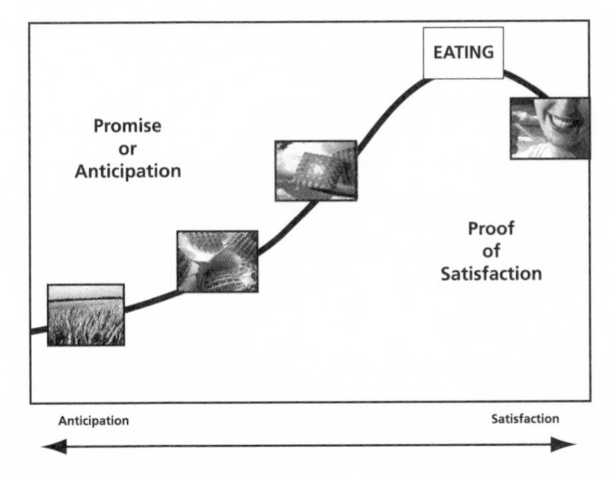

Product Drama Curve for virtual consumption of food product.

Purchase Intent

A common measure of motivation. Most often a five-point purchase interest rating, ranging from "definitely will buy", "probably will buy" to "definitely will not buy," which is usually weighted to count the "definitely will buy" rating most heavily toward measuring the persuasiveness of advertising.

Reach

A media measure reporting the proportion of the target audience that is exposed *at least once* to your advertising message during a given time period. This is the companion concept to media *frequency*. The concepts of reach and frequency account for the breadth and the depth of the advertising media buy.

Reliability
Relates to consistency of measurement. For example, all other things being equal, a commercial that is retested in a given system should receive similar scores on the second test as on the first. Most major pre-testing systems have test-retest reliability scores of over 90%.

Rotation
The practice of varying the order of stimuli so that there is no systematic preference based on what was shown first or last. Ideally, each respondent is shown stimuli in a different random order.

Sample
Those members of a population surveyed in order to draw conclusions about the larger population of which those respondents are members.

Scatterplot
A visual representation of quantitative data shown as points on a plane.

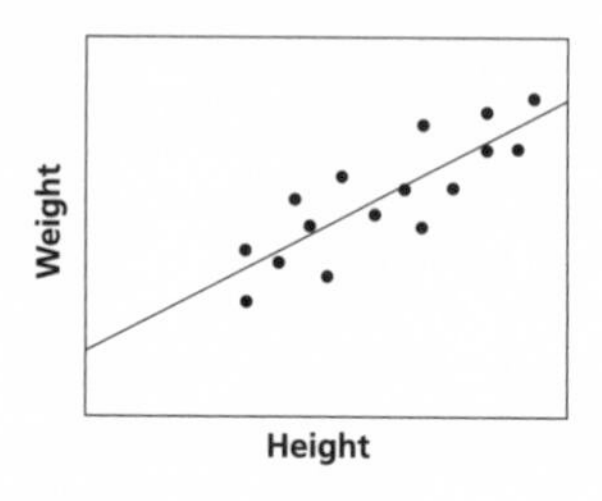

Screening Questions

These are questions asked before the main questionnaire to determine eligibility of the consumer to participate in the research study as a respondent. At the very least, consumers are screened out for "security purposes"—if they work in advertising/marketing or, alternatively, in an industry that relates to the brands, products, consumer research, or services being focused upon in a given study.

Selling-Edge Analysis

A quantitative technique that uses brand ratings from a copytest to identify the degree to which different product attributes or benefits are driving purchase motivation after removing any halo effects. Also used to validate the underlying strategy of the advertising.

Semantic Information

The rational informational content of an ad, such as selling propositions, product facts, or other functional product information. Semantic information is translatable from one channel of communication to another. It is, for example, the part of a picture a respondent can talk about. Consequently, the communication of semantic information can be tested with traditional verbal methods. This is the part of the commercial message that plugs into the semantic memory system.

Semantic Memory

One of several memory systems in the mind. This is the system where logical, structured concepts related to the outside world are stored (in contrast to the Episodic memory system). It is the part of the brain where a brand's place in the world, or positioning, is established. This system is easily accessed via verbal research techniques and is the basis for traditional pre-testing methods.

Semantic Network

A quantitative technique that analyzes the data in a control and test cell to determine how an ad strengthens the linkages between related ideas in a product category. This technique can also be used as a tool for strategy development for identifying different "selling pathways" for motivating the consumer.

Simulated Test Market

A type of concept research study used to predict year one sales or market share for a new product or service based on consumer response to an ad, either in rough or final form, in combination with other marketing and media plan assumptions. The most widely used simulated test market system is BASES.

Single-Minded Branding Moment

A Flow of Attention peak that contains a

single focus of attention on the identity of the brand being advertised. It is distinguished from branding peaks where audience attention may be divided between the brand name and other distracting executional elements competing for attention within the frame.

Skin Conductance

A physiological measure of emotional arousal that is sometimes used to measure the emotional response to advertising. Changes in skin conductivity to electrical currents is also the basis for polygraphs or "lie detectors."

Spontaneous Playback

Respondent mentions of an idea contained in the commercial without prompting or probing by the interviewer. Spontaneous playback suggests that an idea is "top-of-mind." It is a better indicator of commercial effectiveness than ideas extracted from the consumer through probing.

Statistical Test of Significance

This is an analytical method used to determine if the difference you observe between two pre-tests, for example, is a chance difference or a real difference. When the difference is very slight, this method will tell you that it is overwhelmingly due to chance factors. Alternatively, when the difference is very large, this method will tell you that it's not likely due to chance factors. Therefore, it's a real difference. It is customary to conduct two types of statistical tests of significance: (1) between pre-test results for different ads on key performance measures and (2) between a pre-test result for an ad and its corresponding norm.

Stealomatic/Ripomatic
A "rough" television commercial created by joining together "borrowed" pieces of pre-existing film (e.g., from director's reels) for the purpose of testing an advertising concept. This type of commercial may be indistinguishable from a finished film commercial from the viewer's standpoint, but it is far less expensive to produce than film created from scratch.

Stickiness
A diagnostic measure that captures the extent to which readers wish to spend more time looking at or reading a print ad. This measure is used to help understand a print ad's performance on the key evaluative measures of Stopping Power and Brand Linkage. However, there are no absolute levels of stickiness required for advertising effectiveness. For example, a visually simple ad with little copy could be a "quick read," but nevertheless be quite effective.

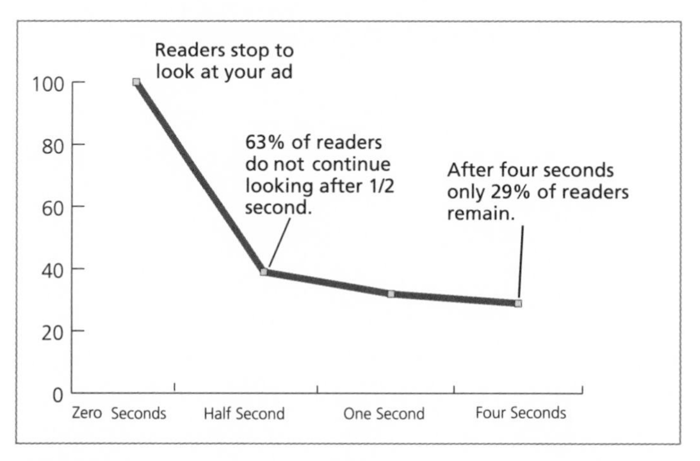

Stickiness is a measure of the decay of readership over time.

Stopping Power

Another name for an Attention Score for print ads. Conceptually, this is the ability of a print ad to break through a cluttered media environment and grab the attention of the reader—i.e., to stop the reader from flipping past the page the ad is on.

Storyboard

A "comic strip" style page consisting of the key frames in a television commercial along with frame-by-frame notations for copy and sound effects.

Stubs

All of the rows that run vertically down the side of a page in a cross-tabulation. The stubs are usually the dependent variables in a study.

Subjective Time

In contrast to mechanical clock time, subjective time is the idea that the perception of time (time flying by us, time dragging slowly) is tied to experience. Subjective time is tied to the rate of information flow in an ad, e.g., cutting speed. Picture Sorts, with a variable number of pictures used to describe the visual information content in different ads, use subjective time as the frame of reference for measuring the ad experience, as opposed to dial-a-meter approaches which use clock time, e.g., every 0.2 seconds, for measurement. This is one reason the two approaches produce fundamentally different insights.

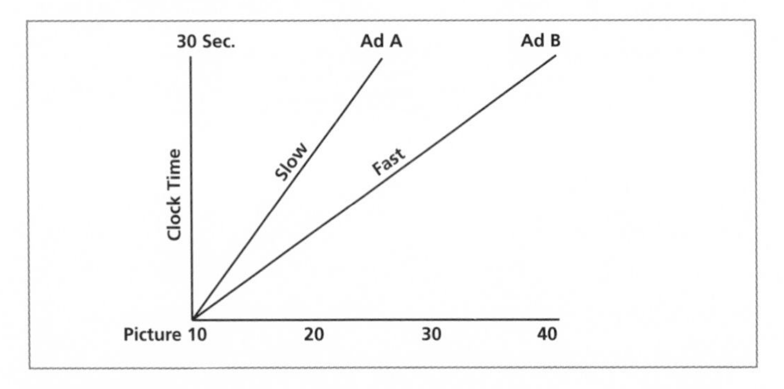

Ad B produces a more energetic, perceived subjective time than ad A because of the higher rate of information flow.

Sustained Emotion

One of four archetypal dramatic structures identified by the Flow of Emotion. It is also known as Producer-type advertising. This dramatic structure is characterized by a high level of continuous positive emotions with no negatives. The brand is usually introduced early in the commercial as the presenter or source of these emotions. Montage commercials with strong music soundtracks are an example of this type of advertising. When the content of the ad is rational product information, rather than emotional content, this type of execution turns into a lecture type of ad.

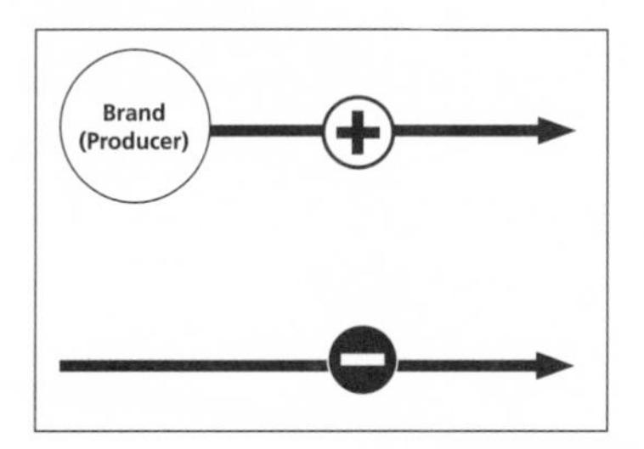

Tab Plan

A detailed specification of the various banner points and stubs to be used in processing cross-tabulations for a research study.

Target Rating Points (TRPs)

Same as GRPs, but the base is the *target audience* you are trying to reach rather than all the households in the market. It's a measure of the total media weight spent to reach this target, measured as the product of Reach and Frequency.

Thinking
The use of cognitive processes (e.g., encoding, storing and retrieving) that are put into service in reacting to stimuli in the outside world, or as a result of other related thoughts that come into consciousness (e.g., beliefs, attitudes and evaluations).

Top Box
The percentage of a sample choosing the highest rating on a scale. Top box ratings are an indicator of the intensity of consumer feelings or perceptions, and generally are more discriminating measures than mean scores. For example, validation research by concept-testing companies has shown repeatedly that top box purchase intent carries the most weight in actually predicting consumer purchase behavior.

Topline
This is also referred to as a topline report. In general, this is a summary of the key performance scores or evaluative measures, without the diagnostics or analysis.

Trace

Millward Brown's moment-by-moment technique using a one dimensional, dial-a-meter response to TV commercials. A number of experiments have shown that Trace and Picture Sorts produce results that are uncorrelated, so the two approaches seem to measure very different things.

Validity

This concept deals with the question of whether or not you are actually measuring what you say it is you are measuring. For example, is day-after recall in advertising research really a measure of breakthrough? These days, all the major copytesting systems claim substantial evidence supporting the relationship between in-market sales effects and their key measures, so validity is a "cost of entry"

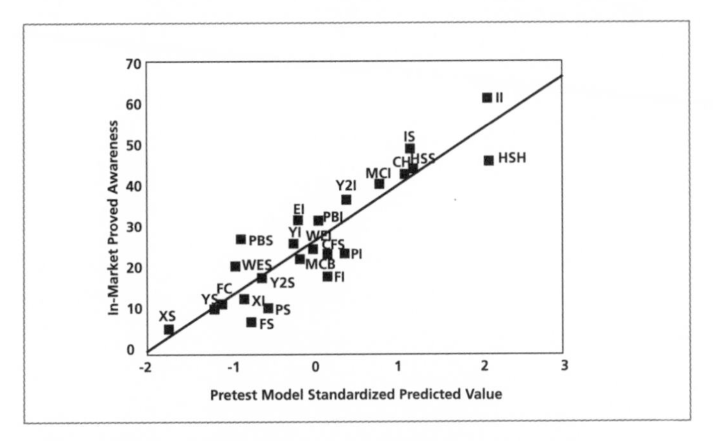

Example of a Validation graph from Ameritest.

criterion for using any pre-testing system.

Values
The axiomatic set of ideas that determine a person's life. Frequently the values people claim to hold are different from their true or underlying values. According to screenwriter Robert McKee, people reveal their true values by the choices they make under pressure. Brands can usually own only one or a few values in the mind of the consumer, usually through the brand-building process of advertising. For example, Coca-Cola tries to own the value of authenticity, the "real thing." Marlboro Cigarettes tries to own the values of freedom and independence through its long-lasting "Marlboro Country" campaign.

Verbatims
The respondent's answers, recorded word for word, to open-end questions in the interview. Selective use of verbatims in the research report can sometimes illuminate insights into how the advertising concept is perceived by the audience.

Video Rhythm
The natural wave-like curve one expects to see in the Flow of Attention that reflects the interaction between audience and film. This curve occurs because the human mind can only process visual information at a certain

speed and so consumes information in meaningful chunks. These chunks are equivalent to peak moments, the fundamental units of structure in film storytelling.

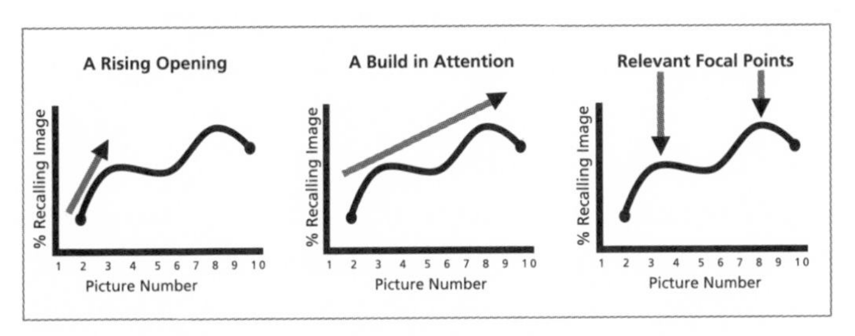

Characteristics of a Flow of Attention curve related to Attention and Recall.

Viral Marketing

Viral Marketing describes any strategy that encourages individuals to pass on a marketing message to others, creating potential for exponential growth in the message's exposure and influence.

Virtual Consumption

A hypothesis about how advertising works that explains the important role that experiential product drama plays. Because memories stored in the episodic memory system are easily re-written or revised, it is hypothesized that the artificial or "false" memories created by advertising are mixed together with the real memories of product experience to create brand loyalty. For example, a consumer who has four real brand experiences in a year and sees advertising for that brand six more times will have memories of ten brand experiences a year. In analyzing advertising, therefore, it is important to understand how the film dramatizes the virtual consumption experience of the brand.

Visual Connectedness

The extent to which the Flow of Attention pattern is smooth and continuous as opposed to scattered, turbulent or disjointed. This is a measure of how well the images in the commercial are glued together in the mind of the viewer. Smooth flows, which indicate stronger connections being made between the images in a commercial, are characteristic of more persuasive commercials.

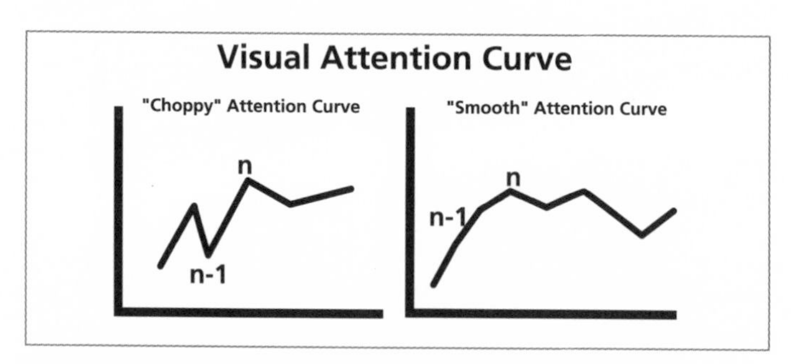

Persuasive ads tend to exhibit smoother flows, or be better connected.

Warm-Up Questions

These are interesting, simple, non-threatening questions (e.g., "What are your favorite television shows?") posed at the beginning of the interview (after the screening questions) and are designed to clear the mind and get the consumer into the "mind-set" of being a respondent. The responses are usually not analyzed.

Wear-In

The notion that up to a point the selling power of advertising *builds* over time and with repeated exposures.

Wear-Out

The notion that after a point, the selling power of advertising *declines* over time and with repeated exposures.

Working Emotion

Also known as aesthetic emotion. The reactions Aristotle says are produced by works of art. An analogy to working energy in physics, this concept divides the emotional content of advertising into two categories: the emotion created by a commercial that is put to work for the brand in selling the product versus borrowed interest, or the entertainment values that work to attract attention to the advertising execution. The strong correlation between the Flow of Emotion and Motivation suggests that the Flow of Emotion is a good measure of Working Emotion.

Resources

Resources

Websites

AAAA American Association of Advertising Agencies, www.aaaa.org

AAPOR American Association for Public Opinion Research www.aapor.org

ACR Association for Consumer Research www.acrweb.org

ADM American Demographics Magazine www.demographics.com

AMA American Marketing Association www.marketingpower.com

Ameritest advertising research firm www.ameritest.net

ARF Advertising Research Foundation www.thearf.org

ASA American Statistical Association www.amstat.org

CASRO Council of American Survey Research Organizations www.casro.org

CMOR Council for Marketing and Opinion Research www.cmor.org

ESOMAR European Society of Opinion and Marketing Research www.esomar.org

McKee, Robert World-renowned expert on storytelling and creator of the Story seminar www.mckeestory.com

MRA Marketing Research Association www.mra-net.org

Quirk's Marketing Research Review Magazine www.quirks.com

QRCA Qualitative Research Consultants Association www.qrca.org

The Santa Fe Institute A multidisciplinary research and education center, pursuing emerging science www.santafe.edu

Tufte, Edward R. Data artist www.edwardtufte.com/tufte

US Census Bureau www.census.gov

WARC World Advertising Research Center, Ltd. Home of **Admap** magazine. www.warc.com

Wikipedia The free encyclopeida of anyone who can edit, http://www.wikipedia.org/. Items of interest are: Advertising Research, Ad Tracking, Ameritest, Copytesting, Global Marketing, Integrated Marketing Communications

Wiktionary A wiki-based open content dictionary http://www.wiktionary.org/. terms of interest are: aesthetic emotion, attention, awareness, top-of-mind awareness, aided awareness, unaided awareness, brand, brand image, branding, brand linkage, brand stretch, branding moment, continuous advertising tracking, copy sort, copy test, day-after recall test, discontinuity in the flow, dramatic structure, emotional build, emotional pivot, emotional structure, entry point for the eye, episodic memory, esthetic information, executional peak, experiential advertising, fit, flow of attention, flow of emotion, flow of meaning, motivation, persuasion, peak visual, Picture Sorts, pre-test, product peak, positive transition, selling-edge analysis, semantic information, semantic memory, semantic network, single-minded branding moment, stickiness, stopping power, subjective time, sustained emotion, video rhythm, virtual consumption, visual connectedness, and working emotion.

END NOTES

[1]Ostlund, L. E., Clancy, K. J., and Sapra, R. Inertia in Copy Research. *Journal of Advertising Research*, 1980, 20(1), 17–23.

[2]Honomichl, J. J. *Honomichl on Marketing Research*. Lincolnwood, IL: NTC Business Books, 1986.

[3]Ross, H. Recall vs. Persuasion: An Answer. *Journal of Advertising Research*, 1982, 22(1), 13–16.

[4]Lodish, L. M., Abraham, M., Kalmenson, S., Livelsberger, J., Lubetkin, B., Richardson, B., & Stevens, M. E. How TV Advertising Works: A Meta-Analysis of 389 Real World Split Cable TV Advertising Experiments. *Journal of Marketing Research*, May 1995, 125–139.

[5]Schwerin, Horace S., and Henry H. Newel, *Persuasion in Marketing*, John Wiley and Sons, Inc., April, 1981.

[6]Blair, M. H. An Empirical Investigation of Advertising Wearin and Wearout. *Journal of Advertising Research*, 40 (November/ December 2000).

[7]Arnold, S. J., & Bird, J. R. The Day After Recall Test of Advertising Effectiveness: A

Discussion of the Issues. In *Current Issues and Research in Advertising*, 1982, 59–68.

[8]Young, C. E. The Eye Is Not A Camera. *Quirk's Marketing Research Review*, 2003, 58–63.

[9]Young, C. E. Researcher as Teacher: A Heuristic Model for Pre-Testing TV Commercials. *Quirk's Marketing Research Review*, 2001, 23–27.

[10]Kastenholz, J., Young, C., & Kerr, G. Does Day-After Recall Testing Produce Vanilla Advertising? *Admap*, June 2004, 34–36.

[11]Kastenholz, J., Kerr, G., & Young, C. Focus and Fit: Advertising and Branding Join Forces to Create a Star. *Marketing Research*, Spring 2004, 16–21.

[12]Moult, W. H. *Selective Success Amid Chaos: Advertising in the 1990s*. Paper presented at Esomar, 1995. In *Selected Papers and Presentations: 1990-1996*, Stamford, CT.: ASI Market Research, Inc., 1996.

[13]Wells, W. D., Leavitt, C., and McConville, M. A Reaction Profile for TV Commercials. *Journal of Advertising Research*, 11(6), December 1971, 11–17.

[14]Schlinger, M. J. A Profile of Responses to Commercials. *Journal of Advertising Research*, 1979, 19(2), 37–46.

[15]Krugman, H. Memory Without Recall, Exposure Without Perception. *Journal of Advertising Research*, July/August, 1977.

[16]Hall, B. F. A New Model for Measuring Advertising Effectiveness. *Journal of Advertising Research*, March/April 2002, 23–31.

[17]Young, C. E., & Robinson, M. Video Rhythms and Recall. *Journal of Advertising Research*, June/July 1989, 22–25.

[18]Young, C. E., & Robinson, M. Visual Connectedness and Persuasion. *Journal of Advertising Research*, March/April 1992, 51–59.

[19]Young, C. E., & Kastenholz, J. Emotion in TV Ads. *Admap*, 2004, 40–42.

[21]Young, C. E. Brain Waves, Picture Sorts, and Branding Moments. *Journal of Advertising Research*, 42(4), 2002, 42–53.

[22]Young, C. E. Capturing the Flow of Emotion in Television Commercials: A New Approach. *Journal of Advertising Research*, June 2004, 202–209.

Publications

Aaker, D. A., *Building Strong Brands*. New York, NY: The Free Press, 1996.

Agres, S. J., Edell, J. A., & Dubitsky, T. M. *Emotion in Advertising: Theoretical and Practical Explorations*. Westport, CT: Quorum Books, 1990.

American Association of Advertising Agencies. Positioning Advertising Copy Testing (PACT): A Consensus Credo Representing the Views of Leading American Advertising Agencies. NY: AAAA, 1982.

Arnheim, R., *Visual Thinking*, Berkeley: University of California Press, 1974.

Arnold, S. J., & Bird, J. R. The Day-After Recall Test of Advertising Effectiveness: A Discussion of the Issues. In *Current Issues and Research in Advertising*, 1982, 59–68.

Blair, M. H., An empirical investigation of advertising wearin and wearout. *Journal of Advertising Research*, 2000, 40(6), 95–104.

Blakeslee, Sandra & Blakeslee, Matthew *The Body has a Mind of its Own, How Body Maps in Your Brain Help You Do (Almost) Everything Better,* Random House, New York, 2007.

Bohm, D., *On Dialogue*, London: Routeledge, 1996.

Booth, W., *A Rhetoric of Irony*, Chicago: University of Chicago Press, 1974.

Brown, G., Campaign Tracking: New Learning on Copy Evaluation and Wearout. Paper presented at the Fourth Annual ARF Copy Research Workshop, New York, 1987.

Brown, G., Insights into Campaign Wear-in and Wear-out from Continuous Tracking. Paper presented at the ARF Advertising Tracking Studies Workshop, New York, 1984.

Campbell, D. T., & Stanley, J. C., *Experimental and Quasi-Experimental Designs for Research*. Chicago, IL: Rand McNally, 1963.

Campbell, J., *Grammatical Man*, New York: Simon and Schuster, 1982.

Csikszentmihalyl, M., *Flow: The Psychology of Optimal Experience*, New York: Harper Collins, 1990.

Ehrenberg, A. S. C., Repetitive advertising and the consumer. *Journal of Advertising Research*, 2000, 40(6), 39–49.

Einstein, S., *Film Form*, New York: Harcourt Brace, 1977.

Eisner, W., *Graphic Storytelling*, Tamarac, Florida: Poorhouse Press, 1996.

Fryer, B., Storytelling that Moves People: A

Conversation with Screenwriting Coach Robert Mckee. *Harvard Business Review*, June 2003.

Gigerenzer, G., & Todd, P., *Simple Heuristics That Make Us Smart,* Oxford University Press, 1999.

Gladwell, M., *Blink.*, New York: Little, Brown, 2005.

Gladwell, M., *The Tipping Point*. New York: Back Bay Books, 2002.

Goffman, E., *The Presentation of Self in Everyday Life*, Garden City, NY: Doubleday, 1959.

Greenspan, S. I., & Shanker, S. G. *The First Idea: How Symbols, Language, and Intelligence Evolved from our Primate Ancestors to Modern Humans*. Cambridge, MA: DaCapo Press, 2004.

Grobe, M., *Emotional Branding: The New Paradigm for Connecting Brands to People*. New York, NY: Allworth Press, 2001.

Haley, R. I., & Baldinger, A. L. The ARF Copy Research Validity Project. *Journal of Advertising Research*, 2000, 40(6), 114–136.

Hall, B. F., A New Model for Measuring Advertising Effectiveness. *Journal of Advertising Research*, March/April 2002, 23–31.

Hall, B. F, On measuring the power of communications. *Journal of Advertising Research*, 2004, 44(2), June, 181–188.

Hansen, F. and Christensen, S.R., *Emotions, Advertising and Consumer Choice*, Copenhagen Business School Press, 2007

Heath, Chip & Heath, Dan, *Made to Stick: Why Some Ideas Survive and Others Die,* Random House, 2007.

Hoffman, D., *Visual Intelligence*, New York: Norton, 1998.

Holland, J., *Hidden Order*, Cambridge, MA: Helix, 1995.

Honomichl, J. J., H*onomichl on Marketing Research*, Lincolnwood, IL: NTC Business Books, 1986.

Janiszewski, C., "Preconscious Processing Effects: The Independence of Attitude Formation and Conscious Thought," *Journal of Consumer Research,* 15, pp.199–209, 1988

Jaynes, J. ,*The Origins of Consciousness in the Breakdown of the Bicameral Mind,* Princeton University, 1976

Jones, J. P., *What's in a Name: Advertising and the Concept of Brands. Lexington*, MA: D. C. Heath Books, 1986.

Jones, J. P., (Editor), *How Advertising Works:*

The Role of Research, Thousand Oaks, CA: Sage Publications, 1998.

Kastenholz, J., Kerr, G., & Young, C., Focus and Fit: Advertising and Branding Join Forces to Create a Star, *Marketing Research*, Spring 2004, 16–21.

Kastenholz, J., Young, C., & Dubitsky, T., Roughing It: Rehearse Your Creative Ideas in Rough Production to Optimize Ad Effectiveness. *Marketing Research,* 2004 (Winter), 16(4), 22–27.

Kastenholz, J., Young, C., A Film Director's Guide to Ad Effectiveness. *Admap*, September 2003.

Kastenholz, J., Young, C., & Kerr, G., Does Day-After Recall Testing Produce Vanilla Advertising? *Admap*, June 2004, 34–36.

Klapp, O., *Heroes, Villains and Fools*, Englewood Cliffs, NJ: Prentice-Hall, 1962.

Krugman, H., Memory Without Recall, Exposure Without Perception. *Journal of Advertising Research*, July/August, 1977.

Krugman, H. E., Memory without recall, exposure without perception. *Journal of Advertising Research*, 2000, 40(6), 49–54.

Kuhns, W., *The Moving Picture Book*. Dayton, OH: Pflaum, 1975.

Leahey, T. J., & Harris, R. J. *Human Learning*. Englewood Cliffs, NJ: Prentice-Hall, 1985.

Levitin, Daniel J., *This Is Your Brain on Music: The Science of a Human Obsession*, Plume; 1 Reprint edition, August 28, 2007.

Lodish, L. M., Abraham, M., Kalmenson, S., Livelsberger, J., Lubetkin, B., Richardson, B., & Stevens, M. E., How TV Advertising Works: A Meta-Analysis of 389 Real World Split Cable TV Advertising Experiments. *Journal of Marketing Research*, May 1995, 125–139.

Malhotra, N. K., *Marketing Research: An Applied Orientation*. (3rd Edition.) Upper Saddle River, NJ: Prentice-Hall, 1999.

Maloney, J. C., Curiosity versus disbelief in advertising. *Journal of Advertising Research*, 2000, 40(6), 7–14.

McCloud, Scott, *Making Comics: Storytelling Secrets of Comics, Magna and Graphic Novels,* Harper paperbacks, 2006.

McCloud, Scott, *Understanding Comics: The invisible art*. New York, NY: Harper Collins, 1993.

McKee, Robert, *Story: Substance, Structure, Style and the Principles of Screenwriting*. NY, NY: HarperCollins Books, 1997.

Meyrowitz, J., *No Sense of Place*, Oxford: Oxford University Press, 1985.

Moles, A., *Information Theory and Esthetic Perception*, Urbana: University of Illinois Press, 1967.

Moult, W. H., Selective Success Amid Chaos: Advertising in the 1990s. Paper presented at Esomar, 1995. In *Selected Papers and Presentations*: 1990–1996, Stamford, CT.: ASI Market Research, Inc., 1996.

Murch, Walter, *In the blink of an eye*, Beaverly Hills, CA, Silman-James press, 2001.

Ondaatje, Michael, *The Conversations: Walter Murch and the Art of Editing Film*, New York, NY: Alfred Al. Knopf, 2002.

Ostlund, L. E., Clancy, K. J., & Sapra, R. Inertia in Copy Research. *Journal of Advertising Research*, 1980, 20(1), 17–23.

Plummer, J. T., How personality makes a difference. *Journal of Advertising Research*, 2000, 40(6), 79–84.

Plummer, Joe, Rappaport, Steve, Hall, Taddy & Barocci, Robert, *The On-line Advertising Playbook: Proven Strategies and Tested Tactics from the Advertising Research Foundation,* Advertising Research Foundation, John Wiley and Sons, 2007

Ries, A., & Trout, J., *Positioning: The Battle For Your Mind*, New York, NY: McGraw-Hill, 2000.

Ries, A., & Trout, J., *The 22 Immutable Laws of Marketing*. New York, NY: Harper Collins, 1994.

Ross, H., Recall vs. Persuasion: An Answer. *Journal of Advertising Research*, 1982, 22(1), 13–16.

Rossiter, J.R. and Percy, L., *Advertising Communications and Promotion Management,* McGraw-Hill, New York, 1997

Schlinger, M. J., A Profile of Responses to Commercials. *Journal of Advertising Research*, 1979, 19(2), 37–46.

Schlinger, M. J., Olson, D., & Young, C., How Consumers React to New-Product Ads, *Journal of Advertising Research,* June/July, 1982, Vol 2, No 3.

Scott, D. R., & Solomon, D., What is wearout anyway? *Journal of Advertising Research*, 1998, 38(5), 19–28.

Senge, P., *The Fifth Discipline*, New York: Doubleday, 1990.

Shannon, C., and Weaver, W., *The Mathematical Theory of Communication*, Urbana: University of Illinois Press, 1975.

Stewart, D. W., & Furse, D. H., Analysis of the impact of executional factors on advertising performance. *Journal of Advertising Research*, 1984, 24 (December), 23–26.

Stewart, D. W., & Furse, D. H., *Effective Television Advertising: A Study of 1,000 Commercials*. Lexington, MA: D. C. Heath Books, 1986.

Surmanek, J., *Media Planning: A Practical Guide*. (3rd Edition.) Chicago, IL: NTC Business Books, 1996.

Sutherland, M., & Sylvester, A., *Advertising and the Mind of the Consumer: What Works, What Doesn't and Why*. St. Leonards, Australia: Allen & Unwin Press, 2000.

Tabachnick, B. G., & Fidell, L. S., *Using Multivariate Statistics*. New York, NY: Harper & Row, 1983.

Tufte, Edward R., *Envisioning Information*. Cheshire, CT: Graphics Press, 1990.

Tufte, Edward R., *The Visual Display of Quantitative Information*. (2nd Edition.) Cheshire, CT: Graphics Press, 2001.

Tufte, Edward R., *Visual Explanations*. Cheshire, CT: Graphics Press, 1997.

Tulving, E., *The Elements of Episodic Memory*, Oxford: Oxford University Press, 1983.

Vaugn, R., "How Advertising Works: A Planning Model," *Journal of Advertising Research,* Vol.20, No.5, October 1980

Wells, W. D., Lectures and Dramas, *Cognitive*

and Affective Responses to Advertising. Lexington Books: Mass./Toronto, 1988.

Wells, W. D., Leavitt, C., & McConville, M. A, Reaction Profile for TV Commercials. *Journal of Advertising Research*, 11(6), December 1971, 11–17.

Young, C., The Advertising Magnifier Effect: An MTV Study, *Journal of Advertising Research*, December, 2006.

Young, C., Aesthetic Emotion and Long-Term Ad Effects, *Admap*, April 2006, 38–40.

Young, C., Brain Waves, Picture Sorts, and Branding Moments. *Journal of Advertising Research*, 42(4), 2002, 42–53.

Young, C., Call the right play, *Quirk's Marketing Research Review*, April, 2008, 34–42.

Young, C., Capturing the Flow of Emotion in Television Commercials: A New Approach. *Journal of Advertising Research*, June 2004, 202–209.

Young, C., Co-creativity, Admap, January, 2008, 24–27.

Young, C., The Eye Is Not A Camera, *Quirk's Marketing Research Review*, 2003, 58–63.

Young, C., Fast editing speed and commercial performance, *Admap*, May, 2007, 2–5.

Young, C., Fast-working advertising, *Admap*, June, 2007, 32–34.

Young, C., A Film Director's Guide to Ad Effectiveness, *Admap*, September, 2003 16–18.

Young, C., Finding the Creative Edge: Research as Flow, *Admap*, December, 2006, 45–47.

Young, C., Minding music and movies, *Admap*, May, 2008, 45–48.

Young, C., Researcher as Teacher: A Heuristic Model for Pre-Testing TV Commercials. *Quirks Marketing Research Review*, 2001, 23–27.

Young, C., Tags are it, *Quirk's Marketing Research Review,* April, 2007, 38–45

Young, C., What is the information in an ad?, *Admap*, November, 2007, 48–50.

Young, C., & Shea Hall, Amy, Case study: BMW movies—Luxury car to movie star, *Admap*, April, 2007, 17–19.

Young, C., & Shea Hall, Amy, Multi-platforming engagement—An MTV case history, *Admap*, October, 2007, 35–38.

Young, C., & Robinson, M., Video Rhythms and Recall. *Journal of Advertising Research*, June/July 1989, 22–25.

Young, C. E., & Robinson, M. Visual Connectedness and Persuasion. *Journal of Advertising Research*, March/April 1992, 51–59.

Young, C., & Kastenholz, J. Emotion in TV Ads. *Admap*, 2004, 40–42.

Zaltman, Gerald, *How Customers Think: Essential Insights into the Mind of the Market.* Boston, MA: Harvard Business School Press, 2003.

Zaltman, Gerald & Zaltman, Lindsay H. *Marketing Metaphoria: What Deep Metaphors Reveal About the Minds of Consumers,* Harvard Business School Press, April 22, 2008.

Note: All Ameritest Papers (Young, et al.) can be found on our website at www.ameritest.net.

ROUGH GUIDE TO STATISTICAL TESTING

One of the questions frequently asked in any research meeting with numbers is, "Is that difference significant?" For example, if your ad generates a 52 Attention score and another ad generates a 40, how do you determine if your ads Attention score is *significantly* different from the other ad?

What follows is a convenient method to determine very quickly (*without* using any statistical formulas) whether certain differences in a pretesting report are statistically significant.

Perhaps the most useful comparison will be between a test cell and a norm. You'll want to know whether your ad scored significantly above or below a given norm for a key evaluative measure. Another useful comparison will be between two ads that have been pre-tested (i.e., between two test cells). For instance, you'll want to know whether one ad is outperforming the other on a key evaluative measure. The chart shown below assumes that the sample sizes for your test cells are equal to 125.

You may also want to determine whether

	Sample Size 1st Ad 125	Norm	Sample Size 1st Ad 125	Sample Size 2nd Ad 125
Approximate minimum percent difference needed for statistical significance at 90% confidence level.	8%		10%	

your ad performs differently for one specific target group segment compared to another target group segment. Listed below are approximate minimum percent differences that would correspond to analysis of subsets of your total dataset.

	Sample Size 1st Ad 60	Sample Size 2nd Ad 60	Sample Size 1st Ad 50	Sample Size 2nd Ad 75
Approximate minimum percent difference needed for statistical significance at 90% confidence level.	14%		13%	

	Sample Size 1st Ad 25	Sample Size 2nd Ad 100	Sample Size 1st Ad 30	Sample Size 2nd Ad 90
Approximate minimum percent difference needed for statistical significance at 90% confidence level.	20%		16%	